George Eliot

George Eliot

A Critic's Biography

BARBARA HARDY

continuum

Continuum
The Tower Building
11 York Road
London SE1 7NX

80 Maiden Lane
Suite 704
New York, NY 10038

British Library Cataloguing-in-Publication-Data
A catalogue record for this book is available from the British Library.

ISBN HB: 0-8264-8515-4
      PB: 0-8264-8516-2

Library of Congress Cataloging-in-Publication Data
A catalog record for this book is available from the Library of Congress.

Typeset by Fakenham Photosetting Limited, Fakenham, Norfolk
Printed and bound in Great Britain by MPG Books Ltd, Bodmin, Cornwall

In memory of Richard Ellmann and Jerome Beaty

Contents

Preface and Acknowledgments

I think of this book as a critic's biography, because in it I concentrate on George Eliot's art and marginalize biographical fact, reversing the emphasis of conventional critical biography, which concentrates on life and marginalizes or excludes literature, and also because I give close readings of her novels, letters and, more selectively, of some of her friends' writing.

My interest in linking her life with her work began in the 1950s. In *The Novels of George Eliot: A Study in Form*[1], I drew on letters and novels for patterns and images – of disenchantment, daylit objects, swamp and river – which dramatized or described affective experience, but I did not discuss genres or biographical implications. I was concerned with her art, which had been neglected – except by FR Leavis, and he was often out of sympathy with her work, especially *The Mill on the Floss* and *Daniel Deronda*[2]. I was influenced by the New Critics' close scrutiny, especially that of William Empson, who combined verbal analysis with an interest in psychological and social contexts, but as I explained in *The Appropriate Form*[3], I came to find the criteria of tight closure and total relevance, argued by Henry James long before New Criticism, inappropriate for analysing and judging the multiple action and overt commentary of large Victorian novels.

Now I have combined criticism with biographical narrative, using both selectively[4]. To treat events thematically involves some narrative overlap but I have avoided it as far as possible; and to treat events sequentially has disadvantages too, making it hard to concentrate on developing characters and relationships, emotion and sensuous experience, let alone observe the moments as they pass.

George Eliot's life-materials are usually assimilated in her art, but while serving immediacy and particularity they may be casual or random, or detached from dominant themes or patterns. But her particulars are important, and have many purposes. She could have been a philosopher, like Rousseau, Comte, Carlyle or Feuerbach, who all helped her thinking, and while she was working as translator and reviewer, she contemplated a philosophical book called *The Idea of a Future Life*, which got as far as Chapman's list of prospective publications and which her friend Sara Hennell assumed she was working on when she stopped writing reviews and essays in the mid-1850s. Released into creative confidence by her loving partnership with George Henry Lewes, she chose to be an artist, to particularize ideas in what she called the 'embodying' process of fiction. Of course, concepts remain powerful and fascinating, and in the last few decades critics have disembodied the particulars of her art, to turn them back into skilfully articulated Comtean, Feuerbachian or Darwinian abstraction. She was a conceptual thinker but she assimilated concepts so thoroughly that she could relax into self-generative and intuitive art. Herbert Spencer, whom she loved for a time, knew better than anyone that 'her philosophical powers were remarkable' but he also knew she had a novelist's 'needful qualifications in high degrees – quick observation, great power of analysis, unusual and rapid intuition into others' states of mind ...' He admired her 'capacity for abstract thinking' but found it went 'along with capacity for concrete representation' (Spencer, p. 397[5]). It was Spencer, whose writing is highly abstract, who emphasized observation and intuition, and not Lewes, whose literary and dramatic criticism is personal and particular.

I want to supplement and not reject conceptual analysis. Using close reading in the interest of selective and thematic biography, I discuss real events and relations in order to look at her 'concrete representation'. It is hard to combine narrative sequence with analytic criticism, and I have followed my chosen themes from life into art, moving backwards and forwards, like George Eliot as she broke narrative sequence in *Daniel Deronda*. I begin with family and the break after she went to live with Lewes, and the consequences for her fiction, like aspects of Adam Bede which recall her father or the tragic wish-fulfilment of *The Mill on the Floss*, and smaller things, too. I discuss her Midlands landscape, romanticized by some scholars – but not Cross – her travels in Europe of which England was a reluctant part, and her need for foreignness. She was not a systematic political thinker but she could think political thoughts, and shaped fiction to experiment with social possibilities and criticize injustice and nationalism. Her partnership with Lewes – biographer, critic and scientist – her friendships with Maria Lewis, Charles Bray, Sara Hennell, John Chapman, Herbert Spencer and Jane Senior, all contribute to her art in affective pattern, relationships, odd images and incidents. Slighter acquaintances get into the fiction, especially the first stories, more completely than people she knew well. My discussion of the important events in her life, treated as far as possible in sequence, includes deaths. Sometimes life gets into art in minute detail, and I look at single words like 'pirouette' and 'fee-fo-fum', and everyday objects like pens and smelling-salts, that turn up as facts and fiction. Such little things are links between living and writing, particulars in her art which can tell us about her life, and the relation between her life and art.

I look at imagery and language in George Eliot's letters, journalism, poetry and fiction as they relate to each other, and at some writing of her close friends – Lewes, Sara Hennell, Charles Bray and Spencer. It is easy for biography to turn the artist's friends into minor characters, as their lives and letters are read for explicit reference to the main subject. In George Eliot's biography, for instance, Frederic Harrison appears as Positivist and legal adviser, Sara Hennell as misguided Deist left behind by a creative genius, Spencer as repressed and jealous object of misplaced affection. (Lewes's role in her creative career and his remarkable achievement in many fields has saved him from this fate: his theatrical criticism and the *Goethe* biography are still readable though his books on Aristotle and Robespierre are probably only read by a few George Eliot scholars.) Sometimes her friends are compared adversely with her, like Bray and Spencer by Haight, who finds one crude and the other ridiculous[6]. (Though Haight became interested in Chapman for his own sake.) It may be easier for a critic than a biographer to read such *dramatis personae* as independent lives and resist the temptation to pick references to the chief character and neglect the rest. George Eliot was observant and intuitive, a good listener to other people, and remembered events in other people's lives, such as Spencer's flight from school and his work as a railway engineer, Bray's boyish spelling, and Harrison's childhood love, transplanting them in her art, often unconsciously.

Her letters, and other people's, are mined by biographers for fact and opinion about family, religion, her love for Lewes or Cross, but also contain a mass of fine detail with inconspicuous but interesting biographical interest, words or phrases like 'Daddy', 'slippery pen', 'Shining Ones' or 'diffuse', first used casually but hooked into memory, to recur purposively in her art.

Thomas Hardy has a wonderful passage about experiencing and losing the present: 'Today has length, breadth, thickness, colour, smell, voice. As soon as it becomes *yesterday* it is a thin layer among many layers, without substance, colour, or articulate sound' (*The Life and Work of Thomas Hardy*, 302)[7]. As Hardy knew, the novelist can give an illusion of the present. It is also this sensuous immediacy and particularity which is often thinned in the layering of biography's retrospect. In my narrative, I hope at times to recover some sounds, colours, and thickness of George Eliot's lost present, the feel of her selfhood.

The novels were central in her life but biographers – since they are biographers not critics – often treat them as mere sources of information about life, or treat them too generally, saying little about language, form and originality, and neglecting critics even if they mention them. I think of this book as a kind of anti-biography, attempting to redress the balance, but it is heavily dependent on the work of biographers like Haight, Cross[8] and Rosemary Ashton[9].

I am interested in looking at aspects of George Eliot's life which show us more about her art, not with re-interpreting the life, but there are some uncertainties and contradictions in the story of her life – her love life, in particular – which have no special importance for her art but which I cannot ignore[10]. For instance, there are gaps in our knowledge of the commitment she made when she went off to Germany with Lewes the married man, evident in letters she wrote about Lewes's separation from his wife, which need more scrutiny than they often get. There is an odd lack of interest in Herbert Spencer's hesitant proposal of marriage to her, perhaps because he tends to be seen as a forgotten Victorian eccentric who made the mistake of not returning the love of a great novelist. The story of her husband John Cross jumping into the Grand Canal in Venice on the wedding journey, once seen as gossip, is now often recorded as fact, even by Haight and Ashton, wise scholars who avoid the speculation that is meat and drink to many biographers. Quite likely Cross did jump, but there is no firm evidence that he did. I raise these problems, not solve them.

I recently returned to Cross's book, which he saw as an experimental mix of biography and autobiography, with attention and sympathy, and my book is indebted to him, as well as to Haight's *George Eliot: A Life*, in which Haight understandably attacked Cross for uxorious censorship. I owe a great deal to Cross and Haight – especially Haight, whom I use on every page – for their editions of the letters, to Ashton's biographies of George Eliot and George Henry Lewes, to Thomas Pinney[11] and Ashton for their selections of essays, Judith Johnston and Margaret Harris for the *Journals*, and the early biographers Mathilde Blind[12] and Oscar Browning[13]. Rosemarie Bodenheimer's *The Real Life of George Eliot* is stylish and original, and her discussion of letter writing valuable, but I find some of her interpretation too abstract and selective[14]. I have learnt from disagreeing with Raymond Williams, Daniel Cottom and Edward Said, hostile or unsympathetic to George Eliot's politics[15], and agreeing and disagreeing with some feminists: Kate Millett, Elaine Showalter and Deirdre David[16]. I discussed the Casaubon marriage in *The Appropriate Form,* and have read with pleasure the many commentators who have identified the original Casaubon, but I refrain from joining them.

Like the analytic interpretations of David Carroll[17] and the philosophical research of Valerie Dodd[18], George Eliot's notebooks throw into strong relief what I say little about in this book – George Eliot's immense learning in mythology, history, language and literature. The research of Anna Kitchel, John Clark Pratt, Victor A. Neufeldt, William Baker, Joseph Weisenfarth and Jane Irwin[19] is very different from my culling of affective detail – though they include detail – but without their work, I could not have made my miscellaneous assembly. Pratt and Neufeldt quote William Lecky, from whom George Eliot may have picked up the idea of using St Theresa, amongst other things: 'Life is history, not poetry. It consists mainly of little things …' (*George Eliot's 'Middlemarch' Notebooks*, xli). I mention only such scholars whom I have consulted for this book or whose ideas have recently been in my mind, and apologize to many others whose diffuse influences I have taken in over the years and not mentioned.

I dedicate this book to Richard Ellmann and Jerome Beaty, whose conversation I have missed while writing it. Gordon and Mary

Haight were hospitable friends to me long ago. I valued encouragement given at an early stage by John Rignall and Rick Rylance who read the first two chapters of my draft. I have been generously helped by Rosemary Ashton, Beryl Gray, Graham Handley, Derek and Sybil Oldfield, Janet El-Rayess, Miranda El-Rayess, Zuhair El-Rayess and Katharine Worth, who read all or parts of the book in draft, and helped by listening, criticizing, correcting, lending books, answering questions and discussing problems. I am additionally grateful to Miranda El-Rayess for careful assistance with references, checking and proof-reading. Some friends spotted errors, blemishes, omissions and redundancies, but I am, of course, responsible for defects that remain. I thank Joan and Richard Michaelis for doing research in Geneva, Sybil Oldfield, author of the forthcoming biography of Jane Senior, and Frances Harris of the British Library, for information and ideas about Jane Senior, Merivan Coles for tracking down 'the oceanic feeling', and Peter Mudford for giving me Herbert Spencer's *Autobiography* and talking about Spencer. I had warm support and help from Isobel Armstrong, William Baker, Michael Baron, Martin Dodsworth, Sue Roe, Michael Slater and Jeremy Worman. My brother, Bill Nathan, and my daughters Julia and Kate Hardy have always taken a loving interest in my work, and Julia and Kate gave me indispensable help with computers.

Parts of Chapters 2 and 4 draw in revised form on two of my articles: 'Rome in Middlemarch: a Need for Foreignness', in *George Eliot – George Henry Lewes Studies*, pp. 24–5, September 1993 and 'Art into Life, Life into Art: Middlemarch and Jane Senior's letters', in *George Eliot – George Henry Lewes Studies*, pp. 44–5, September 2003.

Notes

1 London: Athlone, 1959; see especially chapters 9 and 11.
2 *The Great Tradition*. London: Chatto and Windus, 1948.
3 London: Athlone, 1964; introduction and chapters 1 and 5.
4 I omit many personal and public events, dates and characters normally included in biographies less concerned with texts.
5 Herbert Spencer (1904) *Autobiography*. London: Williams & Norgate.

6 Gordon S. Haight (1968) *George Eliot: A Biography*. Oxford: Clarendon Press.

7 Michael Millgate (ed.) (1984). London & Basingstoke: Macmillan.

8 JW Cross (1885) *George Eliot's Life As Related in Her Letters And Journals*. Edinburgh and London: Blackwood.

9 Rosemary Ashton (1991) *GH Lewes*. Oxford: Oxford University Press; (1996) *George Eliot. A Life*. London: Hamish Hamiton.

10 I discuss these gaps and problems in Chapter 3.

11 Thomas Pinney (ed.) (1968) *Essays of George Eliot*. London: Routledge and Kegan Paul.

12 Mathilde Blind (1883) *George Eliot*. London: John Ingram.

13 Oscar Browning (1890) *Life of George Eliot*. London: Walter Scott.

14 Ithaca and London: Cornell University Press, 1994; see Chapter 3.

15 Raymond Williams (1973) *The Country and the City*. Oxford: OUP; Daniel Cottom (1987) *George Eliot, Social History and Literary Representation*. Minneapolis: University of Minnesota Press; Edward Said (1993) *Culture and Imperialism*. New York: Alfred A. Knopf.

16 Kate Millett (1970) *Sexual Politics*. New York: Doubleday; Deirdre David (1987) *Intellectual Women and Victorian Patriarchy*. Ithaca, NY: Cornell University Press; Elaine Showalter (1977) *A Literature of Their Own: British Women Novelists from Brontë to Lessing*. Princeton: Princeton University Press.

17 (1992) *George Eliot and the Conflict of Interpretations*. Cambridge: Cambridge University Press.

18 Valerie Dodd (1990) *George Eliot: An Intellectual Life*. London: Macmillan.

19 Anna Kitchel (ed.) (1950) *Quarry for 'Middlemarch'*. Berkeley: University of California Press; William Baker (ed.) (1976–85) *Some George Eliot Notebooks: An Edition of the Carl H Pforzheimer Library's Holograph Notebooks. MSS 707,708,709,710,711,* Salzburg: Salzburg University Studies in English literature; John Clark Pratt and Victor A Neufeldt (ed.) (1979) *George Eliot's 'Middlemarch Notebooks. A Transcription'*, Berkeley and London: University of California Press; Joseph Wiesenfarth (ed.) (1981) *George Eliot: A Writer's Notebook* 1854–79. Charlottesville: University Press of Virginia; Jane Irwin (ed.) (1996) *George Eliot's 'Daniel Deronda' Notebooks*. Cambridge: Cambridge University Press.

References and Abbreviations

I reference citations, not every event: if no source is given, I have drawn information from Cross, Haight, and Haight's edition of *Letters*.

I have used the Clarendon text of George Eliot's novels, with chapter references, except for *The Mill on the Floss*, where I give chapter and book. I give chapter and book for Goethe's *Elective Affinities* (Harmondsworth: Penguin, 1971).

Unless a page number is specified, references are to chapters.

In notes and chronology, George Eliot and George Henry Lewes are referred to by intials. Titles of George Eliot's novels and tales are abbreviated in citation-references. The following abbreviations are used for other books often cited:

Ashton	Rosemary Ashton (1996) *George Eliot: A Life*. London: Hamish Hamilton.
Cross	JW Cross (1885) *George Eliot's Life As Related in Her Letters and Journals*, 3 vols. Edinburgh and London: Blackwood.
GEC	John Rignall, ed. (2000) *Oxford Reader's Companion to George Eliot*. Oxford: Oxford University Press.
Haight	Gordon S Haight (1968) *George Eliot: A Biography*. Oxford: Clarendon Press.
Journals	Margaret Harris and Judith Johnston, eds (1988) *The Journals of George Eliot*. Cambridge: Cambridge University Press.
Letters	Gordon S Haight, ed., *The George Eliot Letters*, 9 vols., 1854–78. New Haven: Yale University Press.
NGE	Barbara Hardy (1959) *The Novels of George Eliot*. London, Athlone.
Pinney	Thomas Pinney, ed. (1968) Essays of George Eliot. London: Routledge and Kegan Paul.

Poems	Lucien Jenkins, ed. (1989) *The Collected Poems of George Eliot*. London: Skoob.
SCW	Rosemary Ashton, ed. (1992) *Selected Critical Writings*. Oxford: Oxford University Press.
Spencer	Herbert Spencer (1904) *Autobiography*. London: Williams and Norgate.
ITS	Nancy Henry, ed. (1994) *Impressions of Theophrastus Such*. Iowa City: University of Iowa Press.

An Outline of George Eliot's Life and Writing

This chronological commentary is designed to outline a sequence of events and fill gaps in what is a largely thematic discussion of connections between George Eliot's life and writing, and is primarily intended for readers not fully familiar with the facts and texts.

1819   22 November: GE is born in South Farm, Arbury, Warwickshire, where her father is land agent for Francis Newdigate's Arbury estate.

29 November: Christened Mary Anne in Chilvers Coton church; she and family spell her name 'Ann'. Third and youngest surviving child of Robert Evans and his second wife Christiana, née Pearson. Her siblings are Christiana or Chrissey (1814–59), Isaac (1816–90), the twins, William and Thomas (1821; died when 10 days old), and her half-siblings by her father's first marriage to Harriet or Harriott Poynton are Robert (1802–64) and Frances or Fanny (1805–82).

1820   The family moves to Griff, between Nuneaton and Coventry.

1824   GE goes to Mrs Moore's dame school with Isaac.

1825–7   GE boards at Miss Lathom's school in Attleborough, near Nuneaton.

1828–32   GE boards at Miss Wallington's school in Nuneaton, where the principal 'governess' is the evangelical Maria Lewis, with whom she makes friends. A local evangelical revival is led by John Edmund Jones, who is drawn on for 'Janet's Repentance'.

1832–5   GE boards at a Coventry school run by the Miss Franklins, Baptists; she leaves Christmas 1835. GE sees the Nuneaton riots in 1832. Her mother is very ill.

1836   Her mother Christiana dies of cancer; during her illness her husband has a severe kidney attack. GE apparently starts writing to Maria Lewis.

1837   Chrissey marries Edward Clarke, a doctor; GE is bridesmaid.

1839   GE plans the Chart of Ecclesiastical History and gives up in 1840 when another is published. She sends Maria Lewis a 'Sonnet' (*Letters* 1, 30).

1840   GE studies German and Italian with Joseph Brezzi; later helped with Latin and Greek by head of Coventry Grammar School. Her first publication is a poem 'Knowing that shortly I shall put off this tabernacle' (often called 'Farewell') in *Christian Observer*, signed MAE (*Letters* 1, 27–8).

1841   GE and her father move to Bird Grove, Foleshill, outside Coventry. GE is bridesmaid when Isaac marries Sarah Rawlins and they settle in Griff. GE continues languages and studies chemistry; reads Charles Hennell's critical but tolerant biblical analysis *Inquiry Concerning the Origin of Christianity* (1838) before or after meeting the radical Brays for a second time and begins a lifelong friendship.

1842   January: GE refuses to go to church and is then estranged for a while from her father; unable to respect her views he threatens to sell Bird Grove and live by himself.

In May GE compromises and starts going to church again. During the summer GE meets Cara's sister Sara Hennell and begins a close friendship.

In October GE meets Rufa Brabant and Charles Hennell.

In December the family discuss her association with the Brays, and a quarrel ensues but is settled.

1843   Works on Spinoza translation.

GE goes with Brays for a short trip to Stratford, Malvern and Worcester and in July to Bristol and South Wales.

In London for the marriage of Rufa Brabant to Charles Hennell, where she is bridesmaid. GE visits Dr Brabant and his wife in Devizes, causes jealousy and leaves in a hurry.

1844 Takes over from Rufa Hennell the translation of David Friedrich Strauss's *Das Leben Jesu*.

1845 There is a brief friendship with a young picture restorer who wants to marry her but is refused. GE goes to London, Birmingham and Scotland with the Brays. In London with Bray, has her head cast.

1846 Strauss translation is published anonymously by Chapman: *The Life of Jesus Critically Examined*. She visits Sara Hennell in Clapton. GE writes various reviews and first part of *Poetry and Prose from the Notebook of an Eccentric* for Bray's *Coventry Herald and Observer*. Goes to Dover with her father. Writes a letter about Bücherworm's quest for an ugly learned wife.

1847 Second and third parts of *Poetry and Prose* in Coventry Herald, including 'A Little Fable with a Great Moral', her first contrast of egoism and altruism. Goes to the Isle of Wight with her father.

1848 Goes to St Leonards with her father. His health deteriorates during the year.

1849 31 May: Her father dies.

6 June: Her father is buried.

12 June: GE goes to France, Italy and Switzerland with the Brays; in Geneva for eight months.

July–October: in Plongeon on lake.

1850 October–March: with François and Julie D'Albert Durade, Rue de la Pellettiere, becoming 'passionately attached' to life there. Observes life, walks, rows, reads, translates Spinoza's *Tractatus Theologicus-politicus* (unfinished), studies maths.

1850 March: GE returns to England, escorted by D'Albert Durade. At Griff with Isaac and Meriden with Chrissey, she feels unwanted and rootless. At Rosehill with Brays, where at John Chapman's request she reviews Mackay's *Progress of the Intellect* for the *Westminster Review*, her first powerful analytic critical writing.

1851   GE stays at 142 Strand; but after flirtation with Chapman causing his wife's and mistress's jealousy, returns to Rosehill.

Chapman buys the *Westminster*; during summer GE writes prospectus. Chapman and GE vow platonic friendship, and GE returns to 142 Strand to act as unofficial editor. She reviews for *Leader* and contributes to the *Belles Lettres* section of the *Westminster*. She makes friends with Herbert Spencer.

1852   GE reviews Carlyle's *Life of Sterling* for *Westminster*. Meets the feminist Bessie Parkes. During the summer holiday in Broadstairs, GE tells Herbert Spencer she loves him, and though he cannot love her, he makes a hesitant proposal which she refuses. Through him she makes friends with George Henry Lewes, journalist, novelist and all-purpose writer, who is married to Agnes, née Jervis, from whom he separated but whom he could not divorce because he had condoned her continued infidelity with his friend and co-editor Thornton Hunt. Goes to stay with the Combes in Edinburgh and Harriet Martineau in Ambleside. Death of Chrissey's husband.

1853   GE moves to Hyde Park Gardens, where she probably starts her serious love affair with Lewes. She gives up editing *Westminster* but reviews for it.

1854   Translates Feuerbach's *Wesen des Christenthums*, published under her name Marian Evans as *The Essence of Christianity*: its secularized ethic influenced her fiction, where Christianity is valued insofar as it corresponds with a humanist replacement of Divine Law, Immortality and Providence with social duty and love, work and creativity and ethical self-determinism. She writes 'Evangelical Teaching: Dr Cumming' for the *Westminster* which Lewes thinks shows genius. She goes to Berlin and Weimar with Lewes. Publishes 'Woman in France: Madame de Sablé' in the *Westminster*.

1855   On their return to England she stays in Dover when Lewes goes to London, joins him in Victoria Grove Terrace, Bayswater, then East Sheen. Lewes's *Life of Goethe* is published, marked by scholarship, personal style, detachment, and excellent critical analysis of poems, *Faust, Wilhelm Meister* and Goethe's science; 2nd and 3rd editions in 1864 and 1875. GE writes for *Leader* and *Westminster.*

1856   GE finishes translation (from Latin) of Spinoza's *Ethics,* begun by Lewes; (plans fail and it is unpublished until 1981 in Thomas Deegan (ed.) *Salzburg Studies in English Literature,* 102). GE's 'Silly Novels by Women Novelists', in *Westminster,* is an amusing critique of morally and culturally pretentious popular fiction. GE begins her career in fiction with 'The Sad Fortunes of Amos Barton', the first of a series (the rest not yet written) entitled *Scenes of Clerical Life.* Lewes offers it as the work of a friend to John Blackwood who publishes all her fiction except *Romola* and the story 'Brother Jacob'.

1857   'Amos Barton', 'Mr Gilfil's Love Story', and 'Janet's Repentance', each divided into parts, are published anonymously in consecutive issues of *Blackwood's Edinburgh Magazine* or *Maga.* The stories are consistent with moral principles argued in 'Silly Novels', especially in a critique of 'white neckcloth' novels and appeal on behalf of ordinary tragic lives. Dempster's accident and *delirium tremens* and Janet's sufferings subtly combine outer and inner action; a male narrator, parallelism and contrast, modulations of comedy and pathos, are constructed with skill. Her tales link clerical lives but show a deep concern for the sufferings of women, rooted in her sister Chrissey's troubled life as wife and mother. GE draws on her early life near Nuneaton with more 'portraiture' than in her later fiction. Irked by Blackwood's criticism of 'Janet' she ends the series. She writes to Isaac, Fanny and later Chrissey, that she is 'married', admitting the truth when questioned by the solicitor Holbeche, and her brother and sisters stop writing to her.

1858   *Scenes* published in one volume, 'by George Eliot', reviewed favourably; admired by Dickens who is sure the author is a woman. Lewes publishes *Seaside Studies,* for which the couple did marine research in Ilfracombe, Tenby, and the Scillies. GE and GHL go to Munich and Dresden.

1859   Chrissey writes a letter of reconciliation just before she dies of tuberculosis. *Adam Bede* is a literary and commercial success, selling 16,000 copies in a year. It constructs patterns of growth and deterioration, parallels and contrasts of character: Hetty/Dinah; Adam/Arthur; striking symbolism: mirror/window, finery/quaker garb, carpenter's shop/pleasure ground, oak/larch; and fine detail like a little pink handkerchief in the seducer's wastepaper basket, and an ironically named 'Hermitage'. The narrative commentary becomes more delicate, with Hetty's fantasy and feeling shown in skilful 'free indirect style'. Henry James called her GE's best heroine and does not appreciate Dinah's immaculate virtue, animated by her creativity and passion. Aspects of Adam's life draw on her father's memories. Lewes suggested the active involvement of Adam, and – less happily – Arthur's sensational ride to the scaffold with Hetty's pardon. There is satire and ironic social criticism, emphasizing the class division which precipitates tragedy, and comically articulated in Mrs Poyser's subversion. GE's authorship was identified by her friend Barbara Bodichon but GE had to tell Brays and Sara Hennell she is George Eliot. GE and GHL rent Holly Lodge, Wandsworth and find congenial friends in the Positivists Richard and Maria Congreve. *The Lifted Veil* is published in *Blackwoods,* described by GE as a '*jeu de mélancolie*', a fantastic novella about extremes of egoism and empathy, but in the style of Poe, also about clairvoyance, telepathy and resuscitation, given subtlety by its portrait of the artist, in negative, and moments dramatizing imagination and feeling.

1860   *The Mill on the Floss* is published, a more personally rooted story than *Adam Bede*, with partial portraits in Maggie, Tom, and perhaps the comic aunts, and an artist-figure in Philip, empowered by his wound and his love. There is a subtle pattern of imagery and a tragic but triumphant ending which is much debated. GE and GHL go to Italy; GHL suggests a novel about Florence and Savonarola.

1861   *Silas Marner* is published – an English pastoral which interrupted work on *Romola* – and another story of class difference, with drama of work, rural culture and dissent, a strong working-class heroine and a brilliant plot. Silas – weaver, miser, cataleptic, and foster-father – is one of her finest studies in the 'ordinary' life. The conspicuous patterning, and what she saw as a kind of poetry, play with motifs of two thefts, two villains, and two kinds of gold. She and Lewes return to Florence for more work on *Romola*.

1863   *Romola* published in 14 parts in the Smith, Elder & Co's *Cornhill Magazine*. George Smith's offer of £7,000 (£10,000 for a deadline she could not accept) was irresistible, so with some guilt she left Blackwood, who felt bitter but behaved courteously. *Romola* is one of the most interesting Victorian historical novels: like Dickens's *Barnaby Rudge* and *A Tale of Two Cities,* Thackeray's *Esmond,* and Elizabeth Gaskell's *Sylvia's Lovers,* it merges fact with fiction and uses past to mirror present. GE was used to 'hearing' her characters speak and felt constrained by the 'translated' and archaic English-Italian she adopted. Written with her 'best blood', it is thoroughly researched fiction which does not wear its scholarship lightly, and is found by many readers factually overloaded and too self-consciously willed. But it is deeply felt, balanced and intricate, with imaginative art history and symbolism. The scholars and fathers, blind Bardo and half-mad Baldassare, are fine studies in mind and passion. Romola's self-discoveries in marriage and religion, the deceits of Tito, and the history of Savonarola are analysed dynamically, with social and political detail, but Romola is GE's least animated heroine (mostly because of the artificial style), Tito's deterioration is over-schematic, and Savonarola done too much from the book, lacking interiority. She said she started it as a young woman and finished it as an old one, and drew on her labour and frustration in the character of Casaubon.

1864   'Brother Jacob', written in 1860, is published in the *Cornhill* as a present to Smith because of his financial loss on *Romola*, a feeble story but with some worthy tough crude satire of racism. GE starts *The Spanish Gypsy*, a blank verse tragedy, which she finds agonizing to write; Lewes persuades her to break off for a time.

1866   *Felix Holt* is published by Blackwood, perhaps after it is refused by Smith. It is set at the time of the First Reform Act 1830, with strong scenes of political corruption and unrest which draw on her experience of a mining community and election riots in Nuneaton, and her early experience of class differences. Felix Holt is over-idealized and a very conservative radical, contrasted with the more complex Harold Transome, and Rufus Lyon, her best Dissenter and one of her best virtuous characters. Humiliations, tormenting guilt, Tory politics, energy and ignorance make Mrs Transome a startling and original feminist study, more interesting than the heroine Esther. The lawyer Jermyn stars in a revelation scene which is sensational and moving. The skilfully patterned novel, with fine moments of poetry, some inspired by Dante, is strained by highly technical and tortuous plotting, where legal facts are obtrusive and obscure. GE and GHL travel in Spain.

1868   *The Spanish Gypsy* is published, after much revision. Its theme is the conflict of love and duty, its heroine a woman who sacrifices love and assumes political power. Thought of first as a play, it is a closet drama like Shelley's, Browning's and Tennyson's but without their lyrical power. GE researched prosody but never passed from knowledge to intuition, never wrote verse with the natural speech, free flowing rhythm and particularity of her prose. Her inversions, archaisms, and monotonous smooth regularity are compounded by sentimental and lofty tones like those of her early pious and pompous letters. Blackwood is wry but diplomatic, and the book sells well and is praised, although after her death sharply criticized by Mathilde Blind and Oscar Browning, both sensitive to poetry. 'Felix Holt: An Address to Working Men' is published in *Blackwood's* in 1868 and written at the request of diehard Tory John Blackwood, and promotes her distrust of electoral reform in a style and tone all wrong for an address to the working class, and emphasizes her own growing conservatism.

1869   Travels in Italy, where she meets John Walter Cross, a banker and stockbroker, to whose family Lewes had been introduced by Spencer. She begins the first version of *Middlemarch*, with the Garths, Lydgate, and Vincys, but breaks off.

May: Thornton, Lewes's second son, returns from Natal, (where he and his brother Herbert (Bertie) were sent to farm and led a very hard life). Wasted and agonized by spinal disease, perhaps tuberculosis, he dies in GE's arms in October.

1870   November: Begins *Miss Brooke*.

1871   *Miss Brooke* is amalgamated with the first *Middlemarch*.

December: Eight part-publication of *Middlemarch* begins.

1872   January–December: Part-publication of *Middlemarch* continues;

then as a four-volume publication. A massive novel, with rotating stories of love and vocation, its 'poetry under prosaic conditions' includes ironic and sympathetic analysis, moments of vision, poetic prose, probing and comic free indirect style and flexible dialogue. Its feminist indirection does not show a heroine who enjoys creative success like George Eliot's, but an ordinary woman's life in the fortunes of careerless Dorothea Ladislaw, ancestress of Anna Karenina, Fontane's Effie Briest, DH Lawrence's Ursula Brangwen and Lady Chatterley, and perhaps inspired by the early frustrations and public success of the workhouse reformer Jane Senior. A Finale tidies up destinies but is essentially an open ending, leaving some questions unanswered and dissolving fiction into real life.

1874   *The Legend of Jubal and Other Poems:* Joseph Langford, Blackwoods' London manager, wrote perceptively of 'Lisa Loved the King' that it 'is carefully written … but … reads to me more like one of Leigh Hunt's imitations of Dryden than Dryden himself.' (*Letters* 5, 23n). This is a shrewd response to her artificial style and unspontaneous use of metre and rhyme, which could be extended to 'Jubal', and 'Armgart', and other poems which discuss imagination, poetry, women and politics but too baldly, and less effectively than her light unpretentious 'College Breakfast Party'.

1875   June: Bertie Lewes dies in Natal, leaving a wife Eliza, and two young children, one of whom he never saw. Lewes – and eventually GE – take financial responsibility for them.

1876   February–October: *Daniel Deronda:* eight-part publication.

December: publication in three volumes, her most experimental, political and criticized novel. Deronda is a Jew who discovers his race and vocation, a man of complex imagination, psychic and political needs, Gwendolen Harleth, the heroine, an original study in mind and feeling. Their relation, structural and emotional, inner action and unspoken speech are new for GE and the English novel. The ending is morally clear but 'chipped off' like the Berenice series painted by Meyrick. The love-stories of Klesmer and Catherine Arrowpoint and Grandcourt and Lydia Glasher are skilful compressions. The structural turns and retrospect are ironic, the reader knowing but startled as Gwendolen's enclosed ego is abruptly opened to world politics. There are defects of over-idealized and defensive stereotyping in Daniel and perhaps the poet-scholar Mordecai, almost turning the novel into the *Tendenzroman* GE disliked, but amusing, often muted, satire of the Church, the sexual double standard, the marriage market, English politics and xenophobia. The novel is welcomed by Jews but some Victorian readers, like FR Leavis much later, dislike the Jewish parts, sometimes for a mixture of aesthetic and political reasons. GE's Zionism is tentative but perhaps inevitably blinkered and in our time has been much debated and criticized. The Leweses buy 'The Heights', Witley, Surrey, as a summer retreat.

1878   30 November: Lewes dies. GE works on his *Problems of Life and Mind*; sets up memorial studentship in Cambridge.

1879   *Impressions of Theophrastus Such:* Lewes corrected the proof before his last illness, but on his death GE postponed publication. A return to the semi-fictional form of her *Coventry Herald* sketches, it has been seen both as an experimental novel and fatigued retreat from fiction. It is an interesting fictionalized memoir with clever abstract Theophrastean 'characters' but is more a series of essays or 'impressions' than dynamic and fully particular narrative. Like her verse, it discusses ideas of race, nation, art and imagination. In February she seeks advice from Cross, a family friend she and Lewes called 'Nephew' and a financier who handled their investments. They read Dante and their consoling friendship becomes love.

1880   6 May: GE and Cross marry in St George's Church, Hanover Square. Isaac writes to congratulate her and she replies affectionately. The couple travel to France and Italy where Cross is surprised by her energy. In Venice he breaks down and gossip reports that he jumped into the Grand Canal. He gets medical treatment and he and Marian are escorted part of the way home by his brother.

July–December: he recovers, staying in Witley while planning a move to 4 Cheyne Walk (on 3 December); GE catches cold, suffers from her chronic renal illness, and dies on 22 December. She is buried with Lewes – and their letters to each other – in Highgate cemetery, London.

Chapter One
Scenes of Family Life

...what has it pleased the Almighty to make families for? (*Middlemarch*, 12)

Mary Anne Evans was born in Arbury Farm (also called South Farm), Warwickshire, on 22 November 1819. In March 1820, when she was four months old, the family moved to Griff House just outside Nuneaton. Her father was Robert Evans, who began as a carpenter like his father and brother but became land agent for the Newdigate estates. He was locally famed for strength, integrity and creativity in building, surveying, agriculture, mining, management, forestry and road-building. He was born in Derbyshire, just over the border from Staffordshire, and was agent for Francis Parker. He moved to Warwickshire with Parker when he inherited his uncle Sir Charles Newdigate's estate and took his name. By marriage to Harriott Poynton, Robert Evans had two children, Robert and Frances (or Fanny), born 1773 and 1805 respectively, then five children by a second marriage to Christiana Pearson; Christiana (or Chrissey), born 1814, Isaac, born 1816, Mary Anne, and then William and Henry, born 1821, and who lived for ten days. Robert and Fanny left home early, Robert to follow his father's line and clever Fanny to keep house for him then work as a governess. At five Mary Anne went to the local dame school, then at six to Miss Lathom's boarding school near Griff, and at nine to Mrs Wallington's school in Nuneaton, where she made friends with Maria Lewis, one of the 'governesses', a strict and fervent Anglican with whom she shared pieties and intensities. At 13 she went to a Coventry school run by Baptists, the Misses Franklin, leaving at 16. She and Chrissey nursed their mother, who died from breast cancer in 1836, and kept house for their father and Isaac until Chrissey married Edward Clarke in 1837. For the last 12 years of her father's life, Mary Ann – as she and the family spelt her name – was the housekeeper, supervising servants, cooking, dairying, and feeding family, friends and workers, and his companion, talking, listening, reading aloud and – apart from a short lapse in 1841 – going to church with him.

The home and places of her childhood and youth have been fiction-alized and pastoralized. When her husband and first biographer, John Walter Cross, imagines the Evans fireside, he draws on the novels, featuring 'the little wench' at her book near her fond father, a boy at boyish play, a Mrs Poyser-like pale sharp mother and a neat Chrissey as described to Cross by his wife and Isaac. Reality was less cosy, boarding school when Mary Ann was too small to push for a place near the fire, never-outgrown night fears, and early acquaintance with pain and death. But Cross can keep close to life. He is accurate about places, drawing on stories his wife told him in the summer of 1880. Gordon Haight claims that 'she seldom saw beauty in any terrain that was unsuitable for farming. Romantic views of mountain or sea attracted her less than the meadows with long grass …' (*George Eliot: A Life*, 3–4, and *Letters* 1, xlvii). He is himself taking a romantic view of her feeling for the Midlands landscape, but Cross says the 'country about Griff' was not 'exhilarating':

> There are neither hills nor vales – no rivers, lakes, or sea – nothing but a monotonous succession of green fields and hedgerows, with some fine trees. The only water to be seen is the 'brown canal'. The effect of such a landscape on an ordinary observer is not inspiring … (Cross 1, 7)

The 'brown canal' is from the sixth sonnet in 'Brother and Sister', and echoes the 'brown pond' where a cygnet swims in the Prelude to *Middlemarch*. 'Brown' is often drab: Mary Garth wryly sees her reflection as a 'brown patch' and the Vincys' governess Miss Morgan is 'brown, dull, and resigned' (*Middlemarch*, 12, 16). The motto for Chapter 57 of the novel stresses an unromantic home scene: Scott's grand landscape in *Waverley* makes 'the little world their childhood knew / Large with a land of mountain, lake, and scaur'. As a 'town mouse' in Griff, Mary Ann envies 'the glory of form and colour' enjoyed by Martha Jackson, country mouse and 'Rusticus', apologizes if she seems to value her friend 'for the sake of the landscape' and invents a florid medley of all seasons (*Letters* 1, 85–6). She declines Maria Lewis's invitation to Brighton because she likes nature wild – 'Give me a cliff that no tools have violated from whence to view the great deep, not a crowded splendid pier' (*Letters* 1, 51) – but later envies her a grander sight – 'I think indeed that both my heart and my limbs would leap to behold "the great and wide sea" that old Ocean on which man can leave no trace …' (*Letters* 1, 101). She admired sublime scenery and did not romanticize her home scene, though she could be nostalgic. She told Cross about a life 'very monotonous, very difficult, very discouraging' for 'a young girl, with a full passionate nature and hungry intellect, shut up in a farmhouse' (Cross 1, 34). He repeats her story of ordinary scenes populated by ordinary people, a poor industrial habitat of mines, canals, drink and dirt, and cleverly contrasts George Eliot's transformative art with 'ordinary' observation, to suggest that a narrow field trained her vision:

> … this life, though full of interests of its own, and the source from whence the future novelist drew the most powerful and the most touching of her creations, was, as a matter of fact, very monotonous, very difficult, very discouraging … No doubt, the very monotony of her life at Griff, and the narrow field it presented for observation of society, added immeasurably to the intensity of a naturally keen mental vision, concentrating into a focus what might perhaps have become dissipated in more liberal surroundings. (Cross 1, 34–5)

Haight makes Mary Ann's visits to Astley Castle or Arbury Hall sound cosy: she is 'left prattling with the servants in the kitchen … or in the housekeeper's room' (Haight 4) and 'invited … to borrow freely any books she liked from the great library' by 'Kind Mrs Charles Newdegate, mistress of Arbury Hall …' (Haight 24) but the protégée wrote about her library privilege more coolly. The lady approved her projected Chart of Ecclesiastical History: 'Mrs Newdegate is very anxious that I should do thus and she permits me to visit her library when I please in search of any books that may assist me' (*Letters* 1, 40–1). Cross is more alive to English social difference than Haight and repeats what his wife told him, that contacts with the gentry through her father caused an 'accentuated … difference[s] which had a profound significance for such a sensitive and such an intellectually commanding character, and which left their mark on it', and relates Esther Lyon's susceptible touchiness about luxury refinement to George Eliot's early class-consciousness, no doubt because she did too (Cross 1, 36).

She did not like being 'shut up in a farmhouse' but cherished the home scene when she had to leave. When Isaac decided to marry Sarah Rawlins in 1841, where would everyone live? Would they all live in Griff? Would father and daughter move? Would Robert stay and Mary Ann go to Chrissey in Meriden, by then married to Edward Clarke, a doctor? As Robert wavered and took his time to move to Bird Grove in Foleshill, just outside Coventry, Mary Ann realized her need for continuity – of people, time and place, and the painful need felt by Maggie as she sees empty space where the old bookcase was: 'the end of our lives will have nothing in it like the beginning!'(*Mill* 3, 6). In March 1841, three months before Isaac married, Mary Ann told Martha Jackson 'we are undergoing one the chief among the minor disagreeables of life – that of moving. To me it is a deeply painful incident – it is like dying to one stage of existence …' (*Letters* 1, 86). She hopes to see Maria Lewis in 'scenes which now I am called on to leave them, I find to have *grown in* to my affections' (*Letters* 1, 71). After the move she is relieved her father is settling down so well in retirement but she is homesick, telling Martha in the stiff wordy style she affected at the time, about a 'considerable disturbance of the usual flow of thought and feeling on being severed from the objects so long accustomed to call it forth' (*Letters* 1, 93).

The end of the year brought a more painful break. On 2 November, she announced to Maria Lewis a visit to the Brays, whom she had met briefly in May through her neighbour Mrs Pears, Charles Bray's sister: 'I am going I hope today to effect a breach in the thick wall of indifference behind which the denizens of Coventry seem inclined to entrench themselves' (*Letters* 1, 120). Eleven days later: 'Think – is there any *conceivable* alteration in me that would prevent your coming to me at Christmas?'(*Letters* 1, 121). She was no longer a Christian. She had always read and re-read the Bible, then theology, philosophy and geology, and had recently turned to the higher criticism of the Gospels in Charles Hennell's *Inquiry into*

Christianity (1838). Urged to undertake the study by his sister Cara, a Unitarian whose husband Charles Bray had questioned her faith as soon as they got married, Hennell concluded that the Scriptures were a mixture of fantasy, mythology and history, Christ a human being and morality not dependent on belief in the supernatural. Brought up in the Church of England, Mary Ann came close to Dissent through her Methodist uncle Samuel and his preacher-wife Elizabeth, and her Baptist teachers, the Misses Franklin. She had been encouraged in her austere evangelicalism by Maria Lewis, her kindred spirit until this radical conversion to a kind of deism which became agnosticism.

She probably read Hennell before she made friends with the Brays and Cara's sister Sara Hennell, all progressive in religion and politics. Hennell's tolerant analytic criticism instructed her but she and the Brays denied that their friendship changed her beliefs and in *Phases of Opinion and Experience During a Long Life* (1884), Bray said she may have been influenced by his emphasis on social law in *The Philosophy of Necessity* and his fundamental resignation to the pain of life. The Brays encouraged her confidence and openness, and formed her future in many ways, introducing her to radical thinkers like Emerson, Froude, Robert Owen and Herbert Spencer, and phrenologists, mesmerists or spiritualists like Harriet Martineau and George Combe, in some respects cranks, like Bray, but serious reformers. (Combe was much taken with her, and introduced her to his friends though later questioned her sanity when she went off with Lewes, appalled that she had been his house-guest.) She began writing for *The Coventry Herald and Observer* when Bray bought it, and met Hennell, Dr Robert Brabant and his daughter Rufa, who was to marry Hennell and whose translation of David Friedrich Strauss's *Das Leben Jesu* Mary Ann took over in 1843.

At the beginning of 1842 her literary life lay ahead. Her immediate problems were at home. Maria Lewis arrived to spend Christmas with the family, left to see a school in Nuneaton where she was going to work, and returned for the New Year drama. On 2 and 9 January, Mary Ann refused to go to church. Her father and friend went without her, as Robert records briefly in his diary. He lost no time. Strict Tory and Anglican, he threatened to break up the household and move to a cottage he had in Packington, offering his daughter the prospect of living on her own and earning her living, probably as a governess. Attempts were made to persuade and re-convert her, but she was more instructed than the learned pious instructors, as they ruefully admitted – they included a professor of theology and a Baptist minister.

On 28 February, she wrote her father a remarkable letter of justi-fication – rational, analytic, intense and uncompromising. She was desperate: 'As all my efforts in conversation have hitherto failed in making you aware of the real nature of my sentiments, I am induced to see if I can express myself more clearly on paper ...' (*Letters* 1, 128). She had not become a Unitarian, she admired much – not all – of Christ's moral teaching but found the Gospels a mixture of history and fiction and their doctrine 'dishonourable to God and most pernicious'. Her opinion was supported by some of the best minds in Christendom, like Benjamin Franklin, and she was not willing to join in hypocritical worship even for her father's sake. Isaac had told her that her father kept up an 'establishment' to give 'her a centre in society' so she offered to give up to his other children 'any provision' made for her. She thanked him for tenderness and kindness, assured him of her love, and added a martyr's touch – she had 'no one to speak' for her, and would do her 'duty'. She invoked 'the laws' of a 'Creator' but was no longer a Christian (*Letters* 1, 128–30).

Not surprisingly, Robert did not answer but went on with plans to move. She went back to Griff, now supported by Isaac, who had been summoned to 'school' her but who concluded she was badly treated, and by his wife Sarah who pointed out the stupidity of threatening a conscientious child with worldly sanctions. Mary Ann was restless at having no 'home' and steeled herself to ostracism, solitude and struggle. Robert listened, dithered and, in the end, cancelled his arrangements to move and Mary Ann went to church again in mid-May. She kept up her attendance in her own way: 'I generally manage to sink some little well at church, by dint of making myself deaf and looking up at the roof and arches' (*Letters* 1, 229). After they married, she told Cross 'although she did not think she had been to blame, few things had occasioned her more regret than this temporary collision with her father, which might, she thought, have been avoided by a little management' (Cross 1,

113). She had repented almost at once, writing in March 1842 to kind Mrs Pears who deplored heterodoxy but was a 'guardian angel': 'on a retrospection of the past month, I regret nothing so much as my own impetuosity both of feeling and judging' (*Letters* 1, 134). In October 1843 she wrote to Sara in a new fluent imagistic style:

> The first impulse of a young and ingenuous mind is to withhold the slightest sanction from all that contains even a mixture of supposed error. When the soul is just liberated from the wretched giant's bed of dogmas on which it has been racked and stretched ever since it began to think there is a feeling of exultation and strong hope. We think we shall run well when we have the full use of our limbs and the bracing air of independence, and we believe that we shall soon obtain something positive which will not only more than compensate to us for what we have renounced, but will be so well worth offering to others, that we may venture to proselyte … But a year or two of reflection … must … effect a change. Speculative truth begins to appear but a shadow of individual minds, agreement between intellects seems unattainable, and we turn to the *truth of feeling* as the only universal bond of union. We find that the intellectual errors which we once fancied were a mere incrustation have grown into the living body … (*Letters* 1, 162)

She was to base her novels on a secular morality and an understanding tolerance for religious faith. Her insistence on human love and duty is inseparable from her agnosticism, her emphasis in life and art grounded in Feuerbach's belief that Christianity is a supernaturalizing of natural affections, but it was personally proved in her bondings and continuities.

The next quarrel was more quickly and easily made up. It was about her friendship with the Brays and Sara Hennell. Isaac was afraid that their free spirits and liberal ideas would spoil her chances of a suitable match and encourage dangerous acquaintance. The widening cultural divide between Mary Ann (now often 'Pollian') and the family is clear in his ignorant disapproval of the earnest Rosehill circle. (Bray's sexual life was unconventional but discreet.) In the end Robert admitted that he had no real objection to the new friends and blamed Isaac. He probably saw the advantage of having a single daughter dutiful in domesticity if not in doctrine.

Their life together was marked by her devotion, and relieved by holidays with the Brays and her writing. She had written undistinguished religious poems and now turned to articles for the *Coventry Herald* and her translation of Strauss's *Das Leben Jesu*, published in 1846. But Robert grew increasingly dependent and ill, until his death in 1849.

Deeply depressed, she left England after the funeral to travel with the Brays in France, Italy and Switzerland then stay in Geneva for the winter and early spring of 1850. When she came back she visited her family, felt unwanted and excluded, and made a temporary home with the Brays in Rosehill, where she had a room she could call her own. She wrote an important review of Robert Mackay, visited London, then after a false start settled in the Chapmans' house, 142 Strand, beginning a busy but badly paid career as an editor and journalist. An unsatisfactory relationship with Herbert Spencer was followed by a friendship with George Henry Lewes, with whom she joined her lot. This caused the last family quarrel, which lasted until she married Cross in 1880.

Her choice to live with Lewes in what was technically an adulterous relationship, because he had condoned his wife's infidelity and could not divorce her, meant a final break with the past. It did not happen at once. London was a long way from Nuneaton and no news of her private life reached the family. During the first years of her new life, travelling, settling in London, taking working holidays and starting to write fiction, she corresponded with Chrissey, Isaac, Sarah and Fanny; visited Chrissey, and saw the family when Chrissey's husband died in December 1852, and again at Christmas 1853. During this time she used Chapman's address. Not until the first two *Scenes of Clerical Life* were published and she was finishing 'Janet's Repentance' did she decide to tell – or not tell – her family about Lewes.

Her letters breaking the news to Isaac and Fanny are evasive, ambiguous and untruthful – extraordinary texts (*Letters* 2, 331–3). She uses the words 'marriage' and 'husband' in a way that made moral sense to her, but she must have known they would be read literally by her family. She signs her letter to Isaac: 'Your affectionate sister, Marian Lewes', the name she used defiantly until after Lewes's death when she acquired it by deed-poll to get at her own money. She picks her words carefully, starting with literal but ambiguous truths, then lying: 'You will be surprized I dare say, but I hope not sorry, to learn that I have changed my name, and have someone to take care of me in the world … My husband has been known to me for several years.' She asks Isaac to pay the trust income from her father's estate to Lewes's bank account. Writing herself into the rhetoric of deceit, she re-tells her story to Fanny mentioning 'husband' twice and 'marriage' once: 'marriage is a very sober and serious thing when people are as old as we are …' Haight seems right to surmise that Fanny replied because she took the letter at face-value, though Ashton thinks it was because she was more tolerant than Isaac. The delighted letter George Eliot wrote back to her with 'a thousand thanks' has ironically touching references to Mr Lewes and 'Friends of ours' (*Letters* 2, 336). After hearing from Fanny, Mary Ann wrote to Chrissey, to whom she had postponed writing, but by then Isaac had instructed the family solicitor Holbeche to tell 'Mrs Lewes' he was hurt because she had not communicated her 'intention and prospects', and ask when and where the marriage took place (*Letters* 2, 346). She replied at once that the marriage was not legal but a sacred bond. She wrote to Chapman and Sara Hennell that she had informed her family that she was married, and told Sara she did not think Chrissey would give up writing to her. However, like Isaac and Fanny, she did until she was dying.

It is hard to see what Mary Ann expected. Perhaps she was playing for time by breaking the news in instalments, but her letters are even more unrealistic than the one to her father about her loss of faith; and the second one to Isaac is very self-righteous, considering her position and her equivocation. Even the faithful and liberal Cara and Sara were doubtful about her commitment to Lewes and one letter to Cara makes it plain, in spite of defensive irony, that she expected only an 'unworldly, unsuperstitious person who is sufficiently acquainted with the realities' *not* to find her 'relation to Mr Lewes immoral' (*Letters* 2, 214). Radicals like George Combe and Joseph Parkes, who had sought her company, were astounded, and too attached to the realities of a double standard not to be morally outraged. She could not have expected her provincial family not to find the 'relation' immoral, and it is less surprising that they did, and cut her off, than that she was so unapologetic and uncomprehending. She was a brilliant woman 'acquainted with the realities' from social experience and sociological knowledge, but out of control. Her very lack of common sense and social sensibility speak for her pride, turmoil and raw vulnerability. She used the strong metaphor 'dying to the past' when she left Griff for Foleshill, and the religious quarrel was an agonizing crisis, but these problems had been solved. The new one was not, and she lost what was intensely and peculiarly important to her, her sense of continuity in time, place and feeling. Its loss haunted her memory and helped to shape her art.

How do home and family and loss get into the fiction? Cara Bray said that Fanny Houghton, who had much in common with Mary Ann, also 'regarded the miraculous part of Christianity as purely mythical'. She read Hennell and Strauss, but according to Cara 'had no idea of making herself singular and obnoxious by an avowal of her opinions, and thinks MA very foolish not to keep her notions snugly to herself' (*Letters* 1, 157). On 'the tip-toe of expectation' about *Felix Holt* she wrote to Isaac: 'It is too much to hope that no member of her own family will figure in it' (Haight 394). As far as we know, she never gets into the novels – unless her second name 'Lucy' is pointedly given to Lucy Deane. (Gwendolen Harleth's mother and a half-sister are called Fanny, but without any likely allusion to Fanny Houghton.) But when she read the long comic scene in which Mrs Gregg fails to resist Bob Jakin's 'cheap spots and sprigs', and hard-to-get salesmanship (*Mill*, 5, 2), she may have been reminded of Mary Ann's letters from London in 1851: one asks her to choose a muslin, 'The quality of the spotted one is best, but the effect is chintzy … The one with the reddish flowers would have a better effect but the quality is not so good', and another thanks her, 'The muslin is beautiful in quality and pattern' (*Letters* 1, 362). Fanny kept the letters, and we wonder what she thought.

There may be a trace of her brother Robert, George Eliot's half-brother, in the *Mill on the Floss*. Like his father and Isaac he was a land agent and left home at 14. He spent the last night of his father's life at Bird Grove with him and Mary Ann. After his son Robert wrote to her about his death in 1864, she wrote to her sister-in-law: 'I think there can hardly be one whose memory of the husband you have lost stretches so far back as mine. For in all the years I have lived

I remember nothing that is much earlier than the knowledge that I had a brother Robert, and I have always thought of him, throughout the years we have been separated, as one whose heart had on every opportunity shown its ready kindness towards me' (*Letters* 4, 134). Jane Evans wrote to say that 'the last Book he looked at' was *Adam Bede*, and he had asked her to read 'Dinah's Prayer and Sermon' just before he died (*Letters* 8, 316). He was the furthest removed from her in age and we have no letters between them, but her grateful memory sounds like Maggie's, 'you know, the first thing I ever remember in my life is standing with Tom by the side of the Floss, while he held my hand: everything before that is dark to me' (*Mill*, 5, I). We think mostly of resemblances between Tom and Isaac, and the novel came four years before the letter, so it may have shaped her tribute to Robert, but whichever came first, the words and tone remind us that Maggie had one brother but Mary Ann was a sister to two.

Four, if we count the twins. George Eliot surely remembered their brief lives in the novel which has fewest traces of her lived life, in one of the moments when she makes us look at character with surprise and deepened insight. Monna Brigida says to her cousin Romola: 'For you have never had a baby, and I had twins, only they died as soon as they were born' (70).

And George Eliot was little sister to two sisters. There is an isolated sisterly detail in 'Mr Gilfil's Love Story', when Tina is 'soothed' by 'the air of sisterly equality' in Gilfil's sister Mrs Heron after her breakdown (20). George Eliot claimed 'a very special feeling … stronger than any third person would think likely' for her elder sister Chrissey (Cross 1, 31). When she was placating friends after going to Germany with Lewes, she told Sara that she, Cara and her 'own sister' were 'the three women who are tied to my heart by a cord which can never be broken and which really *pulls* me continually' (*Letters* 2, 182). Chrissey was the one with whom she had least in common: Cross says the relation between them was like that of Dorothea and Celia, 'no intellectual affinity, but a strong family affection' (Cross 1, 31), and Chrissey was constantly in George Eliot's mind as she created Celia in *Middlemarch*. She obviously recalled Chrissey's marriage to a poor provincial doctor, though as unlike Lydgate as Rosamond is unlike Chrissey. Mary

Ann cared for Chrissey's children, and Chrissey was the sibling who wrote after the breach, in self-reproach as she lay dying. George Eliot told Cara, 'I have just had a letter from my Sister Chrissey – ill in bed – consumptive – regretting that she ever ceased to write to me. It has ploughed up my heart' (*Letters* 3, 23). Chrissey is sometimes linked with Lucy Deane through the blonde hair, neat clothes and tidy habits which George Eliot described to Cross and which make the contrast between the girls in *The Mill*, but grown-up Lucy has mind, talents and wit which seem more like Fanny's than Chrissey's, though we don't know if she is like either.

Chrissey's style brightens a sentence about doctrine and may get into *Middlemarch*: 'I shall soon hate heretics as vehemently as any papist can desire, for both their wide uniformity and their narrow differences are as Chrissey would say, *pestering*' (*Letters* 1, 46). The lexically learned stylist enjoying the simple force of her sister's words made Dorothea reject Celia's 'fond' and 'fad' but come to say 'fond' herself. George Eliot listened to the way people spoke and the words they used.

She did not say Chrissey was in her mind when she wrote 'Amos Barton' and there is no character like Chrissey in the story but its pity and sympathy remind us of her short unhappy life. Amos's sad fortunes are his wife's, too. Haight says: 'Milly's six children, so appealingly depicted, remind us at once of Chrissey's six … to whom their Aunt Polly was tenderly devoted' (Haight 2, 2). He leaves out a seventh child, not appealingly depicted but very important: Milly has six children, the last an infant; she is pregnant and miscarries, is almost at once pregnant again, loses the seventh child and dies. Chrissey married Edward Clarke when she was 23, and had nine children, five dying in childhood. When Edward died in 1852 she was 38, with almost no money and six young children, the youngest a baby, the oldest 15. Marian went to her at once, dropping her editorial work for Chapman, desperate to help. She contemplated going to Australia with Chrissey and the children, and coming back after seeing them settled. Chrissey died in 1859, three years after George Eliot began *Scenes of Clerical Life* in September 1856, but she was anxious about Chrissey's poverty, children and health long before her death. She wrote to Maria Lewis, who knew Chrissey well, 'My dear Sister is rather an object of solicitude on many accounts – the troubles of married life seem more conspicuously the ordinance of God, in the case of one so meek and passive ...' (*Letters* 1, 117). Her letters carefully and regularly report Chrissey's confinements, health, ill health, and the illnesses of children she loved, looked after when their mother was confined, and distracted with play when their father died. After his death she is torn by responsibility, telling Cara that she could not live with Chrissey 'in that hideous neighbourhood amongst ignorant bigots' and feels guilty because she is enjoying London life (*Letters* 2, 97). She is anguished by distance, worried about Isaac's attitude, deeply sympathetic as Chrissey's heart is 'wrung' by the prospect of her children going to 'an orphan asylum' and, later, when her 'naughty' son Robert is drowned at sea. While Marian and George are in Scilly during April and May 1857, the *Journals* note family bulletins about Chrissey: 'Since we came here Chrissey has lost her pretty little Fanny, and I am still waiting anxiously for news of Katy and herself – both ill of fever when I last heard'; on 8 April: 'A letter from my brother ... tells me that Chrissey and her Katy are better, but not yet out of danger'; on 11 and 12 April she records that there is no news; on 18 April a letter from Sarah says: 'Chrissey is still very ill, and Katie too'; on 22 April: 'Letter from my Brother saying Chrissey is worse. I am deeply depressed and feeling the ills of life more than the blessings'; on 2 May: 'Received letters saying Chrissey is out of danger and Katie doing well' (*Journals* 68). Chrissey's eldest daughter Emily wrote to her aunt about her mother's illness and death, and George Eliot kept in touch with her and the younger Katie, who died in 1860, visited them at school, had Emily to visit, and found in her a loyal blood-relation – she sent her condolences on Lewes's death and congratulations on her marriage.

Not Chrissey's character, but pity for her as child-bearing wife, mother, poor man's spouse and frail widow, went into the first story then more indirectly into the two that followed[1]. Of course, the novelist was not only an observer. The usual woman's lot was one she must at times have dreaded or hoped for herself, though when she started to write fiction she was with Lewes and had decided to have no children. Of course, Chrissey was not the only woman George Eliot observed. Although she is unlike Jane Austen in putting explicit gender sympathy into novels as well as letters, George

Eliot is like Austen in being a childless novelist alive to the pains of women – successive pregnancies, miscarriages, painful labour, illness and early deaths. Her father's first wife died with her third child after childbirth; her own mother never recovered after the death of the twins. She saw suffering at home and she saw the sufferings of the poor, some of their hovels close to Griff, their wants pitied as she organized clothing clubs and did her share of cottage visiting. But Chrissey was the suffering woman closest to her. She wrote to Fanny from Geneva in October 1849: 'Dear Chrissy also has found time and strength to write to me – very precious her letter was, though I wept over it. "Deep abiding grief must be mine" she says and I know well it must be. The mystery of trial! It falls with such avalanche-weight on the head of the meek and patient' (*Letters* 8, 20).

Meek Milly's all-too-common pains are solicitously presented by the 'male' narrator and charitable Mrs Hackit, like Mrs Poyser often said to resemble the second Mrs Evans. Mrs Hackit's compassion may recall stories Mary Ann's mother told her daughters about poor women. The theme of women is not announced in the series-title but it is developed in repetition and accretion, more subtly than the clerical life, which is a social subject not a moral category. The emphasis on suffering women begins when Mrs Hackit addresses the company at Cross Farm, who are gossiping rather spitefully by Mrs Patten's 'bright fire' on a 'freezing' February evening, about Amos Barton and his plans to rebuild Shepperton church: '*I* like Mr Barton. I think he's a good sort o'man for all he's not overburthen'd i' th'upper story; and his wife's as nice a lady-like woman as I'd wish to see. How nice she keeps her children! and little enough money to do't with; and a delicate creatur' – six children, and another a'coming' (1). No loose talker, Mrs Hackit is led to Milly by her good nature's inclination to 'contradict the dominant tone of the conversation' and speak up for Amos. The only men present are Mr Hackit and the doctor so she can mention pregnancy without offence. Later on, the male narrator can't say 'miscarriage' but puts it decorously: 'It was a sad thing, too, that when the last snow had melted, when the purple and yellow crocuses were coming up in the garden, and the old church was already half pulled down, Milly had an illness which made her lips look pale ...' (5). George Eliot writes decorously about miscarriage to Maria Lewis, 'our dear Chrissey is in a very weak state from a kind of affliction second only to a confinement' (*Letters* 1, 43). Milly is ordered rest and (iron-rich) port-wine, e.g. and this with two couples of fowls, are promptly supplied by kind Mrs Hackit, the wise woman of the story. After weeks pass and Milly 'was almost as active as ever, though watchful eyes might have seen that activity was not easy to her', Mrs Hackit may confide to Mr Hackit: 'That poor thing's dreadful weak an' dilicate; she won't stan' havin' many more children' (5). George Eliot observes who is talking to whom, about what, how, where and when. She may draw, or draw on, her mother, the source of her acquaintance with women's pains, as Mrs Hackit presides with a woman's authority over the scenes of women's lives.

Milly dies of pregnancies, miscarriage, fatigue, malnutrition, anaemia, perhaps puerperal fever. Mary Ann observed and George Eliot recorded not only the relation between malnutrition and death in childbirth which is still a subject of clinical research, but also other pains of women's life. Patty Barton is an anxious child applauded by the moral male narrator but if we attend not to the teller but the tale, she is observed as a woman worn out by womanly exertion: 'She was about thirty, but there were some premature lines round her mouth and eyes ...' Mary Ann Evans had been the self-sacrificing daughter devoting days and nights to her father, putting him first, sleeping on a sofa in his room, pitied by friends as she looked gradually more worn or showed pathetic pleasure when he was unusually kind. She was a devoted and exhausted daughter 'about thirty' when he died. Caterina Gilfil is said to have weak lungs, is weakened by shock, exposure and fatigue, then dies in or after childbirth, with echoes of 'Little blossom' Dora in *David Copperfield*: 'the delicate plant had been too deeply bruised, and in the struggle to put forth a blossom it died' (21). Janet Dempster is beaten up by her husband and takes to drink – it is suggested – because she is a childless wife.

George Eliot wrote about ordinary clergymen, so about their ordinary wives and daughters, too. The impersonation of a male narrator influenced her delicate treatment of women's problems. Her own position as an unmarried woman living with a married man who had children by his wife and step-children fathered by his wife's lover, made the discussion of sex, childbirth and marriage problematic. In none of her other books is the common marriage-tragedy so prominent, and the subject heading of clergymen reticently covered it to suit her personal reserve and her narrative stance. If we look not for portraits but feelings, her experience of family pain, poverty and loss, her sympathy for Chrissey's troubles and her concern for Chrissey's future are strongly and unsentimentally present. Imagining the ordinary woman in a compassionate story about ordinary men meant subduing and understating feminist critique, but it is everywhere implicit.

The feelings of Amos and Gilfil are not strongly dramatized, but there is the striking scene where Amos throws himself on Milly's new grave to revive quick-fading grief – George Eliot was experienced in bereavement. The sufferings of women are more individualized and interiorized. They are important victims in the lives of men. Amos and Gilfil, well-meaning ordinary men, are responsible for the deaths of their much loved wives, and brutalized drunken Dempster nearly kills Janet. Perhaps George Eliot herself only became aware of woman's suffering as a theme when the tales unfolded, perhaps not until 'Janet's Repentance'. Unlike the first scenes, it claims a woman's name for title and lets a woman's life dominate. Its clerical life largely depends on a narrative retrospect in the 18th-century manner, Tryan's confession of seduction and conversion, and the main story is about a bad marriage, a battered wife, alcoholism and death from *delirium tremens*.

Janet is allowed to survive without anyone to lean on – several people lean on her. George Eliot quietly shows that she and Tryan, the third clerical hero, would have joined their lives if he had not died. He is brought into relation with Janet in a love story with sentimental touches, but its religiosity is relieved by an ordinary attachment which makes his celibacy and her widowhood less high-toned and saintly. Like Milly and Tina, Janet is physically presented, a passionate, childless woman who adopts a child.

Haight and others have suggested that Mary Ann did not feel much for her mother or her mother for her, but we do not know what either felt for the other. Writing to Maria Lewis George Eliot speaks of her 'dear mother' in pain and near death. She may be recalling her mother – or father – distanced or troubled by illness in a letter to Sara Hennell about 'the sorrows of older persons which children see but cannot understand' (*Letters* 1, 173) and in a later passage in *Felix Holt*: 'And many of us know how, even in our childhood, some blank discontented face on the background of our home has marred our summer mornings. Why was it … there was somebody who found it hard to smile?' (49). Her remark that her father was 'the one deep strong love' of her life naturally responds to their shared life as it was ending, and it need not put down mother-love. After the other children left, Robert and Mary Ann moved house, furnished, read, ate and drank together, depending on each other as housemates bonded by habit, affection, irritation, disagreement, truce and reconciliation. Her life with her mother was brief and less exclusive.

There are lactation images, 'that prejudice in favour of milk with which we blindly begin', in *Daniel Deronda* (3) and the image of the world 'as an udder to feed our supreme selves' in *Middlemarch* (21) but the first is too ironic and the second too grotesquely abstract for a human breast-memory. But there are some remarkable portrayals of mother-love, a feeling George Eliot only experienced as a daughter. She imagines Mrs Meyrick, Scotch–French mother of four in *Daniel Deronda* who lives in what was unfashionable Chelsea. Like childless George Eliot, she is affectionately called 'little mother'. She says: 'A mother's love … is like a tree that has got all the wood in it, from the very first it made'; other love has 'roots that can be pulled up. Mother's love begins deeper down' (*Daniel Deronda*, 32). In a condolence letter to Sara Hennell, George Eliot wrote sadly and tenderly about losing a mother and her own mother. In 'Self and Life' a strong memory or wish produces a good line, 'I was thy warmth upon thy mother's knee.' There is a moving moment when Mordecai has been angry with the child Jacob and comforts him by pressing his head 'against his breast' 'with a maternal action' (*Daniel Deronda*, 38). The deprived Latimer in *The Lifted Veil* remembers his mother's 'caress as she held me on her knee', and his relaxation on 'wide blue' lake water suggests comfort, security, perhaps pre-birth fluidity, lack of boundary, the oceanic feeling[2]. Mrs Tulliver is sometimes cited as a bad mother, but though she favours her 'boy' (according to Cross, like Mrs Evans) she faithfully supports her daughter at the end. Oscar Browning connects Christiana Evans with Mrs Hackit and Mrs Poyser, and saw 'Poyser' as a conflation of 'Poynton' and 'Pearson'. Mrs Hackit is motherly but not presented as a mother, to leave space for her to cherish the Barton children, and perhaps disguise the model. Mrs Poyser spoils her youngest child and feels for the young. The 'Brother and Sister' sonnets are too free with diminutives and sweetness, but the third particularizes maternal love rather well, quietly observing a mother's tactful care, in touch and gaze which want to protect but must 'lessen' and reluctantly let go:

> Our mother bade us keep the trodden ways,
> Stroked down my tippet, set my brother's frill;
> Then with the benediction of her gaze
> Clung to us lessening, and pursued us still
>
> Across the homestead to the rookery elms …

George Eliot's relationship with her father was long-lasting, troubled and dynamic, unlike life with her mother. Her bonding to him was the first family tie she reflected on as an adult, seeing and needing to see it as a whole after his death. Recognizing its strength, she said she was afraid that without him she might become 'earthly sensual and devilish for want of that purifying restraining influence' (*Letters* 1, 284). This is the first striking mention of the demonic streak, found in Caterina, Maggie and Gwendolen.

Adam Bede was based on stories her father told about his early life. Her hero was energized by her filial pride in his skill and lasting work, which she emphasized when Bray got the facts wrong and reported that he had raised himself from artisan to farmer. Adam's hardness, but not his self-reproach, may well derive from Robert – he was hard on her in the religious quarrel and his portrait shows a stern humourless mouth. The novelist makes a pseudo-autobiographical digression in which the narrator talks to Adam Bede in old age, superficially interrupting the story but joining drama and omniscient commentary at a deep level. The narrator takes the position of friendly listener: 'But I gathered from Adam Bede, to whom I talked of these matters in his old age, that few clergymen could be less successful in winning the hearts of their parishioners than Mr Ryde' and quotes Adam's direct speech about religion 'being something else besides notions' ('In Which The Story Pauses A Little', 17). Mary Ann is unlikely to have discussed 'these matters' with her father in his old age, since they concern a touchy subject. They may have talked about doctrine before they were estranged by it, perhaps discussing Samuel Evans's Methodism, and they may have talked about clergymen even later. But when character and narrator talk about religion being a matter of 'feelings not notions', and about feelings as bonds of affection and fellowship, they sound more like Feuerbach and George Eliot than Robert Evans.

The idea about notions and feelings is repeated with a difference at the beginning of Adam's third long speech, in what is either a mistake in writing, the representation of repetitive old age, Adam's emphasis or a realistic variant in reminiscence. He first says: 'I've seen pretty clear, ever since I was a young un, as religion's something else besides notions' and repeats two pages later: 'But I've seen pretty clear ever since I was a young un, as religion's something else besides doctrines and notions.' This is followed by a definition of doctrine and a comment on the value of knowing names, authorial in interest[3] but dramatized in Adam's dialect and intelligence, and may use something her father may have said about tools: 'I look at it as if the doctrines was like finding a name for your feelings, so as you can talk of 'em when you've never known 'em, just as a man may talk o' tools when he knows their names, though he's never so much as seen 'em' ...' (17).

An earlier, more conspicuous personal memory also involves the rhetoric of 'autobiographical' digression. In Chapter 4 Adam is working on the coffin his father neglected and hears 'a smart rap, as if with a willow wand ... at the house door, and Gyp, instead of barking, as might have been expected, gave a loud howl'. Adam investigates, finds nothing, resumes work, and the rap and howl are repeated. Between the two raps he remembers 'how often his mother had told him of just such sound coming as a sign when some one was dying'. In the morning he tells himself 'it's better to see when your perpendicular's true, than to see a ghost' but when he finds that his father has died in the night he concludes, 'This was what the omen meant, then!' The narrator admits that Adam is rational, 'yet he believed in dreams and prognostics, and to his dying day he bated his breath a little when he told the story of the stroke with the willow wand. I tell it as he told it, not attempting to reduce it to its natural elements: in our eagerness to explain impressions, we often lose our hold on the sympathy that comprehends them'(*Adam Bede*, 4). The words after 'prognostics', added in the third edition[4], merge with the first-person commentary which bridges showing and telling, and may bridge fact and fiction. Adam's superstitious streak does not appear elsewhere in the novel and is inconsistent with his secular values and lack of sympathy with Seth's spiritual life. George Eliot's attempts to reconcile 'peasant' and 'artisan' only draw attention to the probability that she is trying to assimilate memories of her father.

The interview – not developed when she wrote the first draft of Chapter 4, and a back-formation from Chapter 17 – establishes Adam as an elderly father in a narrative action in which he does not age, and extends the novel in time. It is also a sophisticated trope in which a detached narrator affects personal involvement. George Eliot knew the work of Flaubert and Thackeray, and may have got the trope from the narrator's claim to have been Charles' classmate in *Madame Bovary*, and the narrator of *Vanity Fair* turning up in Pumpernickel. These narrators flaunt an intrusion of life. Of course, the 20th century influences the 19th, as we look back from modernist breakings and floutings of realism to these transitions at such naïve to sophisticated form. But naive or sophisticated, Adam's characterization moves out of fiction to touch a real past. George Eliot breaks with realism in an artist's struggle to make art out of life. The narrative digressions are signatures of the author as daughter-donor.

Adam's inner life, developing through crises, continuities, regrets and revisions, also draws from her own life. She writes herself into Adam, as she does with Casaubon, modifying biographical elements to create an inner development close to her own, a pattern repeated with re-imagined particulars for Maggie, Romola and Dorothea. Adam's self-examination is part of the novel's analysis of imagination: Dinah, Arthur and Hetty are companion studies in imagination. George Eliot recreates Robert Evans by bringing him, as Adam, into 'new combinations': with Hetty, whose fantasy-life is restricted to the social surface of coaches, clothes and ornaments; with Arthur, whose dreams of golden squirearchy blind him and have a violent end; and with Dinah, whose creativity is implicit and explicit in her speech-energy. In dynamic comparison and contrast,

Adam's deepening vision contrasts with Hetty's pathetic small fancy and Arthur's fatal power-fantasy, while Adam and Dinah are parallel cases of creative energy trying to imagine otherness. They are all images of imaginative limit, reflecting their author but not autobiographical.

The hero of her most tender story of father-child love, *Silas Marner*, could not be more different from her own father, but the novel has a small, striking link between life and art in an endearment rarely found in the fiction of the time, 'Daddy'. George Eliot's use of this intimate address may not draw attention to itself until we put together its rare use in real life and its rare use in her fiction. There is a connection between the endearments of two daughters – possibly but not necessarily as life-source and artistic result. I find very moving the only two occasions, as far as I know, when Mary Ann Evans calls her father 'Daddy'. The first is in a letter of 1840 to Maria Lewis, when she was 21, broken off because her father wants something or is signalling bedtime: 'Tis now eight in the evening and my Daddy has laid by his papers' (*Letters* 1, 73). 'Daddy' is similarly used in a letter of 1846, when she was 27, to Sara Hennell, who replaced Maria as best friend and confidante of the day-and-night stories: 'I am sinning against my daddy, by yielding to the strong impulse I felt to write to you, for he looks at me as if he wanted me to read to him, so farewell, meine liebe' (*Letters* 1, 223–4). There are other letters in which she feels her father's eyes on her as she writes, but this one is light and playful, exclaiming: 'All the world is bathed in glory and beauty to me now', and written in the autumn of 1846, when Cara Bray told her mother that 'MA looks very brilliant', and they 'fancy she must be writing her novel' (*Letters* 1, 223n). The 'sinning against my daddy' is not too serious and, as on the earlier occasion, the affectionate word comes from intimate writing 'to the moment' – as Richardson called it – and to a dear friend about a dear father. The letter to Maria used the language of flowers, initiated by Mary Ann, 'Veronica' and the one to Sara addresses 'meine liebe'. (Cross left out the address to Sara and corrected George Eliot by capitalizing the German endearment.)

'Daddy' is used again in *Silas Marner*. It is what Eppie calls Silas, though she says 'Father' more often. She first uses 'Daddy' in a flush of happiness as they are going home from church and planning a garden, and then she uses it again in a later scene when she tells Silas that Aaron wants to marry her. Sometimes the intimate conversation is playful but when it becomes solemn she reverts to 'Father' (16). She said 'Dad-Dad' in reported infant speech, and the novel's first and observant use of 'Daddy' comes when Silas refers to himself, not as 'I' but as 'Daddy' in his naturalistic speech to the very young child. George Eliot had observed children learning by listening to their parents talking to them. The word is part of a carefully voiced socialect, and used dynamically, for happy reciprocities of fostering and fostered love.

The rare endearment links two emotionally charged filial relationships, the real blood-bond and the fictional adoption. Mary Ann and Eppie both speak in intimate domestic situations. Silas and Eppie are walking or looking at the furze bush outside the cottage as he smokes; Mary Ann is writing to her best friends who know her and her father, aware that her father is requiring her attention and fully understanding her tone – a little reluctant, a little wry, amused and loving – as she reads his silence and his look to stop writing and give him her time. She is speaking the language they shared, a word saturated in affective and social significance, a word she had used many times, for a long time.

Rosemarie Bodenheimer argues that Eppie is the first of a number of foster-children beginning in 1860 and is based on Marian Lewes's relation with her 'stepsons' – actually foster-sons (Bodenheimer, 230). But George Eliot's interest in fostering goes beyond her role as foster-mother to three adolescent boys, two of whom she seldom saw. She was close to Chrissey's children from their birth; her mother had step-children; she saw Cara Bray fostering Nelly, probably her husband's illegitimate child; and she may reflect on kin who are less than kind. And the interest starts before *Silas Marner*. In *Scenes of Clerical Life* Tina is fostered by the Cheverels, Janet has an adopted daughter, and in *Adam Bede* Hetty is gladly taken into her uncle's family and Dinah Morris brought up by a beloved aunt. Tina's parenting by a patron and patroness is not tender, though Sir Christopher is kind in his way; Janet's child and grandchildren are like Dickens's happy-ending children, born on the last page; Hetty does badly but Dinah does well. Eppie's fostering creates a bond of feeling, as Bodenheimer says, not dependent on blood-relationship. I am sure it is rooted in Mary Ann's intimacy with her father, letting us glimpse good moments in shared domesticity at Bird Grove. One 'Daddy' reinforces the other. Maggie calls Mr Tulliver 'Father', Rosamond Vincy calls her father 'Papa', both using customary middle-class address, but surname-less working-class Eppie – the only really poor and humble heroine, and daughter of the only really poor and humble hero in her fiction – calls Silas Marner 'Daddy', like no other daughter in George Eliot but like her author. 'Daddy' links and illuminates life and art, its happy intimate tone showing how and why Mary Ann Evans's love for her father was 'deep and strong'.

It also shows how fiction drew on life for feeling, relationship and theme. Eppie chooses her foster-father, not her real father, whom she calls 'Sir'; and the simple 'Daddy' speaks eloquently for the complex significance of a social and affective bond. The narrator calls the bond between Silas and Eppie a 'perfect love'. If it derives from George Eliot's reading of Feuerbach, as well as from her filial affections, provincial background and her father's working-class origin, it shows how and suggests why she chose to turn abstractions and concepts into eloquent particulars. She could have been, and nearly was, a Victorian sage like John Stuart Mill, Carlyle or Spencer, but she became an artist who extended and re-imagined her emotional experience, which, as her characters insist, is not separable from the intellectual life.

She insisted that after *Scenes of Clerical Life* she drew no portraits. But her characters sometimes remind us of her relations and relationships. What does Caleb Garth have in common with Adam Bede? Or Robert Evans? The two men inherit their kind of work, skill, pride and responsibility from her father but they are quite different characters. Their children may be a link: Letty and Ben Garth are a pair like Tom and Maggie or Isaac and Mary Ann, bookish clever show-off girl, naughty lazy boy eating raw pastry kept for the pig, ignorant of differences between dictation and dictators. Haight thought Mary Garth the author in the novel, and of course she is a plain girl called Mary who loves Scott and writes a book which gossip thinks is written by someone else. There may or may not be a link between Mary Ann's affection for her father and Mary's for Caleb, unlike the bond between Maggie and Mr Tulliver because their characters are unlike. What gets into Caleb's character from Robert are skills, integrity, independent undeferential ways with his social betters and a deep religious feeling.

There is also a link in speech. Cross said some 'bits' of 'Looking Backward' in *Theophrastus Such* were 'true autobiography'. One bit recalls the father's pronunciation of 'the word "Government" in a tone that charged it with awe, and made it part of my effective religion, in contrast with the word "rebel", which seemed to carry the stamp of evil in its syllables ...' (Cross 1, 5). This is like the way Caleb pronounces 'business' in Chapter 24 of *Middlemarch*: 'it would be difficult to convey to those who never heard him utter the word "business", the peculiar tone of fervid veneration, of religious regard, in which he wrapped it ...'. The phrase 'those who never heard' is like some of the personal-sounding references in *Adam Bede*, seeming to pierce through fiction to fact and may, like them, imply a real-life source equivocated with sly secret pleasure. The caustic 'rebel' sounds like Caleb's contemptuous way with bad work like Fred's educated bad writing: ' "The deuce!" he exclaimed, snarlingly' (*Middlemarch*, 56). As I have said, George Eliot was sensitive to voices and said she heard her characters speaking – one reason for her problems with the dialogue of *Romola*. She may have remembered Chrissey's speech as she heard and transcribed Celia's, and Mary's land-agent father and Theophrastus's clerical parent may both echo the venerating and vehement extremes of Robert Evans's tones.

Her most important relative for fiction was Isaac. Cross met him first at the funeral of the famous sister he had not seen for 20 years. The new husband had already brought about reconciliation between the long-estranged pair. Isaac had recognized the authorship of her first books, and was reported saying there 'are *things*' in *Adam Bede* 'about his Father that she must have written'. When Cara Bray passed on the gossip, George Eliot accepted his version: 'being interpreted, things my father told us about his early life, not a "portrait" of my father' (*Letters* 3, 98, 99). One 'thing' Isaac could hardly miss was Bartle Massey, given the name of Robert Evans's night-school teacher. Another could have been the superstition about the rapping on the door.

Isaac would have kept quiet about other recognitions, in passages carefully generalized and coded for the attention of a very particular reader:

Family likeness has often a great sadness in it. Nature, that great tragic dramatist, knits us together by bone and muscle, and divides us by the

subtler web of our brains; blends yearning and repulsion; and ties us
by our heartstrings to the beings that jar us at every movement. We
hear a voice with the very cadence of our own uttering the thoughts we
despise; we see eyes – ah! so like our mother's – averted from us in cold
alienation; and our last darling child startles us with the air and gesture
of the sister we parted from in bitterness long years ago. (4)

It is a fine piece of prose, wittily reviving metaphor ('heartstrings
that tie'), blending literal and metaphorical (knitted 'bone and
muscle') and neatly apt ('web of … brains'). It is rhythmical,
repetitive, exclamatory, lofty, simple, flexible – moving from Adam
and Lisbeth, who were physically unlike, to Adam and Thias, intellectually and physically alike but morally incompatible. George
Eliot's waning interest in phrenology provides the vivid economy of
a 'well-filled brow', common to father and son. Behind the appeal
on behalf of the story and characters and the generalized address to
a reader lies the reference to a real sister and a real brother, whose
real father inspired things in the book written by a real sister who
perhaps expected and wanted the brother to recognize her hand,
and discover her secret. As he did. The comment on family likeness
and estrangement was a personal appeal under cover of fiction. The
author may really have seen the coldly averted eyes of a mother when
she quarrelled with Isaac, really imagined one of his children recalling
his alienated sister. The voice's cadence is striking because George
Eliot's voice probably resembled her brother's in local accent as well
as tone and pitch: the 'Brother and Sister' in the sonnets 'had been
natives of one happy clime, / And its dear accent to our utterance
clung'. Bray was impressed by her educated modulations, a product
of her last school, so she may have lost the voice-resemblance. Her
tone is appealing but not sentimental, pathetic or nostalgic. She
knew Isaac despised her thoughts. Her tone is complex, variable and
grown-up.

The cluster of coded reference is pointed in the generalizing narratives of *The Mill*. Since this novel draws emotionally on Mary Ann's
relationship with Isaac, in bitterness and affection, and factually
in events and relationship, the narrator's address would be sharply
specific for Isaac and Fanny, as it is now for the informed reader,
'We learn to restrain ourselves as we get older. We keep apart when

we have quarrelled, express ourselves in well-bred phases, and in this way preserve a dignified alienation, showing much firmness on one side, and swallowing much grief on the other' (1, 5). Mary Ann and Isaac had quarrelled on several occasions, and their estrangement did not begin with the Lewes affair. They disagreed after Chrissey's husband died and, as George Eliot tells the story to her Coventry friends, she feels bitter but tries to be fair:

> I had agreed with Chrissey that, all things considered, it was wiser for me to return to town – that I could do her no substantial good by staying another week, while I should be losing time as to other matters. Isaac, however … flew into a violent passion with me, winding up by saying that he desired I would never 'apply to him for anything whatever' which, seeing that I never have done so, was almost as superfluous as if I had said I would never receive a kindness from him. But he is better than he shewed himself to me and I have no doubt that he will be kind to Chrissey, though not in a very large way. (*Letters* 2, 75)

Their differences had shown earlier: she wrote in amused, apologetic self-criticism about shaming him by going about 'like an owl'. On holiday in London she had refused to go out in the evening to enjoy the city pleasures. Isaac expected her to marry someone of whom he could approve, as the other brother and sisters had done, and his attitude is reflected in Tom's role as protector of an unmarried sister, proud or ashamed of her as responsible man is protective of a woman. Isaac's conventional sexism is unpleasantly – and perhaps significantly – heightened into Tom's physical contempt for Philip Wakem.

The Mill speaks after her five-year experience of separation, which at the time probably felt irrevocable. George Eliot's nostalgia and bitterness was no doubt exacerbated by Chrissey's deathbed letter, and the impossibility of seeing her to say goodbye. The novel draws on event and character in Maggie's reading, Tom's love and lore of outdoor things, his ascendency, lack of humour, bossiness and, perhaps, her closeness to her father – though Tulliver seems most unlike Robert Evans. The rigid integrity which is the virtue of Tom's narrowness reflects Isaac's and Robert Evans's, though their uncompromising refusal to tolerate certain behaviour in their employers is more exactly repeated in Caleb Garth. Tom and Maggie quarrel over childish things like neglected pets, an unevenly split jam-puff and spilt cowslip wine. There is companionship in their play, and growing incompatibility as they grew older; estrangement slowly tracked with what Henry James in his preface to *The Tragic Muse* calls the art of preparations.

Life would not go exactly into art. Tom does not imbibe high Anglicanism from his education as Isaac did, widening the gulf between him and Mary Ann. But there were moments of good companionship for Mary Ann and Isaac which are not in the novel. Cross relates their 'habit of acting charades together' before the Griff household and the aunts 'who were greatly impressed with the cleverness of the performance' (Cross 1, 24). It is hard to imagine the Dodson aunts enjoying such a show – they were less like Christiana Pearson's sisters than is often taken for granted. And Tom and Maggie never act together. Acting comes into *Daniel Deronda*, but in *The Mill on the Floss* unimaginative Tom stays stubbornly uncooperative when Maggie invites him to join in make-believe about rescuing her from a lion. He is once allowed clever creative play, when he dresses and makes up for the sword-play with great care and excitement. This may owe something to the old charades, but in the novel the boy acting soldiers mimes a masculine violence which wounds him and terrifies his sister. The children fish happily together in a scene repeated for the 'Brother and Sister' sonnets, but Maggie knocks over Tom's 'wonderful' card-pagoda and he excludes her from toad-tickling and pike-watching at the Pullets. He likes card-building with Lucy because she handles the cards dexterously, unlike clumsy Maggie, but also because she asks 'him to teach her'. The Tulliver children's games are not companionable: they exclude the girl or are led by the boy. The revision of lost childhood exaggerates hostility, adding a bitter drop to nostalgia but significantly politicizing the relationship. In the process, she may have made Tom a more conventional male than her brother. Cross not only shows Isaac's creative side but startlingly reveals his 'most vivid recollection': after Chrissey's departure on her wedding day 'he and his younger sister had "a good cry" together over the break-up of the old home life …' (Cross 1, 30–1). It takes their father's death to make Tom and Maggie join in weeping. Isaac's portrait – and Cross – suggests that Isaac looked more like his sister than Tom looks like Maggie and he may have been more like her in feeling; the 'long silence' may have hurt him too. The novelist was not even-handedly imitating life but recreating it for herself at a variable distance from personal patterns and contrasts, writing out of love and bitterness, hardening difference and incompatibility, and bringing out the politics of family life.

Some memories are involuntary. There is an odd little echo of the past when Mrs Tulliver reports that her stricken husband 'said something once about Tom and the pony' (*Mill* 3, 3). The pony has not been mentioned in the novel before, though in his lonely apprenticeship Tom imagines himself on horseback. In real life Isaac did have a pony and, according to Cross, its arrival meant that Mary Ann was finally cut off from joining in his pastimes. Isaac's riding links him with many young men who enjoy an outdoor life in George Eliot's writing, Godfrey Cass, Fred Vincy, Arthur Donnithorne and Anthony Wybrow, but riding was a sport apparently not open to Mary Ann. She was in a lower class than her riding ladies, Beatrice in 'Mr Gilfil', Dorothea, Gwendolen, and Rosamond Vincy, whose family is in trade but have money and aspirations. Rosemarie Bodenheimer links George Eliot's acquaintance with her foster-sons and the sporty young men in her fiction, but she had long before known a sporty young man whose pastimes she saw and heard about but could not share. Isaac's pony strays out of life into the novel, and because Tulliver's stricken mind is also straying it preserves unassimilated a painful splinter of memory, no doubt unconsciously for author as well as character.

The incompatibility with Isaac was revised by Cross, influenced by man-to-man talks and his own wish to play down unpleasantness. After a warning not to read *The Mill* as biography, Cross says:

> … all that happened in real life between the brother and sister was, I believe, that as they grew up their characters, pursuits, and tastes diverged more and more widely. He took to his father's business, at which he worked steadily, and which absorbed most of his time and attention. He was also devoted to hunting, liked the ordinary pleasures of a young man in his circumstances, and was quite satisfied with

the circle of acquaintance in which he moved. After leaving school at Coventry he went to a private tutor's at Birmingham, where he imbibed strong High Church views. His sister had come back from the Miss Franklins' with ultra-evangelical tendencies, and their differences of opinion used to lead to a good deal of animated argument. Miss Evans, as she now was, could not rest satisfied with a mere profession of faith without trying to shape her own life – and it may be added, the lives around her – in accordance with her convictions. (Cross 1, 32)

Cross never criticizes his wife but is rigorous about Miss Evans shaping 'lives around her'. He turns to illustrate Maggie's austerity, then returns to the discontents and aspirations of Marian Evans, a quotation, which is fascinating whether suggested by her or chosen by Cross, identifying George Eliot with her most subversive artist and woman, 'the Alcharisi', who puts art before sexual love or mother-love: 'you can never imagine what it is to have a man's force of genius in you, and yet to suffer the slavery of being a girl' (*Daniel Deronda*, 51).

George Eliot re-imagines her frustration and ennui for Maggie, but not her fulfilments in work or love. Maggie does not desire Philip, and Stephen is promised to Lucy. No longer children, Tom and Maggie are estranged by her friendship with Philip, then by her compromising river journey with Stephen. Her passionate imagination and Tom's complacent, narrow rectitude mark their quarrels until the scene in which Maggie appeals to Tom on his doorstep and is turned away. The novel plumbs the family conflicts and quarrels Cross smoothed over. The final moral dilemma is a justification of her own experience, after the long, painful sibling disagreements and parting. The breaking-point for Isaac was his sister's co-habitation with Lewes; for Tom it is Maggie's escapade with Stephen.

Fiction allowed George Eliot to do what she could not possibly do in real life – to defend herself. In a fine, quiet stroke, George Eliot makes Maggie's Christian asceticism emerge as unselfish humane love. The defence is made simply and explicitly when Maggie resists Stephen, arguing her moral code, Feuerbachian and deeply personal. Through its plea and wish-fulfillment at the end, the novel lets Maggie live out the fantasy of proving her love, telling her love, and retrieving her love in death. It is a sophisticated form of the common childhood fantasy, 'they'll be sorry when I'm dead', mildly foreshadowed in Maggie's flight to the gypsies. It is a way of saying she understood why she and her family could never be reconciled, as well as a justification. Maggie's ethic speaks for George Eliot's. She tells Stephen that in marrying they would be betraying people while breaking no laws of society or religion. With George Eliot the situation was reversed: she and Lewes broke social and religious laws, but betrayed no-one. She was free: Agnes had given up Lewes for Thornton Hunt and said that she wished Lewes could marry Miss Evans. Maggie's renunciation is Marian Evans's moral defence, based on fidelity, trust, and unspeakable promises. The defence had to be covert, coded, argued indirectly in a fictional form, for a story she was free to tell.

And perhaps the moral sub-text was read personally by stubborn, conventional Isaac. He never wrote to her until she married, but his wife Sarah wrote a sensitive sentence when Lewes died: 'My heart aches for you in your sad bereavement' (*Letters* 9, 247). It reminds us of her tactful intervention during the religious quarrel. It is possible, though it seems to me unlikely, that she would write without telling Isaac, so the letter might have been written, and might have been read, as a message. In thanking her, George Eliot sent her 'love' to her brother. There are two ambiguous actions recorded in a memorandum left by Isaac's son Robert, which Isaac's family interpreted as covert signals, in the end to the living from the dead:

> A small Copyhold Property in Herefordshire was omitted from G Eliot's will. My father was her Heir at law. He gave up his claim thinking she meant all to go to C Lewes. We thought afterwards that GE might have purposely made the omission, knowing as a good lawyer that it would come to IPE and wishing in that way to say, 'No ill will.' My father left GE £100 in his will with the same intention. (*Letters* 9, 357)

Reconciliation came right after Mary Ann Evans Lewes – who had acquired the name by deed-poll in order to get access to her estate after Lewes died – married John Cross. She told her solicitor to inform Vincent Holbeche, family solicitor and a trustee of Robert Evans's estate, who had advised her father to leave her the hundred pounds that paid for her trip to France, Italy and Switzerland, as a temporary cash 'provision' after his death. When she wrote to Holbeche in June 1857 about the exact nature of her relationship with Lewes and to arrange for her income to be paid into Lewes's bank account, she thanked Holbeche for 'thoughtfulness' (*Letters* 1, 350). He had also written to announce Isaac's displeasure and question her about her 'marriage'. His last act as messenger in the family drama was to pass on the news of her legal marriage. On hearing it Isaac addressed his 'dear Sister':

> I have much pleasure in availing myself of the present opportunity to break the long silence which has existed between us, by offering our united and sincere congratulations to you and Mr Cross, upon the happy event of which Mr Holbeche has informed me. My wife joins me in sincerely hoping it will afford you much happiness and comfort. She and the younger branches unite with me in kind love and every good wish. Believe me,
>
> Your affectionate brother,
>
> Isaac P Evans. (*Letters* 7, 280)

She replied in one of her astonishing letters: ' … it was a great joy to me to have your kind words of sympathy, for our long silence has never broken the affection for you which began when we were little ones. My Husband too was much pleased to read your letter' (*Letters* 7, 287).

In 1874 her nephew Robert Evans, son of her half-brother, had written to suggest a meeting with her half-sister Fanny and George Eliot's pride flashed out brilliantly: Fanny had renounced their friendship and it was too late for reconciliation. But to Isaac she expressed gratitude, an affirmation of unchanged, faithful sister-love, in a kind of abasement which shows how much she suffered from their estrangement. (There is the same capacity for self-abasement in her relationship with Herbert Spencer.) Brother and sister were reunited but they never met again. The novel had been prescient, life imitating art not coincidentally but because the art was driven by losses and needs of deep love.

The result, however, was a wonderful but less than perfect novel. I can't entirely agree with FR Leavis's influential reading of the novel in *The Great Tradition*, as self-indulgently uncritical of Maggie, whose character I see as most thoroughly judged and analysed, a fine self-detachment in art. However, self intrudes at the end, which is indulgent. The novelist who rejected Providence acted as her own providence. The wish-fulfilling ending has been crudely read as incestuous fantasy but I believe it expresses a binding love, an unbidden love, a familial love without a sexual element. It is the opposite of that passionate affinity she and Lewes enjoyed, and not in competition with that satisfied reciprocal desire. George Eliot is not the first artist to write about a deep, strong non-sexual love. Sophocles, whom she admired, wrote about and alludes to in this novel, made brother-love the ground for tragic defiance and sacrifice[5]. Antigone reminds the chorus and audience of the rare urgency of unbidden, unique sibling-love, as she gives practical reasons in marvellous understatement:

> Not for a husband, you understand,
> Not even for a son would I have done this.
> If the law had forbidden it, I would have bowed
> My head and let them rot. Does that
> Make sense? I could have married again,
> Another husband, and had more children
> ... But my mother and father
> Are dead. There will be no more brothers.[6]

The longing for division to end, for early years to knit into later life, is in her life and her novel. The author answers Maggie's prayer: she can't give in to Stephen or renounce him, so her conflict is resolved by death. It is not an ordinary death and forgiveness but the perfect understanding she always longed for and sees in Tom's eyes. Like her author, brilliant imaginative Maggie has tried to live without romantic illusion, to reject fantasy and live in and for other human beings. George Eliot answers Maggie's prayer because it is her own, and the answer is in bad faith. She had tried to live without opiates, but her heroine returns to childhood, though the last 'Magsie!' – another significant childish endearment – announces a reunion more perfect than the real childhood companionship, where there was not perfect understanding.

The humanism she strenuously developed and argued is compromised. There is a telltale falter: 'he guessed a story of almost miraculous divinely-protected effort' (*Mill* 9, 5). The 'almost' pulls towards the human side, 'miraculous divinely protected' towards the superhuman. This is Tom's vision but George Eliot creates his imaginative growth and revision: 'it was such a new revelation to his spirit, of the depths in life, that had lain beyond his vision which he had fancied so keen and clear', Maggie's 'wondrous happiness that is one with pain', and after fulfilment for both, unity in death. To call the death erotic is to romanticize and diminish catastrophe, sibling-love, characters, and George Eliot's break with her past. The breach with Isaac was painful, but part of the pain of loosening family bonds. In dying, Maggie is happy at being properly loved, for herself, but also in the magical restoration of unbidden loves, and of the lost past.

Before the wish-fulfilling end, there's no magic in the book. George Eliot put into it, realistically, the harshness of her losses, showing in Maggie that renunciation does not always exalt the spirit but may empty and devastate life. As a convert to Thomas à Kempis, Maggie dramatizes self-abnegation, dressing austerely, doing plain sewing and being patient with her parents – practising small renunciations unlike the real thing. In most of the novel George Eliot makes the real thing as hard and bleak as Isabel's prospect at the end of *A Portrait of a Lady*, but unlike James, she softens. She answers Maggie's prayer for short life, and shows a changed Tom, in a brother-and-sister *Liebestod*. The novel about living without illusion and fantasy ends in an illusion and fantasy of justice and reconciliation. Readers have suggested that Maggie should have called Stephen back but this is not within range of the novel's contingencies. She could have ended her life or put up with it like most of us. But nostalgia and meliorism made it impossible for her author to choose suicide. If she had chosen survival, the point of the novel would have been driven against the reader's breast but would not have healed the author's wound. George Eliot knew that a reunion with her family and past was impossible, and that only answered prayer, flood and an obtuse mass of machinery could create it for her characters[7]. Her novel utters a desperate need and we may prefer it to more objectified art. It is close to life because it struggles with real loss, longing and need. More concentratedly than her other novels, its forms of feeling re-work her patterns and passions. In the characters and the author we see the thinking reed bend and break.

Notes

1 The link is made by Kathleen Adams, 'Evans, Christiana', *GEC*.

2 The 'oceanic feeling' is Romain Rolland's phrase, famously adapted by Freud who never felt it: *A Critical Dictionary of Psychology* (1972). Harmondsworth: Penguin. See also Chapter 3, note 3.

3 On collecting Ilfracombe fauna and flora she wrote: 'The … fact of naming an object tends to give definiteness to our conception of it.' *Journals* 272 (1856).

4 The words quoted: 'yet to his dying day, he bated his breath a little when he told the story of the stroke with the willow wand. I tell it as he told it, not attempting to reduce it to its natural elements …' replaced 'and you see he shuddered at the idea of the stroke with the willow wand' in first and second editions: see Beryl Gray, '*Adam Bede*', *GEC*.

5 *Antigone*: *The Theban Plays* (1986), translated by Don Taylor, Harmondsworth: Penguin.

6 George Eliot (1968) 'The *Antigone* and Its Moral', Pinney; Barbara Hardy, 'Sophocles, Tragedy and *The Mill on the Floss*', *Lectures D'Une Oeuvre*: *The Mill on the Floss* (2002). Editions Du Temps, Nantes; and an earlier version, 'Tragedy Across the Genres', in *Tragedy, Theory and Practice* (1985) Ankara: Middle East Technical University.

7 Tony Tanner says the feeling at the end is incestuous and, like others after him, finds orgasmic significance in the flood and, to my mind ineptly, Tom's 'It is coming …' *Adultery in the Novel: Contract and Transgression*, Baltimore and London: Johns Hopkins University Press, 1979; Kathryn Hughes says GE fell violently in love with Isaac when she was three: *George Eliot: The Last Victorian* (1998) London: Fourth Estate.

Chapter Two
Home, Travel and a Need for Foreignness

O the bliss of having a very high attic in a romantic continental town, such as Geneva – far away from morning callers, dinners and decencies, and then to pause for a year and think 'de omnibus rebus et quibusdum aliis', and then to return to life, and work for poor stricken humanity, and never think of self again.

Mary Ann Evans to John Sibree, May 1848, *Letters* 1, 261

For George Eliot, nostalgia is desire for lost time and past place. Her rooted and uprooted attachment to the Midlands often informs scene, image, character and narrative retrospect, but she knew rootedness was a metaphor, and not always apt. When Theophrastus Such's beloved Midlands plain is disfigured by the railway, she writes of change in 'the speech of the landscape', not of roots being cut (*ITS*, 2, 'Looking Backward'). She knows the feeling of rootedness is relative, and roots are shallow for Hetty, transplantable for Dinah, deep and nourishing for Maggie, ambiguously inherited by Daniel, and belatedly put down by Gwendolen.

As Mary Ann Evans grew in mind and feeling, her personal and political need for foreignness became as strong as her need for home, perhaps more imperative and unsettling. In his very personal biography, Oscar Browning, teacher, scholar, and one of her unconventional friends, speculated on her affection for life outside England[1]. He did not romanticize her roots but wondered why she did not choose congenial foreign cultures and climates, concluding that 'Londonish' Lewes – as she once called him – needed the city for his professional life. As a homosexual Browning suffered from English 'decencies', and his experience may colour his opinion of her preference. John Cross was also alive to her delight in foreign places, amazed by her health and energy on their wedding travels.

On 12 June 1849, six days after Robert Evans was buried, she left for France, Italy and Switzerland with Charles and Cara Bray, then stayed on her own in Geneva for eight months from the end of July till mid-March 1850. She had been her father's companion since 1837; nursing him for the last three years of his failing life as an unmarried daughter was expected to do, with little help from siblings busy with their own families. His death freed her to go abroad for the first time, and she could afford the foreign interlude because of the hundred pounds her father had left her as cash provision. She went with her old friends and came back with a new one, François D'Albert Durade, her Geneva landlord. Between her arrival and departure from Geneva she rested in creative solitude as she had imagined, then left to work 'for poor stricken humanity', though in ways that were not yet clear.

She spent holidays with her Coventry friends in South Wales and Scotland, but the last trip was interrupted by a summons from Isaac to home and duty. Sara Hennell wrote: 'We were all in ecstasies, but Mary Ann's were beyond everything – but here we met with a sad damper to all our pleasure – there was a letter from her brother … saying that her father had broken his leg' (*Letters* 1, 201). Mary Ann's first travels began with childhood trips 'about the neighbourhood, "standing between her father's knees as he drove leisurely"', journeys she remembered in Eppie's short journeys with Marner and the narrator's nostalgia in *Middlemarch* (Cross 1, 18 ; *Middlemarch* 12). An intimate letter to Sara Hennell describes a trip with her father to Brighton and the Isle of Wight where she enjoyed Alum Bay – no preference here for a Midlands scene:

> I heartily wish you *had* been with me to see all the beauties which have gladdened my soul and made me feel that this earth is as good a heaven as I ought to dream of … Fancy a very high precipice, the strata upheaved perpendicularly, in rainbow-like streaks of the brightest maize, violet, pink, blue, red, brown and brilliant white … You might fancy the strata formed of the compressed pollen of flowers … (*Letters* 1, 239)

It is a psychological and sensuous record of reverie, release and stimulus:

> I find one very great spiritual good attendant on a quiet meditative journey among fresh scenes. I seem to have removed to a distance from myself when I am away from the petty circumstances that make up my ordinary environment. I can take myself up by the ears and inspect myself, like any other queer monster ... I have had many thoughts, especially on a subject that I should like to work out 'The superiority of the consolations of philosophy to those of (so-called) religion'. (*Letters* 1, 239–40)

Like Jean Jacques Rousseau, her great inspiration, she saw herself from the outside, freed from self, time and contingency. Her matter-of-fact account suggests an experience less extraordinary than Rousseau's '*extase*' and a reversal of his return, after ecstasy, to self and ordinary surroundings: '*me trouvant enfin ramené ... à moi-même et à ce qui m'entourait*' (*Les Rêveries du Promeneur Solitaire*, Cinquième Promenade). The monster image is one of her self-deprecatory jokes, but what she stresses is the self made strange, freed from routine by 'fresh scenes'. She is stirred to thought not art, but it is a story of inspiration.

Her provincial Midlands culture was not insular. She had few chances to travel but she was a scholarly young woman and, before she went abroad to enjoy more intensely the sense of self, self-loss and creative rebound, she studied history, French, German, Italian, Latin, some Greek and a little Hebrew. Her German was perfected when she took over the translation of Strauss's *Das Leben Jesu*. Sara Hennell was to write nostalgically of the 'German days' and Mary Ann's intense and learned letters to her are lavish with German endearments. At first her spoken German was poor, as she regretted when talking to Strauss on her second foreign journey, but it improved with experience.

French literature was important, and she received a copy of Pascal's *Pensées* as a first-year school prize when she was about 13. In 'The Morality of Wilhelm Meister' she compared Pascal's luminous fragments to cut emeralds or amethysts (Pinney, 74). She must have loved his dark faith, his gamble with disbelief, and his science.

Dinah, Dorothea, Maggie and Daniel are rare brilliant creatures who find isolation congenial, unlike most human beings, who, according to Pascal, cannot bear to be alone in a room. Her frail vessels are Pascal's thinking reeds.

Such links show affinity not influence, and the concept of influence is usually unhelpful when we discuss original art. George Sand, whose tragic and humorous novels of 'passion and its results' inspired George Eliot and who first assumed the English 'George', may have suggested her nom-de-plume but not her books. In 'The Morality of Wilhelm Meister' she praised Balzac as 'perhaps the most wonderful writer of fiction' and, like Scott he disturbingly showed that 'religion was not a requisite for moral excellence' (Cross, 65). She complains that he drags us 'by his magic force' into nause-ating scenes of 'unmitigated vice' (Pinney, 146) but some Balzac novels, *The Country Doctor* for example, tell her kind of story about unheroic obscure lives and secular faith, and share her kind of wide-ranging humane sympathy. *Scenes of Clerical Life*, which links locale and characters, pays homage to Balzac's secular version of Dante, *La Comédie Humaine*: *Scenes of Private Life*, *Scenes of Parisian Life*, *Scenes of Provincial Life*, *Scenes of Country Life*, *Scenes of Political Life* and *Scenes of Military Life*. Just before trying out her own new clerical category, she read Balzac's *César Birotteau*, a fine study of character in society. Marx and Henry James praise Balzac for giving us the creature in its circumstance and George Eliot, the first English regional novelist, followed his example.

The writer who inspired her to 'shape' and to 'make new combinations' – in short, to imagine – was the more eccentric and sentimental French genius Rousseau, as she told Emerson when he asked about influences. If Balzac reflected on social morality, Rousseau told amazing truths about the inner life. He was a deist with a complicated religious history who invented a 'history of the soul' (*Confessions*, Book 2), in candid, subtle discourses unlike anything in his century or the next. Critic of rationality, he confessed or re-imagined his sexual life, fantasies, perversions, loves, friend-ships, enmities, weakness, ambition, response to nature, education, music and writing. He was a wonderfully strange inspiration for an earnest English evangelical Anglican who was to become the first agnostic novelist. She wrote excitedly to Sara Hennell in 1849:

> Rousseau's genius has sent that electric thrill through my intellectual
> and moral frame which has awakened me to new perceptions, which
> has made man and nature a fresh world of thought and feeling to me
> – and this not by teaching me any new belief. It is simply that the
> mighty rushing wind of his inspiration has so quickened my faculties
> that I have been able to shape more definitely for myself ideas which
> had previously dwelt as dim 'ahnungen' in my soul – the fire of his
> genius has so fused together old thoughts and prejudices that I have
> been ready to make new combinations. (*Letters* 1, 277)

Artists who are alien to us can change our perception of the world.
As 'electric' suggests, *Confessions* must have thrilled and shocked
a young, aspiring imagination susceptible to fantasy and scruple.
The sense that her father's death might loosen moral bonds and
she could become 'earthly sensual and devilish' (*Letters* 1, 284) was
something Rousseau may have freed her to articulate then imagine,
more morally, in Maggie and Gwendolen. The passion, thought
and symbols of *Julie, ou la Nouvelle Héloise*, where there is a famous
amorous scene on Lake Geneva, Rousseau's account of rowing on
Lake Bienne in *Les Confessions* and the fifth '*promenade*' in *Les
Reveries* inspired her, as they did many authors[2]. She wrote Maria
Lewis a fragment of fable in June 1841, possibly before she read
Rousseau:

> Somnophilus was rowing his bark down the bosom of a glassy
> stream and saw in the distance a fair garden on its banks whose edge
> presented all manner of bright flowers and luscious fruits … his eye
> … sparkled and he almost forgot his oars, as he gazed and dreamed
> till time and distance vanished and imagination seemed like actual
> enjoyment – when lo! his neglected bark struck against the shore and
> roused the visionary … (*Letters* 1, 87)

It is stiffly and conventionally written, but it introduces the rowing
dreamer who loses a sense of self and time, nearly as often in George
Eliot as in Rousseau.

Paris or Venice are likelier choices for a romantic city but she
probably chose Geneva as it is Rousseau's birthplace, and visited
Vevey (or Vevay), from which her first Swiss letter was written, in

homage to the rowing lovers of *La Nouvelle Héloise*. She made two pilgrimages to *Les Charmettes* at Chambéry, a Rousseau site with no lake, once with Lewes and once with Cross. The lake imagery was reinforced for her by JR Froude, who invoked Rousseau in direct reference and invented an amorous adventure on Lake Como, which somewhat implausibly causes the death of a child. Froude and George Eliot were influenced not only by Rousseau but by Goethe's *Die Wahlverwandtschaften* (1809), which Froude translated. In Goethe's 'novella', Ottilie's distraction causes a child to drown and there are lake scenes straight out of Rousseau, though they are more sentimental. In 1849, Mary Ann Evans enthusiastically reviewed *The Nemesis of Faith*, probably the only Victorian novel before Hardy's *Jude* to be burnt, also by a clergyman. Froude had sent 'the translator of Strauss' a copy via Chapman, a friend of the Brays. Froude almost went on that first foreign journey: he sent a message before they sailed to say he was going to be married. George Eliot praised the 'vitalizing' energy of what, for a modern reader, is an almost unreadable book, and felt inner and outer life transformed by the 'companionship' – probably of his scepticism, candour, wanderlust, ambition and erotic lake-drifting. His style at its best must have appealed to her, too, its abstraction sharpened by particulars, its flexible rhythms and scientific metaphor, though its long baggy generalizations – as bad as Rousseau's in *Émile* – may have warned her to make narration particular and affective.

She rewrote Rousseau consciously and unconsciously, disclaiming any dogmatic influence – 'not by teaching me any new belief'. His ideas about education and society were less important to her than his irrational, subversive fusions and confusions of feeling, relief for reason-crammed mind and food for sentimental appetite. Rousseau is a less sophisticated and solemn moralist than George Eliot, and she may have been critical of his paranoia, defensiveness and vanity, though the very uncertainties are moving. They echoed her guilty fears of introspective fantasy – his experience of a novel-reader's dangerous identifications is very like hers – and she must have loved his scientific, aesthetic, existential response to nature and his blundering, proud, joyful sense of vocation. In time she was to manage her own fusions of nature, sex, and social idealism, in both fact and fiction.

In *The Lifted Veil*, as I have mentioned, Latimer describes an education in Geneva, remembering Rousseau as he images visionary isolation:

> My least solitary moments were those in which I pushed off in my boat, at evening, towards the centre of the lake; it seemed to me that the sky, and the glowing mountain-tops, and the wide blue water surrounded me with a cherishing love such as no human face had shed on me since my mother's love had vanished out of my life. I used to do as Jean Jacques did – lie down in my boat and let it glide where it would, while I looked up at the departing glow leaving one mountain-top after the other, as if the prophet's chariot of fire were passing over them on its way to the home of light. (1)

Benign lake and reverie scenes recur as Latimer describes his friendship with Meunier. It was the name of a preacher George Eliot heard in Geneva, which she uses again for a dismayed name-drop as Gwendolen remembers 'Miss Graves at Madame Meunier's'(*Daniel Deronda,* 21). Latimer recalls how 'in Charles's rare holidays we went up the Salève together, or took the boat to Vevay, while I listened dreamily … to his bold conceptions … I mingled them confusedly in my thought with glimpses of blue water and delicate floating cloud, with the notes of birds and the distant glitter of the glacier … my mind was half absent …' (I)

For solitude or company, the lake is a sacred foreign place for Latimer, and a seat of creativity. It is countered by another foreign scene, this time in Prague, which is made as frightening as it is strange, dissolving into a larger 'presence of something unknown and pitiless', a disappointed, perverted and destructive vision. Relaxed solitude on the lake is associated with early recall of a dead mother's 'surrounding' love, imaging infantile closeness, perfect ease, water and a lack of boundary in desire or memory. (Rousseau calls Nature '*Mère*' in a lake '*extase*' described in the last chapter of *Les Confessions*.) For George Eliot's dreaming artist, whose creativity is a tormenting negation, the lake-drifting is a stimulus and lost paradise.

She grew up by a brown canal, grew to love lakes, and came to imagine the Floss where Maggie and Stephen drift, and Maggie and

Tom drown. Like Rousseau's Julie and Saint-Preux, Maggie and Stephen – chiefly Maggie – are water-lulled to brief, blissful escape from time and duty. Rousseau kills off Julie, his passionate dutiful Héloïse and, like Maggie, she suffers sacrificial drowning and release. If George Eliot went to Geneva because of Rousseau, she accumulated new personal images there for her disturbing novella and her most personal novel.

After the Brays went back to England, she lived in Geneva for eight months, firstly in a pension on the lake at Plongeon, part of the remains of a large estate on the edge of the city. In spite of her isolation from friends and family, lost luggage, her passport being left with the Brays, no books, and wardrobe inadequate for Swiss climate and society, she thinks 'with a shudder of returning to England ... a land of gloom, of ennui, of platitude' though it is the 'land of duty and affection' (*Letters* 1, 336). She admits to a touch of 'Heimweh' (*Letters* 1, 328), giving it its German name, and calls it a longing for people not place.

Geneva was not perfect. Solitude is hard, as Pascal knew. George Eliot was escaping England and trying freedom, but met in Rousseau's Calvinist city a bourgeois if cosmopolitan company which she sketched in sharp characters. She was a '*feme sole*' abroad, more restricted by Geneva's conventions than England's provincial society, free from morning callers and dinners but not 'decencies' (*Letters* 1, 261) and 'sagely settled': 'I dare not look or say or do half what one does in England' (*Letters* 1, 301). Older women pet her, change her hairstyle and, like brother Isaac, point out the disadvantages of heterodoxy for a woman. She writes home for the matronly black velvet dress she wore in London for evening parties to be sent to her. Acquaintances find her single woman's independence eccentric: 'people do not seem to think me quite old enough yet to ramble about at will' and 'I confess I am more sensitive than I thought I should be to the idea that my being alone is odd' (*Letters* 1, 301). Ten years later, writing to D'Albert Durade when she has found her vocation, she reminds him of her old unhappiness in Geneva (*Letters* 3,187).

When she moved to Durade's house, her second lodging in Geneva, a fellow-guest was Jean François de Chaponnière, who funded the *Cercle des Amis de Jean-Jacques* in 1792, which strengthened the

Rousseau connection. She was put off by steep flights of stone steps leading up to the apartment in the rue de Chanoines (now the rue de la Pélisserie) but her room with an alcove for a bed – not an attic as some biographers suggest but opening off the salon on the second floor – was her 'own room' (*Letters* 1, 323): 'one feels in a downy nest high up in a good old tree. I have always had a hankering after this sort of life and I find it was a true instinct of what would suit me. Just opposite my windows is the street in which the Sisters of Charity live … a walk of five minutes takes me out of all streets within sight of beauties …' (*Letters* 1, 321).

François and Julie D'Albert Durade were musical and artistic, and became friends with whom she kept in touch all her life. She called Julie 'Maman', possibly thinking of her having the name of Rousseau's Héloïse and of Rousseau calling his beloved Mme Warens 'Maman'. She was grateful for their kindness and warmth. François painted the only pretty portrait of her, was guide and companion in Geneva and, in a cold March, escorted her across the Jura and sea to England, staying in London for several weeks and visiting the Brays in Coventry. He translated five of her novels. As Mathilde Blind first suggested, she may have remembered his spinal injury, painting and music, in Philip Wakem. The Leweses paid them a pleasant visit in 1860 and Cross visited François when they were both widowers. Julie let Marianne – as she once or twice called herself in Geneva – *tutoyer* François in her early letters from England (which have not survived) and in later letters she always asks affectionately about 'Maman'.

Cross destroyed her Swiss journal but a few letters glimpse lake, shores and mountains. In Plongeon she loves the lake too much to hear anything against it – the location was not thought healthy – and at the end of her life she told Cross about seeing the Jura range across the blue lake (Cross 1, 208). In Plongeon, and later in the town but still near water and mountains, she walked and climbed. From her 'own room' she wrote: 'I am going up the Salève … with M. D'Albert … On one side I shall have a magnificent view of the lake the town and the Jura – on the other the range of Mt Blanc. The walks about Geneva are perfectly enchanting' (*Letters* 1, 319). When she resumed correspondence with D'Albert Durade, she recalled walks with him and his wife. The landscape comes and goes: 'The earth is covered with snow' (*Letters* 1, 325) and 'I am becoming passionately attached to the mountains, the lake, the streets, my own room and above all the dear people with whom I live' (*Letters* 1, 323). Upon returning home, she tells Sara Hennell how she enjoyed 'nature's brightest glories and beauties' (*Letters* 1, 332).

Among descriptions of the Swiss landscape is another account of looking out at nature and into herself, but unlike the Isle of Wight experience, this estrangement seems narcotic. The record is generalized but sensitive and it anticipates images of creativity in her writing:

> This place looks more lovely to me every day – the lake, the town, the campagnes with their stately trees and pretty houses, the glorious mountains in the distance – one can hardly believe one's self on earth – one might live here and forget that there is such a thing as want or labour or sorrow. The perpetual presence of all this beauty has somewhat the effect of mesmerism or chloroform. I feel sometimes as if I were sinking into an agreeable state of numbness on the verge of unconsciousness … The other day (Sunday) there was a Fête held on the lake – the Fête of Navigation. I went out with some other ladies in M. de Herder's boat at sunset and had the richest draught of beauty … The mingling of the silver with the golden rays on the rippled lake, the bright colours of the boats, the cannon, the music, the splendid fireworks, and the pale moon looking at it all with a sort of grave surprize, made up a scene of perfect enchantment – and our dear old Mont Blanc was there in his white ermine robe. I rowed all the time, and hence comes my palsy. (*Letters* 1, 302)

The description is fanciful but her psychic state is clear – an agreeable sinking and dwindling, 'the oceanic feeling'[3]. (The comparisons with mesmerism and chloroform were based on her own experience.) As she took the oars, she must have thought of Rousseau on the Lac Bienne he made famous, and Julie and Saint-Preux on Lac Léman. She went rowing on Lake Lucerne and the Trent with Lewes, on the Serpentine, probably with Lewes, and on the Thames with Lewes and Oscar Browning, but the only record of her taking the oars is this one about Geneva (Haight, 134, 293, 305). The dreamlike experience and its associations return in *The Lifted Veil*; in *The Mill* in the erotic dream of drifting lovers, the night on the Dutch ship, St Ogg's and the Virgin, rescue and drowning; and Daniel Deronda's rowing and meditation on the Thames. Mary Ann's strenuous rowing – 'I have almost lost the use of my arms with rowing' *(Letters* 1, 300) – comes back in the light drawing-room chat when Lucy laughs innocently that Maggie likes rowing 'better than anything' and Philip jokes about her 'selling her soul to the ghostly boatman who haunts the Floss – only for the sake of being drifted in a boat for ever' (6, 13).

Later in the rowing letter, a light-hearted request invokes Keats's amoral poet: 'my nature is so chameleon I shall lose all my identity unless you keep nourishing the old self with letters' *(Letters* 1, 302). The source of 'chameleon' and loss of identity is unmistakable: Lord Houghton's edition of Keats's letters had just been published in 1848, and reviewed for the *Westminster* in January 1849. Keats's 'chameleon poet' who 'shocks the virtuous philosopher', and his well-known anecdote of feeling his identity annihilated, anticipate Latimer's trance, Maggie's dreamy absentness, Deronda's excess of empathy, and the artist's own nature. Keatsian negative capability entered her image-matrix, another idea of liberated creativity[4].

There was a benign return of the experience 11 years later, in a gondola on her second journey with Lewes, during their first visit to Venice:

> Of all dreamy delights that of floating in a gondola along the canals and out on the Lagoon is surely the greatest. We were out one night on the lagoon when the sun was setting and the wide waters were flushed with the reddened light: I should have liked it to last for hours: it is the sort of scene in which I could most readily forget my own existence and feel melted into the general life. (*Journals*, Recollections of Italy, 1860, 365)

She told Herbert Spencer about being tormented by 'double consciousness' (Spencer pp. 386–7) and the driftings of 'forget my own existence' are creative lapses of self. The Venetian experience sounds more socialized and less ecstatic than the Swiss episode. It was not solitary and not new, recorded in her journal where she is generally less relaxed than in her letters, self-conscious even when describing loss of self-consciousness. By this time she was a novelist, practised in departures from self.

In Geneva, for a while, she found creative relaxation in foreignness. She loved the new place and new friends but missed old friends and family. She went to lectures on physics, read and played the piano, but found the winter hard and contemplated the future. She does not write about plans to work or write but they were in her mind. Would she go back home or settle in London? Would she go home for a while and return to Geneva? Would she spend some time with Chrissey and near Fanny, or stay for a while, as she knew she could, with the Brays? She wrote: 'I mean to return to England as soon as the Jura is passable without sledges' (*Letters* 1, 328). The railway had not yet connected Geneva with France so in March she crossed the snows in a sledge with D'Albert Durade, catching the train at Tonnerre. She had suggested that he could not afford the trip but in the end he managed it, so she was escorted, as on all her foreign journeys. She envied the way women went about alone in Weimar, but she depended on support when travelling abroad, like many women of her class and time.

At home she complained that she had exchanged the lake 'to shiver in a wintry flat', repudiating any pleasure in place: 'I am not in England – I am only nearer to the beings I love best' (*Letters* 1, 332). In Coventry, she missed the mountains; in the heart of England when April's there, nature and human nature fail:

> O the dismal weather and the dismal country and the dismal people. It was some envious demon that drove me across the Jura to come and see people who don't want me. However I am determined to sell everything I possess except a portmanteau and carpet bag and the necessary contents and be a stranger and a foreigner on the earth for ever more. (*Letters* 1, 335)

She was isolated amongst relations, except for affectionate Chrissey, and told Cara she was 'delighted to feel that I am of no importance to any of them, and have no motive for living amongst them. I have often told you I thought Melchisedec the only happy man' (*Letters* 1, 336). Her envy of Melchisedec, who had no family, was not sour grapes. She had £90 a year but wanted to be independent, help Chrissey – widowed, hard-up, unwell – but not live with her. She had to find a room of her own in England and work. She had never earned any money (except for £20 for two years' work on Strauss) though she thought of being a governess when her father threatened to turn her out.

When she published reviews and sketches for Bray's *Coventry Herald*, a literary future must have seemed more real. She remembered dreaming of fame while in her mid-20s, and she confided in Cross, in a movingly recalled conversation about her possible autobiography, 'The only thing I should care much to dwell on would be the absolute despair I suffered from of ever being able to achieve anything. No one could ever have felt greater despair' (Cross 1, 36). Her friends seemed to have known her ambitions: as I have mentioned, they had fancied 'she must be writing her novel' (*Letters* 1, 223). Geneva helped her make the move from a dependent, housekeeping daughter to an independent London writer. The re-lived old response to Rousseau was vital: his imagination excited hers, the high nest in his birthplace was her inspiring habitat.

After the foreign city came the thought of stricken humanity. Her need for foreignness was political as well as personal. Before Geneva she had thought feelingly about nationalism and criticized English culture. She was not just tolerant of foreignness but, at times, sounds positively xenophiliac. Disraeli was interesting to her as novelist and politician and though she is scornful of his 'windy eloquence', especially in Sidonia, she approves both his attack on English racism and his belief in superior 'Oriental races'. A distaste for Hebrew history is based on her critique of Old Testament narrative and fundamentalist belief in its authority, but she admits a 'gentile nature' that 'kicks' and uses two 'almosts' before condemning 'everything specifically Jewish':

> … the fellowship of race to which D'Israeli exultingly refers the munificence of Sidonia, is so evidently an inferior impulse which must ultimately be superseded that I wonder even he, Jew as he is, dares to boast of it. My Gentile nature kicks most resolutely against any assumption of superiority in the Jews, and is almost ready to echo Voltaire's vituperation. I bow to the supremacy of Hebrew poetry, but

much of their early mythology and almost all their history is utterly revolting. Their stock produced a Moses and a Jesus, but Moses was impregnated with Egyptian philosophy and Jesus is venerated and adored by us only for that wherein he transcended or resisted Judaism … Everything *specifically* Jewish is of a low grade. (*Letters* 1, 246–7)

It is some way from *Daniel Deronda* but Mordecai is not orthodox and, though Daniel welcomes Jewishness, he remains an Englishman, believing in separateness with communication. The provincial woman of 29 had a detachment from nationalistic feeling rare in her time. Her views are historically and experientially inflected, unpalatable to modern liberal readers but admitting openness and uncertainty:

The nations have been always kept apart until they have sufficiently developed their idiosyncrasies and then some great revolutionary force has been called into action by which the genius of a particular nation becomes a portion of the common mind of humanity … I confess the types of the 'pure races', however handsome, always impress me disagreeably – there is an undefined feeling that I am looking not at *man* but at a specimen of an order under Cuvier's class, Bimana. The negroes certainly puzzle me – all the other races seem plainly destined to extermination or fusion not even excepting the 'Hebrew-Caucasian'. But the negroes are too important physiologically and geographically for one to think of their extermination, while the repulsion between them and the other races seems too strong for fusion to take place to any great extent. (*Letters* 1, 246)

She can think better than this: she prefers aspects of French class and culture to her own, sympathizing with her friend John Sibree's 'happiness about the French Revolution'. She responds to the short-lived Provisional republican Government of 1848 with radical enthusiasm – 'you are just as sansculottish and rash as I would have you' and 'our decayed monarchs should be pensioned off … we should have … a sort of Zoological Garden, where these worn-out humbugs may be preserved' (*Letters* 1, 252–4). Along with an irreverent republicanism, which was perhaps exaggerated for her correspondent, is informed admiration for the French working classes, whose 'revolutionary animus' is celebrated as rural and not only industrial as it is in England. This pre-figures Felix Holt's anxiety about the English working class:

> I should have no hope of good from any imitative movement at home. Our working classes are eminently inferior to the mass of the French people. In France, the *mind* of the people is highly electrified – they are full of ideas on social subjects – they really desire social *reform* – not merely an acting out of Sancho Panza's favourite proverb 'Yesterday for you, to-day for me'.

George Eliot is critical of the English military and the monarchy: no wonder Cross cut her phrase 'little humbug of a queen' from this letter. It was written by the 'sceptical, unusual' woman, whose 'salt and spice' and 'entirely unconventional life' were fondly described by William Hale White in the *Athenaeum* (1885) as he recalled her with her feet over the arms of a chair, her hair over her shoulders and a proof in her hands. He was provoked by reading the Cross biography which Gladstone had called 'a reticence in three volumes' and later revived his Marian Evans of 142 Strand in the kindness and straight pungent talk of Theresa in *Mark Rutherford's Autobiography*.

She sophisticated her internationalism when working as an unofficial editor and reviewer for the *Westminster* under Chapman's ownership. In one letter she candidly re-examines her attitude to America with a willingness to revise her opinion and a warm sense of belonging to a large world with a future:

> The article on Slavery, in the last number … is by WE Forster … I hope you are interested in the Slavery question, and in America generally – that cradle of the future. I used resolutely to turn away from American politics, and declare that the United States was the last region of the world I should care to visit. Even now I almost loathe the *common* American type of character. But I am converted to a profound interest in the history, the laws, the social religious phases of North America, and long for some knowledge of them. Is it not cheering to think of the youthfulness of this little planet, and the immensely greater youthfulness of our race upon it? (*Letters* 2, 85)

This is another blend of bias and openness, with another 'almost' and a refreshing insistence on community and life on a young planet – pre-Darwinian but modern. Her attachment to 'the heart of England' must be seen in the context of this vigorous imaginative internationalism. Her need for foreignness was clear before she set foot on foreign soil.

Her return to England from Geneva was both disappointing and promising. It was one of the transitions she called 'epochs', a significant passage like the one to France, Italy and Switzerland, and many future voyages: the trip to Germany with Lewes; their return to England; the visit to Switzerland in 1859 when Lewes told his sons about her; her meeting with them in 1860; the return with Charles in 1861; and her wedding journey in 1881. The first German visit and her later trips to Florence and Spain were working holidays, for Lewes's *Goethe*, her *Romola* and *The Spanish Gypsy*. Once or twice used for writing – *Adam Bede*, for instance – foreign trips usually came to mark the end of a novel, happy escapes from reviews and town talk.

The journey to Germany with Lewes offered liberation and difficulties. On 20 July 1854, she arrived too early at St Katherine's dock, felt a 'terrible fear' that Lewes was delayed, then saw 'his welcome face looking for me over the porter's shoulder'. They embarked for Antwerp: 'The day was glorious and our passage perfect' (*Journals*, 14). Before she knew Lewes, she had had some limited sexual and emotional experience, with Chapman and Spencer; unhappily erotic and unhappily platonic. Now the attachment which had already made her happy was confirmed and announced by the foreign journey.

There was love, leisure and sightseeing in Belgium and Germany. There was work, too: Lewes had to do some final research as he wrote and re-wrote the biography, in Frankfurt where Goethe was born, and Weimar where Lewes used the modern method of interviewing the subject's friends. The hard-up couple rejoicing in low prices were one day to travel in private carriages and stay in the best hotels but during this time they had to earn money. They were busy professional writers used to helping each other, and energetic Victorian tourists on their special Grand Tour. In spite of headaches and fatigue doing the galleries and monuments, Murray in hand, they enjoyed cheap meals, walks and concerts, testing prejudices and stereotypes. George Eliot mocked Casaubon for doing research in the Vatican on a wedding journey but hers was a working honeymoon, too, though she and her lover found more delight than 'poor Dorothea' and poor Casaubon.

George Eliot had established herself as a successful translator of Strauss from German and was translating Spinoza from Latin. She was a fine reviewer and a great editor – conscientious, practical, firm and tactful in dealing with contributors and with Chapman – and a real writer, who thought and felt in writing. She helped Lewes by translating quotations for the Goethe biography, and contributed editorially and collaboratively in many ways. For herself, she wrote a travel journal which was eventually published as 'Recollections of Weimar', an article on *Woman in France*: *Madame de Sablé* which was a welcome paid commission from Chapman, and another essay on Eduard Veyse. She also translated and abridged for *The Leader* an article on Meyerbeer and Wagner written by a new acquaintance, Franz Lizst.

The brave partnership was accepted by the free spirits of liberal Weimar as it could not be in England. The voyage was the beginning of lasting love and partnership. Working, sight-seeing and socializing at a time of passionate engagement, like the Swiss adventure at a time of alienation and anxiety, added images, themes and characters which were to go into her fiction. New foreign materials and events come into the store of images, to join lakes, émigrés, mountains, rivers and plains: galleries, churches, frescoes, pictures, hotels, beggars, foreign food, research, wedding journeys, music of the future, Italian singing, pianists, composers, grand scandal, princesses and palaces, all to be assimilated, transposed and metamorphosed. These fragments of life are events and images of the present, like water and dreaminess, and also voluntary and involuntary memories which stimulated emotional, intellectual, sensational, symbolic, personal and general associations.

George Eliot drew on rich materials from these early experiences and home-scenes, feeling them more distinctly for being an exile: Joyce left Ireland to imagine it with love and venom and Housman's Shropshire was as fictitious as its Lad, its blue remembered hills seen from a distance, untrodden and untouched, childhood's and dream's horizon. Exile and foreignness are relative. George Eliot is nostalgic not only in foreign places but in London, where there was work, culture and company she enjoyed, but whose streets, dirt and foul air she detested. Much of her hankering after the Midlands lies in her distaste for London. When Celia is horrified at the thought of Dorothea living 'in a street' she shares her author's dislike of bricks and enclosure. Dorothea will learn what 'everything costs' in London, as Marian did in the needy days when she kept the purse and doled out shillings. She always longed for fresh air to breathe, wide skies above her and rough grass underfoot, and she sought them restlessly in the countryside near London.

After she revealed her relationship with Lewes it was impossible to go back to the Midlands. She even avoided visiting the Brays in Coventry, although she occasionally saw them in London, and her Warwickshire became a memory cherished in her writing. But though her novels constantly tap nostalgia, they need foreignness.

Macarthy is her first narrator, a bachelor and wanderer whose papers are edited posthumously by a friend in *Poetry and Prose of an Eccentric*, published in the *Coventry Herald* between December 1846 and February 1847. They contain no scenery but briefly mention Macarthy's love of 'grand organic forms' like rocks, sea and mountains, and the foreign travel on which he spends his patrimony. One sketch is set in Greek fable-land, another describes Rousseau examining a plant, in France or Switzerland, a third is placed in a Paris studio where he likes 'to lounge' and paint a picture of life, 'a home-scene, after Wilkie, a Paul preaching at Athens, or a Brutus passing sentence on his son'. In Pinney's *Essays of George Eliot*, Brutus the father, Paul in Athens, and the plant and child representing Rousseau, get no gloss, but a note on Wilkie suggests that his paintings probably influenced George Eliot's conception of 'the value of ordinary life as a subject for art' (Pinney, 18). This is privileging the home-scene. She valued the ordinary, but needed the exceptional: Adam Bede is not an average man, home life is neighboured by exotic places and people and domestic scenes are made strange by foreignness.

Her last narrator is another wandering bachelor, with a partly foreign name, Theophrastus Such, whose imaginary 'Impressions' draw on his author's foreign travels: he complains that acquaintances forget his travels in the East and his accident in the Alps. He is an internationalist like his author and voices her impassioned and thoroughly reasoned attack on the wicked stupidities of English imperialism and patriotism – on all patriotisms in fact, but criticism must begin at home, especially if home is an empire.

Race was a continuing concern for George Eliot, her critique beginning in letters of the 1840s and 1850s. Ironic Theophrastus deals precisely and uncompromisingly with Englishness, subverting and destabilizing simple notions of nation and race by examining the history of religion, as in 'The Modern Hep! Hep! Hep!':

> True, we are not indebted to those ancestors for our religion: we are rather proud of having got that illumination from elsewhere. The men who planted our nation were not Christians, though they began their work centuries after Christ; and they had a decided objection to Christianity when it was first proposed to them: they were not monotheists, and their religion was the reverse of spiritual. But since we have been fortunate enough to keep the island home they won for us, and have been on the whole a prosperous people, rather continuing the plan of invading and spoiling other lands than being forced to beg for shelter in them, nobody has reproached us because our fathers thirteen hundred years ago worshipped Odin, massacred Britons, and were with difficulty persuaded to accept Christianity, knowing nothing of Hebrew history and the reasons why Christ should be received as the Saviour of mankind. The Red Indians, not liking us when we settled among them, might have been willing to fling such facts in our faces, but they were too ignorant, and besides, their opinions did not signify, because we were able, if we liked, to exterminate them. The Hindoos also have doubtless had their rancours against us, and still entertain enough ill-will to make unfavourable remarks on our character, especially as to our historic rapacity and arrogant notions of our own superiority; they perhaps do not admire the usual English profile, and they are not converted to our way of feeding: but though we are a small number of an alien race profiting by the territory and produce of these prejudiced people, they are unable to turn us out; at least, when they tried we showed them their mistake. We do not call ourselves a dispersed and a punished people: we are a colonizing people, and it is we who have punished others (*ITS*, 18).

This is dry slow irony and surprise: 'they are unable to turn us out; at least, when they tried we showed them their mistake'. This sly accretive figure was a favourite of George Eliot's, used in the unmistakably feminist joke about Sir James Chettam's tolerance of Dorothea's cleverness, 'which, after all, a man could always put down when he liked … Why not? A man's mind – what there is of it – has always the advantage of being masculine …' (*Middlemarch*, 2). *Theophrastus* lacks the psychological particularity of the novels but shares their wit. The smooth synecdoche 'the usual English profile' in that last passage resembles Grandcourt, who has an 'empire of fear' in the home. The ironies move in and out: 'this white-handed man with the perpendicular profile … might have won reputation among his contemporaries' if he 'had been sent to govern a difficult colony' and 'would have understood that it was safer to exterminate than to cajole superseded proprietors …'(*Daniel Deronda*, 48). 'We do not call ourselves a dispersed … people' revises Daniel Deronda's conflation of the English dispersed over the globe and the Jewish diaspora.

Between Macarthy and Theophrastus the novels displace Englishness. Some of her poems are set in foreign parts – and *Romola* is set in Renaissance Italy and uses a consciously constructed language that is neither modern nor English. No wonder its conspicuous research and linguistic self-consciousness was interrupted by her most English story *Silas Marner*, whose rural scene contains one small foreign reference, a suggestion that Dunsey Cass may have gone abroad. In all her other fiction foreignness is present and important. 'Amos Barton' has a character with a Polish name, Countess Czerlaski, whose friendship with the Bartons causes scandal, and Farquhar, a minor character who lisps scornfully that Barton 'believth the whole theory about her Polish huthband and hith wonderful ethcapeth' to be told drily by his host that her 'common' brother is 'knowing about the king of the French. The locals do not believe the lady is a countess but they are wrong: her husband was a count with whom she lived in France and Germany amongst other émigrés 'with large title and small fortunes'. Foreignness is not dignified by the glimpse of Czerlaski the dancing-master but nor is Milby gossip. The Polish story exposes the ignorant small-minded English parish, and George Eliot's fresh experience of English scandal-mongers[5].

Foreignness is developed in 'Mr Gilfil's Love Story'. Set in 1788 just before the revolution, it compares the turmoil of France with the little tragedy of Caterina Sarti, using the political allusion for a critique of class power and injustice in England. There is sly irony about the declension and renovation of the Cheverels since the 'brilliancy' of the first 'Chevreuil who came over with the Conqueror' (2), but Italy is the important foreign country in the story. The plot is operatically sensational: a father's death, an orphan, a dagger, jealous murderous intent, a lover's death, desperate flight, sickness and the heroine's death, all set to Italian music. Sir Christopher Cheverel and his wife need foreign places: he studies the architecture of Milan cathedral for his Gothic restoration, she has her music. The singing heroine's father is a *primo tenore* who loses his voice – like Daniel Deronda's mother but without her genius – and earns a living by copying music, like 'Jean Jacques'. There is also a scattering of Italian words like '*poveraccio*' and '*Padroncello*', the 'wonderful linked sweetness' of Gluck's '*Che farò senza Eurydice?*' and Paesiello's '*Ho perduto il bel sembiente*'.

There is a running joke about English xenophobia in Mrs Patten's ladysmaid experience of 'furriner's' 'victuals and nasty ways', Mrs Sharp's worries about Italian workers 'colloguing' with maids and her distaste for 'gibberish', garlic, 'hile', and pictures in 'furrin churches' of men and women 'a-showin' themselves just for all the world as God made 'em', and Mr Bate's tale of a thieving French valet who 'stool silk stookins, an' shirts, an' rings, an' iverythin' he could ley his hans on … They're all alaike, them furriners. It roons i' th' blood' (4). Mr Bellamy the butler prefers a good English tune like 'Roy's Wife', sung 'staccato' by Mr Bate, over 'all the fine Italian toodlin' – he's obviously heard Tina's '*Ho perduto*' in the drawing-room. Dim-witted Lady Assher has been to Italy for her wedding journey: 'All Italians sing so beautifully. I travelled in Italy with Sir John when we were first married … we went to Venice, where they go about in gondalas, you know' (5). The infant vindictiveness and impulsiveness of the Italian heroine may draw on a stereotype, but English Gwendolen Harleth strangles a canary, outdoing Tina's ink-spilling and vase-breaking, and if Tina's is the first murderous wish and handy dagger she is unambiguously guiltless.

'Janet's Repentance' is an almost enclosed English story but it has glimpses of a bigger world: Tryan mentions travelling to 'unnamed territory', he might go south for his consumption, and his cousin thinks of 'going out' as a missionary. Foreignness rebukes English provincial culture in jokes about Milby ladies with small French and less German; Mrs Pettifer and Mary Linnet read Klopstock's *Messiah* together; and a future generation will amaze their mothers by reading 'a selection' of German poetry and expressing 'admiration for Schiller' (2). A passing reference echoes the anti-imperial letter to Sibree: the Milby parishioners expect Evangelicism as little as 'the innocent Red Indians expected smallpox' (2). The spots of foreignness are less superficial than they may seem at first, strongly subverting nationalism and criticizing xenophobia.

Craig, the know-all Scotch gardener in *Adam Bede*, finds Napoleon 'a bit cliver' because he is Corsican not French, but he is weak because he is backed by 'mounseers': you 'may skewer half a dozen ... at once as if they war frogs'. He tells an anecdote about fitting French regimentals on a monkey: 'you couldn't tell the monkey from the mounseers'. Mr Poyser has never 'heard tell' of the 'French being good for much' but Adam draws on the Rector's travels and his own unbiassed intelligence:

> Come, Craig ... You don't believe that ... It's all nonsense about the French being such poor sticks. Mr Irwin's seen 'em in their own country ... And as for knowledge, and contrivances, and manifactures, there's a many things as we're a fine sight behind them in ... Nelson and the rest of 'em 'ud have no merit i' beating them, if they were such offal as folks pretend. (53)

Bony is a vivid ogre in the novel as he was in popular rumour, the stuff of gossip and jokes – Nelson's defeat of Napoleon is nothing compared with Mrs Poyser's routing of the Squire. But the Napoleonic wars are more than background: Arthur's seduction of Hetty and her lonely desperate journey are shaped by it, and so is Arthur's nemesis when he becomes a colonel in the regular army, his old dreams of golden squirearchy vanished, his life given up to foreign marches and battles. Beyond the novel's small, self-celebrating community where class is divided from class with fatal consequence, and where the Poysers are deep-rooted for better and worse, lies a larger map, which we perceive in glimpses. Some of its foreign places exist on real maps but the fictional map has blank spots, and Hetty, whose tiny fantasy-life is fostered in a class-fractured community, is wiped out in one of them, in some foreign place. Her brief existence after transportation is a virtual one, outside the novel, even vaguer than the after-lives of Dickens's fallen women. (George Eliot is too conservative and too realistic to exile Arthur or Adam with her.)

Foreignness defines and undermines the rural community so often romanticized, though not by George Eliot. Her scenes of provincial life expand in *The Mill on the Floss* where foreign allusion becomes sophisticated. Here the foreign map is detailed, sharply focused. We begin in a seaport: St Oggs looks away from inland life; Holland and the North Sea (originally 'the Northern sea', cut in proof to 'the sea') are not far off. Bob Jakin, Tom, and Mrs Glegg do a little foreign trading. The firm of Guest and Co, in which Mr Deane becomes a partner and Tom a shareholder, makes us aware of the foreign trade which shapes the lives of Tulliver the miller, Wakem the lawyer, Riley the auctioneer, Stephen and Philip – the expensive young gentlemen spending their less genteel fathers' profits on foreign culture. It is not a new theme but it develops George Eliot's earlier refusal to be contained by Englishness. The novel plays with images of breadth, in the first sentence a 'wide plain' and 'broadening' river, then the classical 'black ships' carrying timber, oil-seed and coal, compounding the sense of coast and voyage, and recalling ancient voyages, Ulysses or the Argonauts. We travel beyond the western European coast to Greece and Africa, and by structural and thematic implication, the novel involves a larger geography and economic history. The globe is spun into motion.

The fourth book resumes the foreign emphasis in 'Journeying down the Rhone', and an excursus occupying a whole chapter where the narrator halts the story and calls attention to foreign landscape and history. Book 4 takes its title 'The Valley of Humiliation' from Bunyan's homely and exotic landscape, and its first chapter's wide-ranging heading, 'A Variation of Protestantism unknown to Bossuet', challenges readers to whom Bossuet is unknown. The Floss and its tributary Ripple are displaced by real rivers in Germany and France, and readers are tactfully addressed as 'perhaps' travelled, observant and meditative, who 'have perhaps felt' and 'may have thought', like the narrator, 'Journeying down the Rhone on a summer's day you have perhaps felt … Strange contrast, you may have thought, between the effect produced on us by these dismal remnants … and the effect produced by those ruins on the castled Rhine … (4). Once more the map is enlarged; we move from comparison of feelings for sordid ruinous Rhône and romantic Rhine to comparison of Lincolnshire floods and Rhône floods, and three rivers are linked by the pagan image of 'an angry destroying god'. The shift takes just a paragraph but in it, the mill on the Floss and it are placed, historically and geographically.

Sublime inhuman nature rebukes ignoble human nature:

> you are stifled for want of an outlet towards something beautiful, great or noble; you are irritated with these dull men and women, as a kind of population out of keeping with the earth on which they live – with this rich plain where the great river flows for ever onward, and links the small pulse of the old English town with the beatings of the world's mighty heart. (4, 1)

The traditional image of the heart (to be quoted from Drayton's 'heart of England' in *Felix Holt*) is 'the world's heart' in this novel's metaphorical pattern. The local river literally becomes part of ocean but the cunning narrator forces expansion only to switch our sympathies back home again: we are made to think and feel as inhabitants of a region and of a planet.

In *The Lifted Veil* Latimer begins and ends in a Devonshire 'nest' – harsh echo of the attic room – but tells a European story. Like Mary Ann Evans he travels to Geneva for his benign lake experiences, then to Austria, Venice and Prague, where foreignness seems malignant and imagination turns pathological. The symbolism is set in the mind and then developed as a process over time. Foreignness arrives in a word, 'Prague', spoken by Latimer's father, a *fiat* which leaves his son's mind 'resting on the word … with a strange sense that a new and wondrous scene was breaking upon me: a city under the broad sunshine …' (1). The clairvoyant vision is compared to a dissolving view, pictured in optical terms as 'minute in its distinctness down to a patch of rainbow light on the pavement, transmitted through a coloured lamp in the shape of a star … a strange city … unfamiliar'. The defamiliarization is both confused and clear, but explicitly recognized. Then the fantasy of foreignness changes to solid specific city-scape as Latimer finds he is in Prague.

'Brother Jacob' is concerned with foreignness but the experience of travel is almost parodied, in a crude vehicle for the critique of English xenophobia. The dishonest David Faux goes abroad because he is not appreciated at home, his imagination circling 'round the utmost limits of his geographical knowledge' to light on America, of which he has a general idea 'as a country where the population was chiefly black' so a 'propitious destination for an emigrant who … had the … easily recognizable merit of whiteness'. After six years in the West Indies (which was baldly reported), he settles in a provincial town to charm 'Grimworth Desdemonas' with tales of sharks, hectic rescues, fevers, breadfruit, landcrabs biting toes and broken-hearted Creole heiresses. Prettyman the grocer is xenophobic like other minor figures, 'not fond of people that have been beyond seas, if they can't give a good account of how they happened to go' but he sensibly dismisses David's traveller's tale about 'a life of Sultanic self indulgence'. David did not have a brilliant career among 'the blacks' 'either because they had already seen too many white men, or for some other reason' and sees a lady of submissive temper likely to wait on him 'as well as if she had been a negress': the weak little story has the merit of conflating racism and sexism.

What is outlined here is finely imagined in *Felix Holt*. It begins with a motto from 'Polyolbion' by the Warwickshire Drayton, whose 'shire' is carefully placed, 'which we the heart of England well may call', then further distanced from patriotic interpretation as the stagecoach traveller of the Introduction observes 'this was the district of protruberant optimists' sure that 'England was the best of possible counties'. (We 'are pleased to call Merry England' is another cool placing in *Silas Marner*, a more romantic but not uncritical represen-tation of an English community[6].) Such subtle touches make it plain that patriotic traditions are styles and constructions, and the initial irony prepares a critique of English patriotism and xenophobia. We start with the heart of England, used and revised in *The Mill*, and, again, the metaphor points to national limits.

The story insists that England is on the map of Europe and Asia. Both parts of the plot are rooted abroad, one in France and one in Smyrna. Esther is the child of a French–English marriage and Rufus Lyon marries a French refugee and exile whose English husband has fought in foreign wars. George Eliot has fun with Harold's hookah and sauces, and she sympathizes with nuances of Mrs Transome's conservatism but places it in class and gender. Again she conflates sexism with racism: Harold assures Esther that his love for her is not like his feeling for his child's slave-mother.

The critique becomes central in the novel with an English place-name for a title. After George Eliot's long experimentation with spots of foreignness, we arrive at Rome in *Middlemarch*. An important character is of mixed race, the outsider Will Ladislaw, continuing George Eliot's Polish interests. An English education was not enough for Will or, indeed, Dorothea. (Her Swiss education sounds less experimental than that of the Lewes boys at Hofwyl, a progressive Swiss school near Berne that did not do them much good – even compliant Charles was hampered in his Post Office job by his knowledge of French and German being better than his English.) Mr Brooke had done the Grand Tour, keeping journals and souvenirs like his author; and Casaubon needs the Vatican library, and so he chooses Rome for a wedding journey. When Ladislaw is charmingly showing off as dinner-guest in the Via Sistina and jokes that Rome gives him a new sense of history, stimulating imaginative construction by fragmentariness, or as Casaubon gives his bride a standard account of the Farnesina frescoes once thought to be by Raphael, the novelist brilliantly draws on her own Roman disenchantments for her invented minds and personalities (*Journals*, 341–7).

She does this when Dorothea aspires to lead 'a grand life here – now – in England' but finds her stay in Rome with her scholar-bridegroom less luminous but no less dangerous than Psyche's marriage. In Rome Will's wit and aestheticism meet her ignorance, confusion and puritanism, and he offers an answer through art, but more than art is needed. George Eliot conflates culture shock with sexual disappointment and Will becomes the novel's mild version of Eros. Dorothea sees Rome 'as a bride' in Casaubon's words, as 'a lamp-holder' in her own. The sterile historian gives a clue she cannot grasp when at their first meeting he describes his mind as 'something like the ghost of an ancient …' trying mentally to construct the world 'as it used to be, in spite of ruin and confusing changes' (2). Dorothea, like her author, tries to know the past *because* of ruin and change. In her vastation, George Eliot remakes her own response but also revises images from *Romola* and *The Lifted Veil*. Casaubon is a perverted version of the Florentine spirit in *Romola*, a fantastic link between the written past and writing in the present. Prague brought Latimer the 'death' of all that was 'personal', a 'deadening' of human relations, and a raw 'quickening' of 'the inanimate, in bright, vast, strange shifting imagery'. Dorothea's Rome is written in similar sensations and dynamic form, dissolving and dislocating narrative and image, inside and outside:

> The weight of unintelligible Rome might lie easily on bright nymphs to whom it formed a background … Ruins and basilicas, palaces and colossi, set in the midst of a sordid present, where all that was living and warm-blooded seemed sunk in the deep degeneracy of a super-stition divorced from reverence; the chiller but yet eager Titanic life gazing and struggling on walls and ceilings; the long vistas of white forms whose marble eyes seemed to hold the monotonous light of an alien world: all this vast wreck of ambitious ideals, sensuous and spiritual, mixed confusingly with the signs of breathing forgetfulness and degradation, at first jarred her as with an electric shock, and then urged themselves on her with that ache belonging to a glut of confused ideas which check the flow of emotion. Forms both pale and glowing took possession of her young sense, and fixed themselves in her memory … preparing strange associations … (20)

For the reader this vertiginous and panoramic confusion, gigantism and inhibition is a sensuous and structural correlative, an appro-priate blur and rush, a local instability and shock characteristic of the novel's whole form and motion. At the end of Book 1, 'Miss Brooke' gives way – chance serving choice – to wider and other interests. In the end, the old stable ego of character and story splinter, with 'many Dorotheas'.

In Rome, Dorothea's breakdown is constructed for a reader who is also denied clarity, stability and information by a reticent author not wanting to say precisely what happened. *Middlemarch* forces absences, fragmentariness and doubt on us. George Eliot, the keeper of secrets, does not say exactly what Dorothea thought of her 'wedding journey to Rome'. We cannot know what she might have done instead of becoming 'assimilated' in family life. Timothy Cooper never gets an answer to the question he asks Caleb Garth about injustice, nor do we. We know what happened to Dorothea's son, but not her daughter. Rome is not the only image of instability and doubt but its presence ensures that Middlemarch is displaced. The internal and external disorder of Rome's foreignness is a synecdoche. George Eliot is one of the first novelists to individualize historical consciousness and Dorothea's inability to relate past and present is a failure of that consciousness.

George Eliot's political bias was conservative but she recognizes the limits and defects of national pride and prejudice, she anticipates some aspects of colonial and post-colonial awareness, and it shaped her last novel's development of what is present in all her fiction. Daniel Deronda's sense of history, and his own history, contemplate a form of Zionism unpalatable to the modern mind, but his novel articulates internationalism and a fusion of nations – briefly and brightly in the Meyricks' questioning of Mirah's Jewish separatism, vaguely and solemnly in Daniel's hope, which was inspired by Mordecai and his own grandfather, for separateness with communication. The novel continues the critique of Anglocentricity by negative images of class, state, and church in the English establishment, and positive images of European and Jewish cultures. Theophrastus Such has doubts about racial fusion because of 'the negro races' but George Eliot introduces the West Indies, the Jamaica rising, Governor Eyre and the American Civil War. In a cleverly summarized lunch conversation where all the trivial remarks have political (and personal) undertones, Daniel Deronda anticipates modern post-colonialist discussions, interpreting Caliban as a rebuke to colonialism: he answers Grandcourt's view of 'the Jamaican negro [as] a beastly sort of Baptist Caliban' by saying 'he had always felt a little with Caliban, who naturally had his own point of view and could sing a good song' (*Daniel Deronda*, 29).

The ideals and prospects of Charisi's grandson are also formed by his mother, whose attempt to subvert race and gender is not wholly frustrated. The Princess Alcharisi is one of George Eliot's most interesting foreign characters. She was her one portrait of woman's genius (much more profound than the heroine of 'Armgart'), and her one questioning of maternal and familial vocation, for which Dorothea, though not her author, had to settle. Daniel's mother is also a means of respectfully but strongly criticizing Jewish sexual politics – and sexual politics in general. The novel makes her accept a punishment for denying the son his birthright, but she articulates and represents a woman's problems as no Englishwoman in any of the novels is ever allowed to do. For George Eliot, she had to be foreign. The real feminist questions she raises are left unanswered, but we feel the author's imagination pressing against historic limits and personal restraints. It is true that Gwendolen, and Gwendolen's life, also raise the questions of frustrated ambition, discontent with woman's conventional lot and a woman's enslavement but unlike Daniel's mother, the English heroine is not creative, and her questions are at once too abstract and too personally petulant. She is alone at the end, but in an ambiguous solitude.

Near the end is a doubled return to the domestic and pastoral scene. The return is at first dramatized as fantasy, with the English heroine – like the foreign diva a victim of patriarchy – travelling for the second time from Italy to England. The journeying train is a seat for her imaginative crisis (as it was to be for Anna Karenina, Isabel Archer and Yuri Zhivago).There is a stop between stations, 'one of those long unacountable pauses often experienced in foreign trains … a dreamy, sunny stillness'. Gwendolen's dissolving view is not traumatic like Latimer's or Dorothea's: 'this mingled, dozing view seemed to dissolve and give way to a more wakeful vision of Offendene and Pennicote … She saw the grey shoulders of the downs, the cattle-specked fields, the shadowy plantations with rutted lanes …' She remembers her family's welcome long ago, and *nostos* is literal and metaphorical: 'All that brief experience of a quiet home which had once seemed a dullness to be fled from, now came back to her as a restful escape, a station where she found the breath of morning and the unreproaching voice of birds, after following a lure through a long Satanic masquerade …' (64).

The English idyll is not naive: it is a symbolic transformation, that is internalized and motivated. Gwendolen has lost touch with her self, is menaced by her demons in London, on a luxury yacht, in a small boat. After her murderous wish and belated recoil, she is disturbed but calmed. She has never been in touch with the large world, being no Odysseus but an uneducated young woman, and her return home becomes a shocking encounter with foreignness: Daniel shatters her social ignorance with news of Jewishness and his political mission. The public world that has waited in newspapers and other neglected reading breaks into her imagination.

The English idyll is not isolated. It is the other side of Daniel's journey. He takes the family with him into foreignness, in both fact and symbol – his grandfather's chest and his devoted wife – as Gwendolen takes home guilts and alienations. At the end there is a distant view of foreign shores but George Eliot does not erase Englishness. It is put in its place, thematically and geographically, and revalued, if selectively and comfortably. Daniel's voyage East keeps the novel strange and open – dangerously so, as it turns out – and the English homecoming earths his longer journey. Both parts of the ending are uncertain, both are futures, doubling openness. One stresses a tentative politics: 'I may awaken a movement in other minds …' (69)[7]; the other suggests Gwendolen's growth and independence, while faithful Rex hovers as a fictitiously and historically plausible possibility, in a hint too subtle and shadowy for anti-climax.

'I may awaken a movement.' The insertion of this sentence, which is not in the manuscript, shows George Eliot's care in wording 'pre-Zionist' ideas. Not that these are clear: Mordecai speaks of an 'organic centre' and dismisses Gideon's 'our people have inherited a good deal of hatred' (now more pertinent than ever) and Daniel speaks of 'a national centre, such as the English have', conflating Jewish diaspora and English colonial dispersion (*Daniel Deronda*, 42, 69). These political thinkers are fictitious characters in a public-house discussion and a troubled private conversation, the novelist's medium for ideas which may not be her own, but some of which are presented with suggestive sympathy. But Theophrastus Such's 'Impression' that the English do not call themselves 'a dispersed … people', which I have already mentioned, revises Daniel's facile conflation, and suggests unsteadiness in her concept of his mission, and second thoughts.

The novel most concerned with foreignness turns from the English politics presented in earlier novels, usually by indirection, always with conservative anxiety. When she set *Daniel Deronda* in the present, social unrest in England, seen in trade union protest and the Hyde Park riots, was perhaps too menacingly close for the ironies of *Felix Holt* and *Middlemarch* – 1832 Reform novels placed in the past. Or perhaps she had grown more socially pessimistic about the condition of England after two Reform Acts. English society is pungently satirized but the critique is negative, and her early mild social meliorism is re-directed to foreign shores she had not visited. George Eliot was no friend to English radicalism but even the conservative anti-ballot-box Felix Holt and the well-meaning first Reform MP Ladislaw sound less abstract and romantic than Daniel. It is not surprising that High Tory John Blackwood praised the 'grand … vague' end of his best novelist's aspiring, evasive and nervous political imagination (*Letters* 6, 272).

We read fiction with double consciousness, placing art in its time but aware of historical change, and the two concerns can be incompatible. We approve of *Daniel Deronda*'s critique of racism, concentrated as it was in the Jewish case, and its critique of English society, but we know the terrible past and present of Zionism, Palestine and Israel. Thinkers and activists like Edward Said are urged by political passion to hybridize texts, to judge the past in the light of present. Such readings change the nature of literary response. While we see prudence in 'I may awaken a movement', George Eliot's wary approval of Daniel's politics begs questions and seems dangerously irresponsible, though the revision in *Theophrastus* suggests that she may have come to see this. For us, Charisi's ideal of separateness with communication has changed its meaning[8].

Life and art are intertwined, but are not the same. Ideals are easier to promote in art than life. George Eliot's investments made her complicit with Grapnell & Co, her gambling capitalists. Her shares were not ethical, she invested in the Empire. She implicitly criticizes the romantic colonial fantasies of Rex and Anna Gascoigne, but she and Lewes were also ignorant, like many others, when they sent prospectless sons on African colonial adventures. We can be pretty sure that Thornton and Bertie, joining skirmishes and cattle raids against the Zulus in Natal, farming and failing, drudging as store-keepers and waggoners, did not think about 'the little Mutter's' sincere attack on colour prejudice in 'Brother Jacob'. George Eliot was horrified by the Kaffir and Zulu wars, and when writing to John Blackwood about her disapproval of Sir Bartle Frere's demands and policies, she says: 'it seems to me that we cannot afford either morally or physically to reform semi-civilised peoples at every point of the compass with blood and iron' (*Letters* 7, 109). We do not know but may imagine what she thought when Lewes's daughter-in-law Eliza wrote about the 'nasty dirty black' police in her house for her protection (*Letters* 9, 241).

Her politics are not only the politics of her time but they disappoint our liking for consistent matching of theory and practice with adequate knowledge and foresight. She was not Anglocentric, she learnt Hebrew and tirelessly researched the history of Florence and Spain, but she knew little about 19th-century Palestine. She and Lewes thought of going to the East but never did, and the journey might not have changed her tentative sympathy with the beginnings of Zionist ideas. She was a child of her time, guilty of historical ignorance like most of us, but she fixed hers in famous fiction to be judged in ways she did not anticipate.

But not wholly condemned. George Eliot's internationalism and hatred of racism were rare in her time and relevant now. The critique of Gwendolen's ignorant common self-condemning '*You* are just the same as if you were not a Jew' (69), a critique developed through fictional character and idiolect, is directly put, and politically generalized, in a letter to Harriet Beecher Stowe, a fellow novelist and anti-racist. Colour prejudice is linked with what was not yet called anti-semitisim, as she assumes in her correspondent a common cause and humane sympathy: 'because I felt that the usual attitude of Christians towards Jews is – I hardly know whether to say more impious or more stupid … I therefore felt urged to treat Jews with such sympathy and understanding as my nature and knowledge could attain to'. The argument broadens: she finds the prejudice typical of English superiority 'towards all oriental peoples … a spirit of arrogance and contemptuous dictatorialness … a national disgrace' (*Letters* 6, 301).

Notes

1 Oscar Browning (1890) *Life of George Eliot*. London: Walter Scott.

2 Lamartine, admired by George Eliot for politics not poetry (*Letters* 1, 253), relocates '*Le Lac*' and sentimentalizes Rousseau's ecstasy. Henry James may recall Rousseau as he images the lake for his hero's fancied starlit gliding in a skiff with Daisy Miller and their 'escapade' by steamer to Chillon, locating the free delights at Vevey and contrasting it with Geneva's 'little metropolis of Calvinism'.

3 See Chapter 1, note 2.

4 She quotes Keats' *Letters* in her notebooks: Pratt & Neufeldt, 83, 162.

5 See Tom Winnifrith's 'Subtle Shadowy Suggestions: Fact and Fiction' in *Scenes of Clerical Life*, *George Eliot – George Henry Lewes Studies*, Nos. 24–6, September 1993. When John Gwyther informed John Blackwood he was also a widowed curate sacked to make way for a Rector's connection, and Amos's prototype, George Eliot admitted his was a 'portrait' drawn when her 'hand was not well in – I did not know so well how to manipulate my materials' (*Letters* 3, 99); see Chapter 3.

6 I think QED Leavis exaggerates the harmony of Raveloe's 'organic community' by underplaying, though noting, George Eliot's critique of class. See Introduction, *Silas Marner* (1961). Harmondsworth: Penguin.

7 See Edward Said (1993) *Culture and Imperialism*, New York: Alfred A. Knopf and *Critical Inquiry* (Winter 2005) Vol. 31, No. 2, especially Saree Makdisi, 'Said, Palestine, and the Humanism of Liberation'; Jane Irwin (ed.) (1996) George Eliot's '*Daniel Deronda Notebooks*'. Cambridge: Cambridge University Press; Joan Bennett (1948) *George Eliot: Her Mind and her Art*. Cambridge: Cambridge University Press.

8 See Said, op.cit ; and Nancy Henry (2002) *George Eliot and the British Empire*, Cambridge: Cambridge University Press, which discusses post-colonialist critiques of *Daniel Deronda* as well as George Eliot's colonial investments.

Chapter Three
Three or Four Love Stories

'It is a great experience – this marriage!' George Eliot to Cara Bray[1]

George Eliot was passionate, brave and intelligent enough to find and keep a love as good as human loves can be. One of her deep metaphors calls such love 'the permanent chosen treasure of the heart', (*Daniel Deronda*, 7, 50), precisely describing her love for Lewes – lasting, deliberately chosen and treasured. The lovers shared high intelligence, beliefs, tastes, rational passion and creativity, but were temperamentally different enough to complement and delight each other. She dedicated the manuscripts of her novels to him in loving gratitude.

She called herself 'a queer three-cornered awkward girl' (Haight, 10), Henry James described her as 'horse-faced' and 'massively plain', and Lewes was dubbed 'the Ape' by the mocking Carlyles but reminded Charlotte Brontë of Emily. Most people found them ugly but no one denied their vitality and brilliance. In a society where the double standard ruled, Mary Ann Evans needed nerve for the co-habitation. He was married and could not divorce Agnes. He had condoned her adultery with his friend Thornton Hunt, by whom Agnes had four children, with an earlier four by Lewes, one who died in infancy, then Charles, Thornton and Bertie, regarded by Marian as her foster-children, though only Charles was really domesticated with her and his father. She and Lewes lived together for over 25 years in what they regarded as an indissoluble union, and though it cut her off from her family and most of polite society, her fame ended the social ostracism of the early days.

Eighteen months after Lewes died, when Mary Ann was 60, she married John Cross, who was 41. She and Lewes had known him and his family for years, and Edith Simcox, one of several women excessively devoted to George Eliot, called him 'the fatal Johnny' in a jealous premonition some time before Lewes died (*Letters* 9, 212). Folk wisdom says the happily married are quick to re-marry, and George Eliot was not unusual in loving and marrying Cross, though some people were scandalized. Positivists disapproved of second marriages but though George Eliot admired Comte and let the Positivists use her poem 'O May I Join the Choir Invisible' for a hymn, she never joined the Positivist Society. Not that it was a second marriage – some intellectuals were surprised that after her marriage of minds with Lewes she should be so conventional. Enemies dug up the old scandal about her breaking up the Lewes marriage; friends were hurt because she had not told them she was going to marry, though Barbara Bodichon, who had no use for conformities of any kind, wrote saying she knew all love was different, there was no infidelity to Lewes, and she would have done what Johnny Cross had done if she had been a man and Mary Ann willing (*Letters* 7, 273).

The resilience of George Eliot was an old story. She was a woman of strong and elastic desires, and as a young woman was usually in love, one way or another. She attracted women but preferred men, as she told Edith Simcox, who was cast down by the declaration though it was only telling her what she already knew. There were immature infatuations, and in her 20s and early 30s she became attached to several men, showing a capacity for rebound. Susceptibility and resilience have survival value but romantically sexist friends and biographers proposed that she had a peculiar need for support. Impressed by her large skull and its contents, Charles Bray took her to have her head read and cast, pronouncing: 'She was not fitted to stand alone.' His judgment was varied by Cross, perhaps excusing her for loving him so soon after Lewes's death: 'She showed, from the earliest years, the trait that was most marked in her all through life – namely, the absolute need of some one person who should be all in all to her, and to whom she should be all in all' (Cross 1, 15).

There was a counter-story. When she went to Germany with Lewes in 1854, John Chapman, with whom she had some kind of brief affair and who was personally acquainted with her sexual susceptibility, was not exactly discreet and let it be known that Lewes was unlikely to have made all the running. The town gossips, including the Carlyles, spitefully dubbed her 'the strong-minded woman of the *Westminster Review*'. Some friends – Spencer, Mark

Rutherford and Oscar Browning – gave the impression of a strong, independent woman. She needed the men in her life but they needed her, too. Bray needed her humour and company; Brabant needed her young adulation and good German; Chapman needed her susceptibility, good sense, criticism, editorial skills and professionalism as a journalist; Spencer needed her company, mind, and vitality; and Lewes needed everything she could give, her mind, sexuality, creativity, fun, collaboration, support, fidelity, commitment, courage and love – everything he lost when his marriage fell apart, or had never known. Cross needed her motherliness, which he called 'womanliness', her company and 'high calling'.

Her family relations do not bear out the dependency fiction. As a child she was fond of all her siblings, and needed Isaac as a playmate. Later on she was needed by Chrissey and her father. Most of her women friends needed her at least as much as she needed them, some like Sara Hennell finding it hard when she left them for new friendship and enterprise. The adoring Elma Stuart and Edith Simcox liked to call her 'Mother', and their dependence was gratifying in some ways, trying in others. Like Daniel Deronda, she grew tired of being a mentor or ideal and, when she repeated Dorothea's 'less than ideal' decision to marry Ladislaw and married Cross, she asked Charles Lewes 'if she hadn't been human with feelings and failings like other people how could she have written her books' (*Letters* 7, 284).

We know next to nothing about the young loves or fancies glimpsed in letters to Maria Lewis and Martha Jackson, her early confidantes. Her personal allusions sound arch and pompous because of the high-toned religiose manner, polysyllabic diction, and heavy periodic sentences she affected at the time. She wrote to Martha, a school-friend who shared her taste for study, 'I am just now perturbed by circumstances that have called forth much emotion of a kind not favourable to the progress of the soul, either in earthly or heavenly acquirements' (*Letters* 1, 39). In March she hints away to Maria, rather ludicrously:

I feel that a sight of one being whom I have not beheld except passingly since the interview I last described to you would *probably* upset *all*; but as it is the image now seldom arises in consequence of entire occupation and, I trust in some degree, desire and prayer to be free from rebelling against Him whose I am by right ... I endeavoured to pray for the beloved object to whom I have alluded, I must still a little while say *beloved*, last night and felt soothingly melted in thinking that if mine be really prayers my acquaintance with him has probably caused the *first* to be offered up specially in his behalf. But all this I ought not to have permitted to slip from my pen. (*Letters* 1, 46–7)

In May Mary Ann writes to her about Joseph Brezzi, her tutor in German and Italian, whose tuition, she had told Martha in the letter just quoted, she was looking forward to 'ardently'. She glances at present, past, and future emotions:

I am beguiled by the fascinations that the study of languages has for my capricious mind ... My pilot too is anything but uninteresting, all external grace and mental power, but 'Cease ye from man' is engraven on my amulet. And to tell you the truth I begin ... to have such a consciousness that I am a negation of all that finds love and esteem ... (*Letters* 1, 51)

The confusion of sex and religion is plain and gets plainer when, after putting Isaiah on her amulet, she goes on to say she is re-reading Byron's 'Childe Harold' and quotes his injunction to suppress 'personal sorrows' and remember the troubles of the world. In June she mentions 'little troubles' and 'already detailed perplexities' (*Letters* 1, 52). She wishes for homeless and unsettled Maria's sake to be 'in the noose of matrimony' (*Letters* 1, 54), anticipating Mr Brooke's bachelor complacency, 'It *is* a noose, you know' (*Middlemarch*, 4). In October her words to Martha echo Helen Burns's to Jane Eyre, 'You think too much of the love of human beings':

Every day's experience seems to deepen the voice of foreboding ... 'The bliss of reciprocated affection is not allotted to you under any form. Your heart must be widowed in this manner from the world ... a consciousness of possessing the fervent love of any human being would soon become your heaven, therefore it would be your curse.' (*Letters* 1, 70)

The heavy style is not appealing but the conflict between profane love and sacred love was a real worry for Mary Ann Evans, as it had been for Charlotte Brontë. Human relations diminished and threatened her sense of God, as did her reading of Balzac, Scott and Bulwer Lytton, where goodness is found in characters who are not religious, unsettling the belief or assumption that morality depends on Christian faith. But her immediate problem as she grew up was love and marriage, which was every woman's lot.

About a year later, in August 1841, when she was beginning to move away from Christianity, George Eliot writes to Maria about isolation. She had no one who can enter into her 'pleasures or . . . griefs', no one with 'the same yearnings the same temptations the same delights', and 'no time for sentimental sorrows' (*Letters* 1, 102–3). Her style had freed up a little and she was writing more spontaneously, with simpler syntax and less Biblical diction. Her old friendship with Maria faded away after her refusal to go to church and the beginning of her new friendship with the congenial Brays. Her first close male friend was Charles Bray, a radical and wealthy ribbon-maker – who later lost his fortune when the trade declined and who was a philanthropist, educational reformer, supporter of trades unions and phrenologist. He started the story about her inability to 'stand alone', and perhaps she leaned on him, just a little, for a while. In conversation after George Eliot's death, Maria Lewis told Edith Simcox that he and Mary Ann used to walk together, 'lover-like'. She was fond of him, but far too attached to Cara to flirt with her husband, even though he was an attractive man, who was nicknamed Don Juan. If she knew he had a mistress and illegitimate children, one of whom, Nelly, was brought up by Cara, it is even less likely she would have flirted with him. Her friendship with him may have been an *amitié amoureuse*, the friendship with erotic undertones for which the English have no word, and which poor narrow-living and narrow-minded Maria was unlikely to have been able to discriminate, especially in the vulnerable state in which she met her best friend's interesting new friends. As George Eliot wrote: 'In the wonderful mixtures of our nature there is a feeling distinct from that exclusive passionate love of which some men and women (by no means all) are capable, which yet is not the same with friendship nor with a merely benevolent regard, whether admiring or compassionate . . . ' (*Daniel Deronda*, 50).

Mary Ann loved all three, but when she went away with Lewes, she could confide in Charles more easily than in Cara and Sara. After she had moved from Coventry to London, she reminded him that she was the person who most appreciated his jokes, and called him 'the dearest, oldest, stupidest, tiresomest, delightfullest, and never-to-be-forgotten-est of friends to me' (*Letters* 2, 82). (She used the same comic compound and joking tone in letters to Sara Hennell, and 20 years later for Gwendolen's rare teasing, 'you dreadfully careless-about-yourself mamma' (*Daniel Deronda*, 44).) A reviewer's quip, 'Fitly art thou called Bray', is sometimes meanly quoted without the source – Bray in his autobiography telling a good story against himself. Their friendship did not end; she offered to lend him money when he was hard up, and left Cara an annuity. He visited her and Lewes when they set up house in London, but the men never liked each other, and Bray was touchy about Lewes's lack of belief in phrenology. She was tactful, describing Cross's coronal arch to her old head-reading friend when she sent news of her marriage, and Bray was one of the last people she wrote to.

He may have informed *Middlemarch* by his experience of public health and committee politics, and perhaps bequeathed to Dorothea his blend of practical benevolence and Utopianism. He certainly contributed a nice detail to the home-teaching in the Garth household: Ben hates grammar and when his mother instructs him in its social advantage and rashly asks, 'Should you like to speak as old Job does?' of course Ben would – 'it's funnier' (*Middlemarch*, 24). His superior sister Letty cites Job's confusing pronunciation of 'sheep' as 'ship', but he rejoins that nobody would mistake Job because you don't get ships in gardens. On one of their walks and long talks 'about everything under the sun', Bray must have told Mary Ann that as a Coventry boy he laughed when someone said 'ships at sea': ' "Why a ship's on the common, a'ettin the graas" for such is the local pronunciation' – a detail of dialect and childhood she would not forget (*Phases of Opinion*, p 2). People were struck by her sympathetic listening, and Lewes said she missed nothing that came within 'the curl of her eyelash'. What she called a 'Quarry' is a notebook full of history, literature and fact, but her memory of people's stories was a quarry too.

Her first love story that is more than hint and allusion concerns a nameless young artist and picture restorer. She met him through Fanny Houghton and her husband, and he was smitten by her charms and accomplishments. She thought him very interesting and told the Brays that they were likely to be engaged, then had misgivings about his professional and social standing and cooled off. When her letter ending the acquaintance crossed with his formal offer of marriage, she was contrite and ashamed of her stupid impulsiveness, then felt flat because it was over. Cara reports the episode sympathetically, and the story shows her friends' and family's feeling that plain, clever Mary Ann was in need of matchmakers. Cara took her to visit two eligible cousins, but the one she hoped might be interested was not. The Brays introduced her to Froude, of whom she had written provocative words in her review of *The Nemesis of Faith*, and who had responded promisingly – again raising Cara's hopes. She was pleased Mary Ann should have the excitement but it came to nothing.

Two people she met at Rosehill were Dr Robert Brabant, who was interested in Strauss and biblical criticism, and his daughter Rufa, who had been given her glamorous nickname by Coleridge. Rufa had started to translate David Friedrich Strauss's influential *Das Leben Jesu, kritisch bearbei*t (1835–6) and when she married Charles Hennell in 1843, after opposition from her father because of Charles's tuberculosis, Mary Ann took on the Strauss, her first major publication. Rufa was a long-lasting friend, the first woman to call after she set up house with Lewes. After Rufa's wedding, at which she was bridesmaid for the third time, Mary Ann went to visit Brabant as second daughter, so nicknamed Deutera. She dangerously anticipated Dorothea in finding a little heaven with Brabant as archangel, and may have aroused the jealousy of his blind wife and sister-in-law and seems to have left in a hurry. She played it down later, claiming to have been silently laughing at the learned doctor up her sleeve, scattering incense because she found no better altar, and she and Brabant remained on good terms after she settled in London. According to Eliza Lynn Linton, who found him 'disgusting', Brabant did 'make love' to other young women, and she gives a jealous and unfriendly version of George Eliot's susceptibility in her novel, *The Autobiography of Christopher Kirkwood* (London,

1885). Mary Ann may have been more responsive and Brabant more exploitative than she liked to remember or tell. When Rufa told the story to Chapman, she criticized her father for blaming the quarrel on Mary Ann, though Haight and Ashton think the story may have been embroidered. As well as engaging the admiration of clever young women, Brabant was busy with a never-written work on mythology, so he has been seen as a Casaubon.

Out of this encounter came the first love story Mary Ann wrote, in October 1846. It takes the form of a wedding invitation to Charles Bray, beginning with her friend Mary Sibree announcing Professor Bücherworm, a grotesque scholar in search of an ugly 'strong-minded' blue-stocking to translate for him and support him. He finds Mary Ann ideal, though she is disappointingly beardless, and she jumps at the chance: 'For you must know, learned Professor … that I require nothing more in a husband than to save me from the horrific disgrace of spinster-hood and to take me out of England' (*Letters* 8, 14). There is no arguing about the sense of humour, and her biographer Mathilde Blind was not the last to admire the spoof as Carlylean wit and promising narrative – I find it an unpleasant self-deprecation of her plainness, which serious truths about single women and a wish to leave England make more painful. She laughs so that she may not weep, but the laugh is defensive, strident and bitterly self-humiliating. Bücherworm, too, anticipates Casaubon, but when she wrote *Middlemarch* George Eliot had lived with Lewes for 20 years and no longer paraded anxiety about her looks. As early as June 1857, she sounds unperturbed when telling Cara about her appearance: 'You wonder how my face has changed in the last three years. Doubtless it is older and uglier, but it ought not to have a bad expression, for I never have anything to call out my ill-humour … ' (*Letters* 2, 340).

She probably met Chapman, bookseller and publisher, when she was visiting Sara Hennell in Clapton in 1846. Her first impression, in retrospect, is critical, 'He was always too much of the *interesting* gentleman to please me' (*Letters* 1, 231). But she succumbed to his good looks and charm. In 1850, Chapman and Robert Mackay came to Rosehill and persuaded her to write her first big review, of Mackay's *Progress of the Intellect*, for the *Westminster Review*, the radical journal Chapman was hoping to buy with the help of wealthy acquaintances. He published her translation of Strauss, the translation of Feuerbach, and announced the publication of a book on *The Idea of a Future Life*, which she never wrote.

In November 1850, she briefly visited the Chapmans' boarding-house over the publishing offices in 142 Strand, and took up residence there in January 1851. Like other English novelists – Defoe, Dickens, Thackeray – she started her career in journalism. Through Chapman's contacts, she wrote reviews for the *Leader*, a progressive weekly edited by Lewes and Thornton Hunt. The Chapman household included his wife Susanna, their children, the governess Elisabeth Tilley, who was also Chapman's mistress, and a variety of boarders, visiting intellectuals and refugees. After Marian, as she now called herself, moved in, Chapman stirred jealousies in his household by listening to her play Mozart on the hired piano in her room, taking German lessons from her, going for walks with her and, once, being caught by his wife holding her hand. Cryptic words and signs in his coded journal suggest some lovemaking, and he notes that Susanna and Elisabeth, bonded in opposition, believe that he and Miss Evans are in love. There must have been physical contact but it probably stopped short of actual seduction, given her later high-minded defence of her commitment to Lewes. Once more, she left in a hurry. As she and Chapman parted at Euston and she pressed him to say what he felt, he admitted he felt affection for her but loved Susanna and Elisabeth, and she burst into tears.

But she had work to do for him, including a catalogue of publi-cations, and he was soon visiting her in Rosehill to discuss his purchase of the *Westminster* from William Hickson, who in turn had bought it from John Stuart Mill. There was another scene, in the grounds of Kenilworth Castle when, either tactlessly or unkindly, he praised beauty in nature and people, she took it personally and once again wept. However, they made up, and she was contrite about causing jealousy. They took a vow of renunciation, which they kept. He persuaded Susanna and Elisabeth to let her return, and the relationship – whatever it was – cooled to a friendly collaboration.

She wrote the prospectus for the *Westminster* and, though she once called herself 'something less than half an editor', it flourished under her unofficial editorship, to become again the great liberal paper it had been under Jeremy Bentham and John Stuart Mill.

Chapman could not afford to pay her a salary, so she worked for board and lodging and little more. (His lack of money and her need for it were her reasons for giving up the editorship in 1853.) She sought, rejected and advised contributors, scrupulously reading abstracts and specimens of their work. She managed the technical side of cutting, revising and proof-reading, and cleverly discouraged Chapman – who was not much of a writer – from contributing written work for the journal, but defended him and sympathized with his money troubles. She wrote reviews and parts of the 'Belles Lettres' feature, but no more long articles until she gave up editing. She thought about lay-out and political consistency, contributors' social seriousness, style and competence, and – most valuable to her as a novelist – mind and thought, which she began to analyse and discriminate. She worked enthusiastically for the journal whose radical and sceptical values were her own, in a full-time profession which was demanding, stimulating and instructive.

She was drawn into London life. She was the only woman at an historic meeting of the Booksellers' Association at 142 Strand about the price-fixing, chaired by Dickens, for which she and Spencer listed resolutions. She went to quiet dinner parties in the black velvet worn by matrons. She made friends with Bessie Parkes, feminist and poet, and heard Haydn's *Creation* with her. She visited galleries, the theatre and the opera, walked in the park or by the Thames, enjoyed the zoo and Kew Gardens, met people in Chapman's office and his dinners and evening parties. She persuaded Mazzini, a refugee from Italy, to write about freedom and despotism; argued with Pierre Leroux, a refugee from France after the *coup d'état* of 1851, about ideological differences with the anarchist Proudhon and another French exile, Louis Blanc, about George Sand, and Strauss's neglect of Christ's connection with the Essenes. In spite of her need for continuities, she must have looked back at the awkward puritan girl outraged by fiction, theatre, music, oratorio, London pleasures and its human spectacle, as belonging to another life – though in less than a decade that girl was to come back as Maggie Tulliver.

In that other life she lamented the multiplication of mortal relationships. Now her sentimental education was taking its course. Recovering what she had lost of her heart to Chapman, she made a new friend, Herbert Spencer, five months her junior, congenial, good-looking, clever and unmarried, a railway engineer turned philosopher and psychologist living at the *Economist* offices across the road in the Strand, where like her he was an assistant editor. Chapman had published his first book *Social Statics* (London, 1850). She sent Bray a copy, commenting that Sara was reading it by her fire in 142 Strand, 'with many interjections' (*Letters* 2, 11). Spencer's blend of egocentricity and detachment is at its most fascinating in a model review he wrote of his own book for the *Autobiography*, which he composed with such anguished consultations that his friends, including Marian, ridiculed him. But that was in the future.

Miss Evans and Spencer took to each other, meeting at the Chapman *soirées,* walking and talking, taking advantages of his free press tickets for the opera and plays, laughing at Thornton Hunt's reports of Louis Blanc's howlers in spoken English. On 27 March she writes a melancholy confiding letter to a new radical friend Clementia Taylor, significantly quoting Margaret Fuller, whose memoirs she was reviewing for the *Westminster*: 'I shall always reign through the intellect, but the life! the life! O my God! shall that never be sweet?' (*Letters* 2, 15). Three days later she is happily joking to Cara, in one of her frequent references to Spencer, that he has proposed 'not marriage' but Rossini's *William Tell*. She sees Lewes's adaptation of a French play, *The Chain of Events*, with Spencer, covers her eyes and screams at a shipwreck on stage.

They agree they are not in love and 'there is no reason why they should not have as much of each other's society as they like'. Enjoying 'the deliciously calm *new* friendship', they see each other every day, 'have a delightful *camaraderie*' and, she complains complacently, 'he runs away with a great deal of my time' (*Letters* 2, 29). She accepts Cara's invitation to Rosehill for him but thinks they should not arrive together as everyone is imagining they are engaged. She was protesting too much. She was in love but he was not.

While Cross was drawing on recollections of friends and making selective extracts from her letters for his biography, Spencer worried about being thought a rejected lover jilted for Lewes. He wanted Cross to say they had not been engaged and he had not loved her but reluctantly accepted a refusal. He sometimes gets credit for this but he made sure posterity would see him righted by writing it in his posthumously published *Autobiography*: 'There were reports that

I was in love with her, and that we were about to be married. But neither of these reports was true' (Spencer, 399).

She loved him more than anyone before Lewes and was unfortunately insensitive to his lack of libido. (One reason why I think she was probably still a virgin.) He was not in love with her and seems never to have been in love with anyone, but after Chapman she probably attributed a man's lack of desire to her undesirability. Spencer did, too, claiming to need beauty in women. Four of her letters to him imply or declare her unrequited love and longing. (Lewes's letters were buried with her, as she had planned, and there is only one real love letter to Cross.) The story of the letters could be by Henry James. Seven letters to Spencer were placed in the British Museum in 1935, on condition that their existence should not be made public for 50 years. They caused much vexation to Haight, who looked for them from 1937 to 1954, when he was told where they were and when they could be seen, and sworn to silence. They were published by Richard Schoenwald, a Spencer scholar, in the *New York Public Library Bulletin* of Spring 1976, and it was disclosed that a covering note read, 'Not to be opened for fifty years from the present time (August 1935), without the permission of the Trustees of the British Museum', 'some of whom', Haight complained 'were my friends' (*Letters* 8, vii). Haight published them in a two-volume supplement to his edition of the *Letters*. In his biography he had predicted that the letters would show that Spencer 'was adored once too'. It's a good joke, but Spencer was not Sir Andrew Aguecheek, and Haight admits in his preface to the supplement that the letters show 'an astonishing intensity of passion'.

We have the man's side of the Chapman affair but for the Spencer story we have both sides, confirming each other, each voicing distress with candour. Spencer confided to an American friend, EL Youmans, in 1881 that he had begun to have qualms 'as to what might result' from his 'constant companionship' with Miss Evans (*Letters* 8, 42). He felt a 'decided' 'feeling of friendship' and admiration for her 'morally and intellectually' but could not 'perceive' in himself 'any indications of a warmer feeling' and feared 'mischief would possibly follow' if the friendship continued. He wrote to her indicating his fears as 'delicately' as possible, then felt he had suggested she was in danger of falling in love with him and wrote to apologize (*Letters*

8, 43–3n). Her reply on 21 April 1852 bears out his report that 'she took it all smilingly': she discouraged more explanation, feeling 'disappointed rather than "hurt"' that he had not 'sufficiently divined' her character to see she was not in the habit of imagining anyone was 'falling in love' with her *(Letters* 8, 42). What he feared came about. She did fall in love with him – no doubt she had done so and disguised her feelings: 'Her feelings became involved and mine did not. The lack of physical attraction was fatal. Strongly as my judgment prompted, my instincts would not respond' (*Letters* 8, 43n).

Her next letter jokes about his coldness in the high temperatures of that summer: 'No credit to me for my virtues as a refrigerant. I owe them all to a few lumps of ice which I carried away with me from that tremendous glacier of yours.' After arch remarks about being glad he is 'uneasy' in her absence, and saying she won't ask if he 'longs most' for her society or sea-breezes, she ends with a black joke about her looks: she loves the sea so much that if she could stay all the year round she would soon be 'on an equality … with the star-fish and sea-egg – perhaps you will wickedly say, I certainly want little of being a *Medusa*' (*Letters* 8, 50–1). Spencer had discussed Medusae in 'A Theory of Population' (*Westminster* 62, 1852, pp 468–501) and there may be a reference to this, but her physical self-consciousness is painful[2]. In the summer of 1856 she and Lewes went on a boat in search of marine specimens, and she records a transformation of the Medusa, like the Ancient Mariner's benign vision of the shining water-snakes: 'This evening G and I have been out in a boat for an hour, and have caught about 20 Medusae. The western light on the rippled water as we went out was glorious, and on our return we saw the lovely green phosphorescence about the net and the oars' (*Journal*, 63). Medusa is recalled for tragic Hetty Sorrel: 'that wondrous Medusa-face, with the passionate, passionless lips' (37)[3].

In the third letter to Spencer, dated 16 July, she says it all: she is ill, she is wretched about him, she must go on seeing him. She knows the letter will make him angry and she begs him to wait till he is not:

> I want to know if you can assure me that you will not forsake me, that you will always be with me as much as you can and share your

thoughts and feelings with me. If you become attached to someone else, then I must die, but until then I could gather courage to work and make life valuable, if only I had you near me. I do not ask you to sacrifice anything – I would be very good and cheerful and never annoy you … Those who have known me best have always said, that if I loved anyone thoroughly my whole life must turn upon that feeling, and I find they said truly. You curse the destiny which has made the feeling concentrate itself on you – but if you will only have patience with me you shall not curse it long. You will find that I can be satisfied with very little … (*Letters* 8, 57)

No wonder she ends it, proud of her self-immolation, 'I suppose no woman ever before wrote such a letter as this.' Desire, pride and abjection are knotted like passions in Shakespeare's sonnets, though without their tormented wit. Or hers. She writes artlessly, with no jokes, no irony, no self-deprecation and no biting metaphor, only plain-spoken longing. No wonder he kept the letters.

He may have lacked sexual passion or desire for women, but he was a man of feeling, and he felt miserable, angry and helplessly sorry for her. In desperation he did something which has hardly been noticed, he 'hinted at the possibility of marriage'. She wisely refused, seeing that it 'would lead to unhappiness' (*Letters* 8, 43n). He was more caring and she more controlled than we might think. He did what she asked; he was patient and continued to see her, until she – not he – became attached to someone else. It did not take long. Her whole life did not turn on her feeling for him.

Haight's sharp pen fixes Spencer as a minor character, simplifying his bad health and hypochondria, reading his hyper-rationality as an abherration, and his breakdown as a wilful withdrawal, a perverse and self-punishing rejection of George Eliot: 'At this price he bought safety from the perils of marriage.' But his neurosis is more likely to have been the cause rather than an alibi, and was scarcely in his control. His contribution to social science and psychology and his development theory and ideas about natural law, have fallen into the background of intellectual history but he was an important figure in his time and more sympathetic than he appears in George Eliot's biography.

He was more than a figure of fun, or a Casaubon, in her story. Just as she walked and talked with Bray, and remembered his stories, so she walked and talked with Spencer, at the Chapmans' dinners and parties, on the embankment at the back of 142 Strand, less happily by the summer sea at Broadstairs. She teased him for arrogance when he said his brow was unlined because nothing puzzled him, but if we read beyond the anecdote, we find an observant account of the relaxed generation of ideas (Spencer, 399–401). It is not as eloquent as William James's analyses, but it is close to George Eliot's ideas about the creative process, which are implied in her imagery of 'simmering' and elaborated in Cross's account of 'a "not herself" which took possession of her', of feeling 'her own personality to be merely the instrument through which this spirit, as it were, was acting' (Cross 3, 424–5).

Spencer took himself too seriously and behaved eccentrically – plugging his ears if conversation got too exciting, for example – but he had stories to tell, and George Eliot listened to him. They both came from what he called lower middle-class families, Anglican with Methodist connections. Like her, he was miserable in adolescence, like her capable of rebellion. When he was 13 and being educated at his uncle's house 120 miles from home, unhappy with fellow-pupils and teaching arrangements, he impulsively ran, or rather walked, back to his parents, 'yearning for home'. He completed an 'immense journey' in three days, walking, getting a free ride in a coach and a lift from a kind waggoner who let him lie on soft straw in a covered wagon, staying in small taverns, making two shillings go a long way, counting it, offering a coachman coppers which he refused, and living on bread, rolls, a little milk and beer, exhausted, indifferent to landscape, and finally, startled by a man with a knife, frightened and tearful.

Hetty Sorrel's 'desperate journey' took seven days, and she too travelled on foot, by coach, getting a lift in a covered wagon, lying on packs of wool, was scared by a drunken postillion, stayed in small inns, making a little money go a long way, counting it, offering a shilling tip, asking for change and getting it all back, living on buns and water, exhausted, indifferent to landscape, startled by a rough man, and frightened and tearful. Her journey is a masterpiece of subtle simplicity and consummate art, a virtuoso narrative in indirect and free indirect style, crucial in the character and action of a great novel. Spencer's circumstantial story was truly artless and crucial to him. She was a vulnerable, frightened pregnant woman, he was a vulnerable, frightened boy. He quotes letters from his father and uncle about the crisis in the *Autobiography*: it was a story told, recalled, read and written. He surely told Marian stories of his childhood, and I think his 13-year-old self helped her imagine Hetty's forlorn fatigue and fear.

She repeated the desperate plea for him not to 'forsake' her in Gwendolen; 'if you … forsake me … .will you forsake me ?'; '*I* shall be forsaken' 'Die – die – you are forsaken'; 'assure me that you will not forsake me' (*Daniel Deronda*, 56); 'I said I should be forsaken … And I am forsaken' (*Daniel Deronda*, 69). But she has her own back when she gratuitously slips a sly parenthesis into a passage I quoted earlier, 'In the wonderful mixtures of our nature there is a feeling distinct from that exclusive passionate love of which some men and women (by no means all) are capable … ' (*Daniel Deronda*, 50) and in Casaubon's surprise at 'the moderation of his own abandonment' (*Middlemarch*, 7). Such detached perception is just in the style of Spencer's abstract introspective, 'I could not perceive in myself any indications of a warmer feeling' in the 1881 letter to Youmans (*Letters* 8, 42n). He may have blundered into such awkward excuse as he backed anxiously away.

However, he may have brought the railway to Middlemarch, 20 years after those London walks. George Eliot's essay 'The Natural History of German Life' suggests, 'The word *railways* … will probably call up, in the mind of a man who is not highly locomotive, the image either of a "Bradshaw", or of the station with which he is most familiar, or of an indefinite length of tram-road … ' (Pinney, 267). She distinguishes such vague associations from knowledge 'whether of navvy, engineer, director, shareholder' or 'landed proprietor in treaty with a railway company'. Her father had dealings with the new railway in his land management, but it is not a responsibility George Eliot ever mentions. She read books about railways, such as Samuel Smiles' *Life of George Stephenson,* but her personal expert was Spencer. He worked as an engineer on the new London and Birmingham railway, and he later took on wider responsibilities as designer, inventor and administrative secretary for the Gloucester and Birmingham line. His *Autobiography* discusses line-laying, levelling and bridge design. He had a grasp of railway economics and politics, dealings with landed proprietors and the profits and perils of railway speculation, which he advised his father and uncle about. His experience and George Eliot's assimilative imagination may animate a chapter of fiction and railway history in which small-landed proprietors wheel and deal, farm labourers attack railway surveyors, and Caleb Garth conducts profitable negotiations offstage on Dorothea's behalf. As a fact-informed railway narrative without a whiff of research, Chapter 61 of *Middlemarch* is rivalled only by *Dombey and Son*, which is symbolically dramatic and less technical, and Gaskell's quietly knowledgable *Cousin Phillis*[4].

Haight was sceptical of Spencer's claim that he suggested fiction to Marian, but Spencer was as well known for truth-telling as George Washington, hopeless at dissembling, and too unimaginative to lie: 'I thought I saw in her many, if not all, of the needful qualifications in high degree – quick observation, great power of analysis, unusual and rapid intuition into others' states of mind, deep and broad sympathies, wit and humour and broad culture' (Spencer, 398). This is confirmed by Lewes in a conversation with Lady Holland: 'Our friends – Herbert Spencer – and others used to say to me – Why doesn't she write a novel? And I used to reply that she was without the creative power' (*Letters* 9, 197). If Marian had accepted Spencer's rash proposal she would still have been encouraged to write fiction, and might still have been one of its stars. She might not have been George Eliot, since she said 'George' was a tribute to Lewes, though it must also honour George Sand. If Lewes loved the fun and the pathos in *Scenes of Clerical Life*, Spencer laughed and cried over *Adam Bede*:

> And now that I have read it what am I to say. That I have read it with laughter and tears and without criticism. Knowing as you do how constitutionally I am given to fault finding, you will understand what this means. That I who am so little given to enthusiastic admiration, should not know how adequately to say how much I admire, will give you some idea of my feeling respecting it. (*Letters* 8, 245–6)

The appreciation is humorous and intimate. He says he admired the genuineness, the true ring of dialogue, the large moral effect, and the details – did he recognize any? He felt better for having read it. No wonder she told friends about his praise. This was a peace-making letter after a rift, and said he would 'feel it as a serious misfortune if anything were to dissolve' the friendship. She had been angry with him for not denying her authorship to the coaxing Chapman, though he later explained ingenuously that when asked point-blank he could not dissemble his voice or facial expression. They had thought his manner changed. Lewes wrote in his journal for 24 March 1859: 'He used to be one of our friends on whom we most relied, but jealousy, too patent, and too unequivocal, of our success, acting on his own bitterness at non-success, has of late cooled him visibly. He always tells us the disagreeable things he hears or reads of us, and never the agreeable things' (*Letters* 3, 49n). Such weaknesses and criticisms are native to friendship, and Spencer would have been less than human had he not felt some envy of these close friends of his, who had so much more than he did. The old friendship with Marian troubled him all his life, as his fuss about the Cross biography shows. Lewes was grateful for his companionship and stimulus, and taxed him about the coolness, eliciting the explanation – or evasion – that he was not aware of a change. Spencer was grateful, too, and said his interest in philosophy and psychology began with Lewes. He was one of the few people not to be spiteful about Lewes's manner, size, looks or morals, and praised his generosity and conscience: 'he discharged the responsibilities which devolved upon him with great conscientiousness, and at much cost in self-sacrifice, notwithstanding circumstances which many men would have made a plea for repudiating them' (Spencer, 378). If his style lacks warmth it is not because he finds emotion hard to express – he cannot go into details about Agnes, Hunt and their children.

After the hot summer of 1856, autumn brought new affections. To help him over a difficult time, Spencer would take Lewes with him when he called on Marian, still seeing her as she had asked. One evening, when he got up to go Lewes said he would stay and Spencer dated their intimacy from that evening. Doomed to be go-between, he brought them together and, years later, introduced Lewes to Cross.

In the end, Marian did not have to make do with 'very little'. She had someone else to take her to the theatre and the opera, and with whom to fall in love. Lewes was ideal. He was too intelligent and experienced to aestheticize love – as is evident in his cool comments on plain and good-looking actresses in his theatre criticisms – and his marriage to a beautiful woman had gone badly wrong. (If we think of Mary Ann's small eyes, big nose and heavy jaw, we should note Bessie Parkes's admiration of her figure, supple and of 'almost serpentine grace' – like Gwendolen Harleth's.) By the winter of 1852 or early spring in 1853, George Eliot and Lewes were probably more than friends. She had known him for two years, first describing him as 'a sort of miniature Mirabeau'. His name comes into her letters before the break with Spencer. In December 1851, she describes him with her and Spencer, making fun of a production of *The Merry Wives of Windsor*, and in February 1852 she comments that he has asked after Sara, with whom 'he was charmed' (*Letters* 1, 377; 2, 13).

Now he took up her time, as Spencer had done. One evening in November 1852, she was busy with proofs when he dropped in and stayed until the second dinner bell; in March 1853 he was 'as always, genial and amusing' and 'had quite won my liking, in spite of myself'; by early April he had become quite a 'pleasant friend'; and later in the month was called 'a man of heart and conscience wearing a mask of flippancy' (*Letters* 2, 68, 94, 97, 98). In January 1853 she thought of leaving the Chapmans and changed her room instead, but in October she moved to 21 Cambridge Street, Hyde Park Square. Oscar Browning thought the affair started then but Ashton thinks it may have been in spring 1853 when, having 'left his family home in Bedford Place, Kensington, some time after July 1852, never to return …', Lewes could use his friend Frederick Ward's flat in Cork Street (Ashton, 104).

Lewes was ill in April 1854 and Marian told Cara she was doing some of his work – reviews for the *Leader* – and complains: 'No opera and no fun for me for the next month!' (*Letters* 2, 151). In May she wrote to Cara about everyone being an island, and said 'this seclusion is sometimes the most intensely felt at the very moment your friend is caressing you or consoling you' (*Letters* 2, 156). She had a caressing friend, whose name crops up a few lines later: Lewes was better and she expected him back. It is surprising that the comment about the caress was not censored by Cross, but if he did not make the connection, Cara surely did. The elopement could only have taken her Coventry friends by surprise if they were expecting her to have a secret affair. (I'm sure Ashton is right to think Lewes's name was carefully dropped as a way of preparing them [Ashton, 106].

On 10 July, Marian told Sara she was leaving London, 'I shall soon send you a good bye, for I am preparing to go to "Labassecour" ' (*Letters* 2, 165). Nine days later her goodbye began: 'Dear Friends – all three' and gave Poste Restante addresses as Weimar and Berlin (*Letters* 2, 166). Reading them, Cara and Sara must have guessed that Marian was not going alone, even though she did not confide in them directly.

In a letter to Ward, in which Lewes says 'L'amour va son train', which Ashton spotted as a likely reference to Marian, he also uses 'Labassecour' for Belgium so either of them may have used the place-name in lover's mimicry (Ashton, 104). He was a great admirer of Charlotte Brontë and Marian a great admirer of *Villette*, thinking it a novel of 'almost preternatural' power, and asking the Brays excitedly '*Villette* – *Villette* – have you read it?' (*Letters* 2, 87, 92). She could identify with a plain, clever heroine in love with an ugly, brilliant man in a plot that did not have a wish-fulfilling end or turn on the marriage morality she hated in *Jane Eyre*. She protested to Bray: 'All self-sacrifice is good – but one would like it to be in a somewhat nobler cause than that of a diabolical law which chains a man soul and body to a putrefying carcase' (*Letters* 1, 268). She could admire Jane striking out for herself but not the absolute Christian condemnation of adultery. Calling her destination 'Labassecour' flouted the omens, boldly or carelessly, because *Villette*'s rites of passage end unhappily for love, if not for brave independence. Marian was luckier than Charlotte Brontë or Lucy Snowe, and more radical than Jane Eyre, saying yes to her Rochester though his wife was alive.

When she met Lewes at St Katherine's Dock on 19 July, she was embarking on a voyage down the Thames to the sea, from London to Antwerp, a passage more decisive than on her earlier journey to Geneva. On the steamer Ravensbourne, the lovers found themselves in the old, small world, meeting Robert Noel, who had just been staying with the Brays; and after a few days in Antwerp, Brussels and Liège, they met Brabant on the train to Cologne. He introduced them to Strauss and Marian records the meeting with her usual self-deprecation, 'my deficient German prevented us from learning more of each other than our exterior which in the case of both would have been better left to imagination' (*Letters* 2, 171).

They chose Germany because of Lewes's research on Goethe, and Weimar also offered an easy society with liberal views and liberated examples, like Liszt and his Russian mistress, Princess Wittgenstein. Her robe 'of some semi-transparent white material lined with orange-colour' (*Journals*, 21) ' is adapted for Daniel's mother, another Russian princess, and another free spirit though twice respectably married. On 16 August, Marian emphasized the friendly, relaxed society in a letter to Bray, 'I have had a month of exquisite enjoyment, and seem to have begun life afresh' (*Letters* 2, 170), and she told Chapman: 'People are wonderfully kind to us ... I am happier every day and find my domesticity more and more delightful and beneficial to me. Affection, respect and intellectual sympathy deepen, and for the first time in my life I can say to the moments "Verweilen sie, sie sind so schön"'; and she also comments: 'The day seems too short for our happiness, and we both of us feel that we have begun life afresh – with new ambitions and new powers' (*Letters* 2, 172–3, 190). Perhaps she expected Chapman to have profited from the German lessons in 142 Strand, but her deep connection is with Lewes – the quotation from the end of Part 2 of *Faust* (an ending Lewes deplored), where Faust is talking about his redemptive land conservation. Lewes, in an interesting negative, describes Faust's 'feverish' and 'transitory' feeling for Gretchen, 'who has no power to make him say to the passing moment, "Stay, thou art fair"' (*The Life of Goethe*, 6, 7). As she helped with *Goethe*, they must have read the line in mutual consciousness of a love neither feverish nor transitory. Her letter to Chapman – an old flame – is naturally a touch exultant, and an earlier letter to him, dated 6 August but published later, was marked by her 'sisterly interest', 'Some day, I hope, you will have as much happiness, and of the same kind, and will let me share it by telling me of it' (*Letters* 8, 116)[5]. She is glad to hear from him, and sorry he is in financial trouble, and she suggests that she should review Victor Cousin on Madame de Sablé. She values her old ties but they were weakening, and her sense of the unknown future is energetic.

During the past year, while deciding her own future, Marian had been worrying about Chrissey, and she fantasized about going to Australia with her or returning to the Midlands. It was only a matter of time before her new life with Lewes would cut her off from her family, and even friendships were threatened. Her goodbye letters look like broad hints, especially after months of name-dropping references to Lewes, but she seems to have been uncertain how much Cara and Sara had guessed or knew. In a loving letter to Bray, she wrote: 'I am quite prepared to accept the consequences' (*Letters* 2, 179). She declares her love for Cara and Sara but her best love for Lewes: 'I love Cara and you with unchanged and unchangeable affection, and while I retain your friendship I retain the best that life has given me next to that which is the deepest and gravest joy in all human experience' (*Letters* 2, 182).

Every pleasure she experienced was an image of love – Liszt's music, the first real piano-playing she had heard; *Nathan der Weise,* an anti-racist play that matched her sympathies; and unpretentious hospitality with Bratwurst and Küchen. The couple enjoyed doubts too and took in their first Wagner, *Der Fliegende Höllander,* which Marian wrote about at length, and remembered when Gwendolen sailed with Grandcourt, *Lohengrin* which Lewes did not sit through, a bad *Fidelio*, in which the 'divine music' triumphed, and Gluck's *Orpheus and Eurydice* with 'Greek shades' looking 'like butchers in women's chemises' (*Journals*, 41). On the Goethe trail of memories and monuments, they visited a small Schloss in Ettersburg with Keats and a picnic, and Goethe's small wooden house in Ilmenau where they wrote their names on a window. In Berlin they visited friends or dined alone, reading and supping in their hotel room. They were a couple, happy in solitude, at ease in society, having fun and working hard. For the time being.

There were bad moments when they got news of spiteful scandal and distorting rumour, and once home, first alone in Dover, then together in Bayswater, life was not easy. They were well known enough to be objects of London gossip. Not everyone knew that Agnes had broken up the marriage, and it was not a subject Marian and Lewes could talk about in public. A year later, after dining with the Brays on one of their London visits, Marian wrote to tell them to forget what she had said about 'poor Agnes'. Some friends who knew the truth, like the uncharitable Carlyles, had no intention of meeting them socially as a couple, and the Brays did not care for Lewes. Bessie Parkes had to be told that the partnership was not a flaunted free union, and that she should restrain her feminism and refer to Marian as Mrs Lewes, not Miss Evans. In June 1856, engaged in a new collaborative research among the rockpools of Tenby for Lewes's *Seaside Studies*, they were joined by Barbara Leigh Smith, whom they had not seen for three years. She had ended a relationship with Chapman, who had wanted to live with her and have children, and they were upset to find her 'older and sadder' (*Journals*, 62). Barbara wrote to her friend Bessie Parkes, who had introduced her to Marian, that she had changed her mind about Lewes and he was a considerate lover: 'It is plain to me that he makes her extremely happy', and the couple used some kind of contraception, not wanting children out of wedlock (Haight, 205). Barbara herself was the illegitimate child of a well-to-do father and a working-class mother. She was a gifted painter, revolutionary, and rich enough to brave society. The lifelong friendship between her and Marian began because they were kindred spirits – brave, creative, but fallible – and there could be a friendship between the three of them. *Felix Holt* says: 'all of us – whether men or women – are liable to this weakness of liking to have our preference justified before others as well as ourselves' (46).

The lovers were journalists, and it is in the *Westminster* that their love first gets a significant, if indirect, mention. In this genre her writing is at its most impersonal and generalized, but it finds room for personal emotion. Her review essay entitled 'Woman in France. Madame de Sablé' discusses women's creativity and marriage with scathing and ironic references to English society and institutions. After discussing marriage and gender in France, the androgynous or masculine narrator suggests that one reason for the greater influence of women's writing in France is 'laxity of opinion and practice': 'Heaven forbid that we should enter on a defence of French morals, most of all in relation to marriage! But it is undeniable, that unions formed in the maturity of thought and feeling, and grounded only on inherent fitness and mutual attraction, tended to bring women into more intelligent sympathy and relation to men' (Pinney, 56). Every word had a personal application, and the cool sophisticated comparisons, polite critique of English marriage, and lively narrative about Madame de Sablé and her circle, can end with a burst of social feeling which is also a private celebration:

> Let the whole field of reality be laid open to woman as well as to man, and then that which is peculiar in her mental modification, instead of being, as it is now, a source of discord and repulsion between the sexes, will be found to be a necessary complement to the truth and beauty of life. Then we shall have that marriage of minds which alone can blend all the hues of thought and feeling in one lovely rainbow of promise for the harvest of human happiness. (Pinney, 81)

There is a flowering of language: the poetry of her prose is alliterative and rhythmical, mixing metaphor in Shakespearean style, not so much allusive as assimilative. She chooses a poem where Shakespeare's rhetoric happily promotes ideal affinity and demotes a legal bond, and she trims 'true' from 'Let me not to the marriage of true minds' without loss. Her essay on Cumming convinced Lewes that she possessed genius but 'Madame de Sablé' looks ahead to her merging of analysis and moments of vision in her novels.

'Three Months in Weimar' is one of two essays adapted from her journal for *Fraser's Magazine*. It withholds personal reference, but keeps sensuous particulars, like the chequered shade, the little stream on which they imagined boating, and a park seat where they chatted or listened. There are emotional moments, such as when the narrator looks through Goethe's window through mists of tears, or tries out the keys of Schiller's piano, which has his guitar on it: 'its tones, now so queer and feeble, like those of an invalided old woman whose voice could once make a heart beat with fond passion ...' (Pinney, 91–2). In the *Journals* (234), Schiller's keyboard is a 'little claveçin' (the French for harpsichord), also with a guitar on it, and so it was changed to a loose 'little piano' for *Fraser's* readers. The lovers' happiness is implicit, their heartbeat and fond passion not imaginary.

This visit was recalled in Lewes's third edition of the *Goethe*, when it was revised for the last time, (Smith, Elder and Co, 1875) and when he felt free to write about the wedding journey and to name her: 'Very memorable to me is one summer afternoon when

George Eliot sat at that harpsichord, and lightly touched its plaintive jingling keys, which sounded like the quavering of an old woman's voice. Never did the duet from Grétry's *Richard Coeur-de-Lion* seem more touching!' ('the duet' is one where the minstrel Blondel and the king discover each other). Lewes complained about the 'wearisome' labour of updating his book for a second time, having done so once in 1864 and, after 20 years of free union, scandal, ostracism, and slow acceptance, he took a tactful liberty[6].

But there is more in the allusion than the pseudonym, unthought of when the *Goethe* came out in 1855. Lewes is not describing Schiller's house in Weimar but '*das teutsche Haus*' in Wetzlar, an old Teutonic Knights' residence and a tourist attraction as the steward's house occupied by Herr Buss, father of Charlotte, the original of *Werther*'s bread-and-butter-spreading heroine, and it was her harpsichord in her room at which George Eliot sat. Conflating or correcting memories, Lewes named George Eliot and, deliberately or unconsciously, quoted the old woman's voice. Did he show her the last revised edition with her name? Was he correcting her conflation? Did she play on two harpsichords? Who first thought of the simile? Had she forgotten the Weimar piano? In any case, she would have welcomed the tender text from the tomb in the two weeks between 28 April and 15 May 1879 when she re-read the book on which they had worked together in the old days 'with great admiration and delight' (*Journals*, 172–4). Whatever the source, it is a fond bit of intertextual dialogue.

Other writers speak for her happiness. Her review of Browning's *Men and Women* for the 'Belles Lettres' section of the *Westminster* is conventionally lavish in quotation, and each choice is telling. 'How it Strikes a Contemporary' quotes the poet's alert scrutiny of life; 'Fra Lippo Lippi' celebrates exuberant secular creativity; and the great lyric 'By the Fireside' shows surprising joy and increasing love in apt imagery of obstructing rocks, and lovers whose affinity speaks not only for Robert and Elizabeth but Marian and Lewes, too:

> At first, 'twas something our two souls
> Should mix as mists do: each is sucked
> Into each now; on, the new stream rolls,
> Whatever rocks obstruct.

She was right about fresh powers. George Eliot came into being soon after Marian Evans went to live with Lewes, and it was on their first stay in Germany that she mentioned her fiction to him. She had dreamed of writing a novel but never got beyond 'an introductory chapter describing a Staffordshire village and the life of the neighbouring farmhouses' ('How I came to Write Fiction', *Journals*, 289). When she read it to Lewes in Berlin he was struck by its 'concrete description' but they both had doubts about her dramatic power. They were wrong, as they realized when she finished 'The Sad Fortunes of Amos Barton', the title which came to her in the drowsy half-dream of creativity, in what Spencer called 'the almost spontaneous way, without strain' (401). Lewes sent it to Blackwood, for whom he had often written – he even brings him and *Blackwoods* into *Ranthorpe*.

At first they rejoiced or frowned over the reviews, but gradually he came to protect her from the stupidities of bad reviewers and criticism of good ones. He developed a routine of going through *The Times* and cutting out passages that might upset her. His elaborate defence system involved persuading her publisher and friends to protect her, and not to tell her about reviews unless they were likely to be very gratifying, although critical responses did filter through. We can see why he did so. Experience and maturity never cured her despairs and self-doubt, each new start brought new fears of failure.

The fresh start with fresh powers was a gift of their relationship for him, too, although he was a practised writer in many genres and needed no screening. He was unlike George Eliot in being truly detached about his work, seeking and accepting criticism, and also detached in his criticism of other people. He would help Bessie Parkes and Sara Hennell by reviewing their work, which neither he nor George Eliot rated highly, but he evaluated it sincerely and impartially. His shrewd judgment of poetry is clear when he criticizes the fables of his friend Robert Bulwer Lytton (Owen Meredith) or reviews Robert Buchanan. Perhaps it is not surprising that taste or candour failed when he read George Eliot's poetry, in which she never found individual voice or natural speech-rhythm but is artificial in language, line-bound and unvaried – at best dull, at worst bad. To adapt Klesmer, poetry was dear to Lewes but George

Eliot dearer. He made her stop *The Spanish Gypsy* – 'George has taken my play from me' – but later advised her on revision and gave her 'delighted' praise.

George Eliot jokes about novelists twanging the old troubadour strings, and argues the importance of other things in life, such as work and politics, but all her novels are love stories. However, she never tells the love story at the centre of her life. Esther Lyon chooses love before money and rank, and the hardship of her choice is emphasized, though it is not all that hard; and Klesmer and Catherine Arrowpoint prefer a marriage of minds to wealth, though they do not have to make a sacrifice for long. These are nothing like Marian's hard choice. Her critics have softened her choice by using euphemisms like 'husband', 'consort', and – inaccurately – 'common-law marriage', but her great love was illicit and outside marriage. She defended it as a sacred, permanent bond, and in her novels the only outlaw affections are shallow, shamed and severely punished. Unlike Thackeray, Dickens and Charlotte Brontë, she puts little of her sexual life into her novels. She was reticent about the chosen treasure of her heart. And with good reason. By Victorian and later English standards, she led a life of scandalous impropriety while she wrote novels of immaculate morality, and the discrepancy was spitefully pointed out by Eliza Lynn Linton in *Women Novelists of Queen Victoria's Reign* (London, 1897).

There is a puzzle about the date of their commitment. A letter from Lewes to Carlyle on 19 October 1854 makes it clear his separation from Agnes was decided long before he fell in love with Marian Evans, 'at a time when I was hypochondriacal and hopeless about myself' (*Letters* 2, 177). However, two letters from Marian, one to Chapman on 15 October and one to Bray on 16 October, imply that a permanent relationship was not definitely agreed when she went away with Lewes: 'Since we have been here, circumstances (in which I am not concerned) have led to his determining on a separation' (*Letters* 8, 124) and 'Circumstances, with which I am not concerned, and which have arisen since he left England, have led him to determine on a separation from Mrs Lewes' (*Letters* 2, 178). In her letter to Chapman she comments that Lewes is 'worthy of the sacrifice I have incurred' but does not yet speak of the attachment as a sacred bond or a marriage. Haight quoted the letters to Bray and Chapman in his biography and in a note to Chapman's letter of 15 October in the *Life* he suggests that the 'circumstances' refer to news of Agnes's pregnancy, evidence that she was still unfaithful. He quotes what Cara Bray told Edith Simcox after George Eliot's death – that George Eliot did not finally commit herself till Agnes said reunion was out of the question and she wished Lewes could marry Miss Evans, but Haight is curiously untroubled by the discrepancy between what Lewes and Marian say about separation, writing as if a permanent relationship and prospect of 'a settled home' was determined before the German journey (Haight, 178–9). He is fully alive to her depression and anxieties in Dover but, like Cross, elides the elopement and the sacred bond. We do not know, but she may have felt less secure and confident than Lewes at the start of her very brave journey[7].

George Eliot never wrote about an attachment like her own, which is understandable not only because of the need for privacy and fear of social stigma, but also because of her moral and political preference for keeping to historical norms. She wanted to show not the extraordinary but the ordinary life. This is why some feminists have complained about her lack of revolutionary and subversive heroines. For her, the best propaganda was historical evidence, reimagined in accumulated particulars – Carlyle's history made up of innumerable biographies. More than most novelists, she was inhibited in telling her own story, but life has a way of insinuating itself into art, refusing to be completely kept out by conscious or unconscious repression.

The conventional three-decker novel, with its masculine, omniscient or nearly omniscient narrator, offered opportunities to a subtle writer preoccupied by personal passions writing under the pressure of a secret life, and needing to tell while at the same time not to tell her true story, concentrating on everywoman and everyman but making room for her subversive self. She used indirection and allusion as she did in her essays, but in the voluminous drama and narrative of novels, they appear as miniature narratives and images. I mentioned a possible hit at Herbert Spencer's incapacity for exclusive passionate love in *Daniel Deronda*, and there is another resonant allusion in that novel to a satisfied love like her own. A positive is introduced by a negative, in one of the strong contrasts of the wonderful chiaroscuro where aesthetic structure is inseparable from character, feeling and story (as in Caravaggio's 'Adoration' and 'Annunciation'):

> While Gwendolen … was hoping that Grandcourt … was not going to pause near her … some woman under a smoky sky, obliged to consider the price of eggs in arranging her dinner, was listening for the music of a footstep that would remove all risk from her foretaste of joy; some couple, bending, cheek by cheek, over a bit of work done by the one and delighted in by the other, were reckoning the earnings that would make them rich enough for a holiday among the furze and heather. (54)

The allusions mix fiction and actuality. The housekeeping, earnings and work are autobiographical, drawing on the frugality and penny-paring Marian joked about in the early days with Lewes, when she doled out money like a miser, or when a landlady's present of game made them realize they had not been eating properly and decide to have beer with their luncheon. A memory of planning and enjoying her Scottish trip with the Brays joins with her holidays with Lewes in Germany, Ilfracombe, Scilly and Tenby, and with their habitually shared work. There is a particular image of touch: 'cheek by cheek'. There is pointed gender reference: in the first vignette the woman is the planner and food-purchaser, but in the second we do not know if the work is the man's or the woman's, because in the life-source it could be either. The details combine to form an image of shared everyday happiness.

In *Romola* there is another animating miniature as the narrative shifts from particular to general. The half-mad, betrayed Baldassare demeans himself by begging, in a will to survive, for which the word 'hope' will not quite do: 'it was only that possibility which clings to every idea that has taken complete possession of the mind: the sort of possibility that makes a woman watch on a headland for the ship which held something dear, though all her neighbours are certain that the ship was a wreck long ago' (67). The image of shipwreck is fantasy, but historically neutral, cleverly linking the historical Florentine past with the reader's present, and an eloquent evocation of love's dread and hope, also present in the earlier extract's blend of risk and joy. She wrote to Cara: 'even untroubled love is overhung by the shadow of death' (*Letters* 4, 7), and to Barbara Bodichon: 'Those only can thoroughly feel the meaning of death who know what is perfect love' (*Letters* 4, 14).

The only character with any resemblance to Lewes is Ladislaw. They share an immature dilettantism, a love of poetry, art and music, an unconventional bright vivacity, a foreign education; journalism and editing; radical politics; and, perhaps, a Shelleyan connection. But Ladislaw is good looking, gives up journalism, goes into the first Reform Parliament, and marries a woman quite unlike George Eliot. Lewes played with 'Dorothea' as an affectionate nickname for Marian, like 'Madonna', but it was play. One aspect of Ladislaw's emotional life almost certainly derives from Lewes. Cut off from Dorothea and compromised by Rosamond, Ladislaw is drifting, wasting time, passive, and indifferent to present and future. It is one of the most daring and unromantically truthful details in the novel's psychological action:

> … it seemed to him as if he were beholding in a magic panorama a future where he himself was sliding into that pleasureless yielding to the small solicitations of circumstance, which is a commoner history of perdition than any single momentous bargain.
>
> We are on a perilous margin when we begin to look passively at our future selves, and see our own figures led with dull consent into insipid misdoing and shabby achievement. Poor Lydgate was inwardly groaning on that margin, and Will was arriving at it … he dreaded his own distaste for his spoiled life, which would leave him in motiveless levity. (79)

The context is negatively erotic. Ladislaw does not desire the beautiful, blonde, musical Rosamond but feels the clutch of her need, *ennui* rather than desire on her part, turning to *ennui* on his part too, threatening them both. The generalization cleverly covers Lydgate, too, veiling the erotic suggestion and the unpalatable truth about sexual life in Will's passive dread of automatized yielding. He hears Lydgate mournfully look forward to his company if they go to London with a sense of doom. The implicit prospect of joyless adultery is one of those unacted possibilities George Eliot inserts so subtly, to give density to characters and actions.

We have no details of Lewes's sex life before or after his marriage broke up, only rumours of free love and open marriage in the Hunt circle, his early condonation of Agnes's affair with Hunt, episodes in *Ranthorpe*, and whiffs of scandal and a tarnished reputation. Elizabeth Gaskell thought him too 'soiled' for George Eliot (Haight, 312), and Barbara Bodichon told Bessie Parkes she had thought him a 'sensual man' until she knew him better. The Faustian 'single momentous bargain' and 'motiveless levity' in the account of Ladislaw are links with Lewes, and his journal for January 1859 records his lack of motive, energy and self-respect in the bad days after he left Agnes and before he got to know Marian, and which he must have confided to her. 'I owe him [Spencer] a debt of gratitude. My acquaintance with him was the brightest ray in a very dreary *wasted* period of my life. I had given up all ambition whatever, lived from hand to mouth, and thought the evil of each day sufficient.' A little later he commented: 'I owe Spencer another, and a deeper debt. It was through him that I learned to know Marian – to know her was to love her – and since then my life has been a new birth' (quoted in Ashton, *Lewes*, 120, 143).

Lewes wrote about a new birth, George Eliot about fresh powers. Love and creativity are subjects in her poem 'Self and Life'. Abstract, archaic, high-flown and intense, it outlines George Eliot's attachment to home and to nature, her early fears, reading in heroic literature, of discontent and frustration, and the triumphant last words of the speaker 'Life' connect love with imagination:

> But then I brought a love that wrote within
>   The law of gratitude, and made thy heart
> Beat to the heavenly tune of seraphin
>   Whose only joy in having is, to impart:
> Till thou, poor Self – despite thy ire,
>   Wrestling 'gainst my mingled share,
> Thy faults, hard falls, and vain desire
>   Still to be what others were –
> Filled, o'er-flowed with tenderness
>   Seeming more as thou wert less,
> Knew me through that anguish past
>   As a fellowship more vast.

In July 1857, George Eliot wrote about past pains and inspiring love more lucidly to Rufa Call, who was not yet in the secret of the 'special work' she mentions: 'I am very happy – happy in the highest blessing life can give us, the perfect love and sympathy of a nature that stimulates my own to healthful activity. I feel, too, that all the terrible pain I have gone through in past years, partly from the defects of my own nature, partly from outward things, has probably been a preparation for some special work that I may do before I die' (*Letters* 2, 343).

But the most interesting statement of love as creative inspiration is made in one of her rare portraits of an artist. Philip Wakem's physique and vocation may have been suggested by François D'Albert Durade, but his imaginative experience is George Eliot's. The intellectual, as well as the artist, of the novel, he writes tentatively about the disparity between Maggie's character and Stephen's, and the subject is not simply misplaced affection: 'I have felt the vibration of chords in your nature that I have continually felt the want of in his. But perhaps I am wrong; perhaps I feel about you as the artist does about the scene over which his soul has brooded with love …' (7, 3). Using images from painting and music – his arts – he meditates on inspiration, love and fresh powers:

> You have been to my affections what light, what colour is to my eyes – what music is to the inward ear; you have raised a dim unrest into a vivid consciousness. The new life I have found in caring for your joy and sorrow more than for what is directly my own, has transformed the spirit of rebellious murmuring … . I think nothing but such complete and intense love could have initiated me into that enlarged life which grows and grows by appropriating the life of others … I even think sometimes that this gift of transferred life which has come to me in loving you, may be a new power to me. (*Mill*, 7, 3)

In a visionary scene when Maggie thinks of 'taking her stand out of herself', like Philip feeling an 'enlarged life', she wants to look 'at her own life as an insignificant part of a divinely-guided whole' (*Mill*, 4, 3). George Eliot first wrote 'immeasurable', appropriate for her own agnosticism, then replaced it with 'divinely-guided', appropriate for her heroine's Christianity: there was a moment in writing this very personal novel when she almost forgot she was not Maggie. Perhaps she almost forgot she was not Philip, whose desires are not gratified but sublimated. Her characters speak the language of feeling used by George Eliot and Lewes to express their ideas and feelings about their love and power.

Philip touches on another point in George Eliot's artistic growth, the loss of the 'double consciousness' she told Spencer about, and which he relates to her release from creative inhibition: 'She complained of being troubled by double consciousness – a current of self-criticism being an habitual accompaniment of anything she was saying or doing; and this naturally tended towards self-depreciation and distrust. Probably it was this last trait which prevented her from displaying her powers and her knowledge' (Spencer, 386–7). Ideas like these are assimilated to her characters and their feelings. Maggie's and Philip's are individual experiences, formulated as ideas by Philip, the more abstract thinker.

In George Eliot's letter and Lewes's journal the lovers write personally, but in her novels their feelings and ideas are de-personalized and developed outside the self, then assimilated to her fiction. In Philip, who speaks for the artist, the idea is more specifically defined and analysed than in Maggie. Unlike her, he is allowed to survive; unlike her, and like George Eliot, he had art for which to survive.

There are direct and indirect signs of Lewes in the novels, including his well-known suggestions for Adam's active involvement in *Adam Bede* and less happily for Arthur's ride with Hetty's pardon, and the plan for *Romola*. The East End debate in the Hand and Banner scene of *Daniel Deronda* is also known to owe its social authenticity and some of its characters to a club Lewes used to attend. The technical detail of Klesmer's lecture to ignorant Gwendolen on the training of actors derives from Lewes, an amateur actor and fine theatre critic and is all there in *On Actors and the Art of Acting,* the essays Anthony Trollope begged Lewes to publish as a book. And when Gwendolen jeers at Mr Middleton, 'If he had to say "Perdition catch my soul, but I do love her", he would say it in just the same tone as "Here endeth the second lesson"' (6), George Eliot reflects Lewes's interest in actors' renderings of Othello's speech.

In Chapter Seven of *Life and Works of Goethe*, Lewes discusses the scene where Faust hears of Gretchen's infanticide and death: Mephisto coldly says she 'is not the first who has so died'. Faust breaks forth: Not the first! Misery! Misery! by no human soul to be conceived! That more than one creature of God should ever have been plunged into the depth of this woe! That the first ... should not have atoned for the guilt of all the rest.' Lewes is puzzled by Goethe's rare choice of prose in the scene but, with his usual openness, leaves the question to the 'ingenuity' of the 'critic'. He and George Eliot must have discussed the crux, and Cross says she was more moved by Gretchen than by anything in Shakespeare. So Faust and Gretchen may have inspired the pity and anger which rack Adam's imagination in another tale of seduction and infanticide: 'O God ... and men have suffered like this before ... and poor helpless young things have suffered like her ... ' (*Adam Bede*, 42). (The agnostic novelist avoids the critique of God which the enlightened dramatist may imply.)

On 30 November 1878, after several painful weeks – and a longer history of suffering – Lewes died of what his death certificate states as 'enteritis', perhaps colon cancer. Among the condolences was Spencer's, touched by Marian's loss and his own lack of such human connection, 'I can but dimly conceive what such a parting must be, even in an ordinary case. Still more dimly can I conceive what it must be in such a case where two lives have been so long bound together so closely, in such multitudinous ways' (*Letters* 8, 87).

On Lewes' death, Marian broke down, screaming. She shut herself off from everyone but Charles Lewes. Unable to hope like *Romola*'s woman on the headland, she copied out griefs and longings from Tennyson and other writers, but she gradually composed herself for his memorial, the completion of Lewes's last book, *Problems of Life and Mind*. Until he was too ill, he was working on this and proofs of *Impressions of Theophrastus Such*, an experiment in factual fiction, and George Eliot's last book. (Its publication was held back a little in respect for his death.) Once again, life imitates fiction: her reasons for finishing Lewes's work are the reverse of Mrs Casaubon's for not finishing the *Key to All Mythologies*. Dorothea refused to finish a book in which she has no faith, and by a husband she did not love; George Eliot worked in admiration and faithful love. She was helped by scientists and developed the idea of organizing a memorial studentship for Lewes in Cambridge, energized by hearing praise from these professionals.

George Eliot never wrote about her last love, John Cross. She wrote nothing of her own in the months after Lewes died, and nothing at all during the ten months of marriage to Cross, a time 'so much divided', Cross said, 'between travelling and illness' (3, 424). In unofficial widowhood, she depended on Cross, a banker and manager of the Lewes investments, for financial advice, especially when people asked for money, including Lewes's nephew, to whom he had been generous, and Bessie Parkes for some good cause. He had been a frequent visitor and fervent admirer of George Eliot, knowing her books better than any other literature; and he was bereaved, too, having lost the mother to whom he was very close ten days after Lewes died. In 1867, Spencer had introduced Lewes to Mrs Cross in Weybridge during one of their walking trips, then Cross's sister Elizabeth, who wrote poetry, called on 'the great author'. Two years later, the Leweses met Cross in Rome and after that they often stayed with the family, especially for festive Christmases. Cross describes how family friendship deepened to intimacy in 1869 when Thornton and his sister Elizabeth both died.

Why did she marry him? It's a hard question to answer about anyone. Biographers have speculated creatively, repeating the story about needing someone to lean on, or, like Bodenheimer and others, spinning a complex psychological interpretation of her actions. He was 20 years her junior, tall, dark, handsome, admiring and newly motherless. There's no smoke without fire, and sharp-eyed Edith Simcox had long ago asked her idol if she was 'afraid of my poisoning Johnny's shirts?' (*Letters* 9, 199). Why not assume that she found him attractive? She had done similar and sillier things, like falling in love with Chapman and Spencer. She was not quite 60 and in an intensely emotional state, ready to be attracted without really understanding the new object of desire. A tender, lyrical letter of 16 October 1879, less than a year after Lewes died, is as amazing as her earlier letters to Spencer:

> Best loved and loving one – the sun it shines so cold, so cold, when there are no eyes to look love on me. I cannot bear to sadden one moment when we are together, but wenn Du bist nicht da I have often a bad time. It is a solemn time, dearest ...
>
> ... Through everything else, dear tender one, there is the blessing

of trusting in thy goodness. Thou dost not know everything of verbs in Hephil and Hophal or the history of metaphysic or the position of Kepler in science, but thou knowest best things of another sort, such as belong to the manly heart – secrets of lovingness and rectitude. O I am flattering! Consider what thou wast a little time ago in pantaloons and back hair. (*Letters* 7, 211–2)

While apparently comparing Cross's virtues with Lewes's philosophy and science and her learning, the letter is embarrassing in its back-handed compliment, for which condescending is too harsh a word. The archaic second-person singular harks back to her effusive letters to Maria Lewis, and the playful German to Sara Hennell. Another letter to Cross is full of jokes and ends fondly but this is her only real love letter to him. She often quotes and alludes to Dante in her novels, but she ends 'thy tender Beatrice' because when Cross said he was reading *The Inferno* in John Carlyle's translation, she enthu-siastically joined him but in Italian, and they could soon have been identifying with the reading lovers Paolo and Francesca.

She kept their engagement a secret except from his family, and wrote to his sister Eleanor of a 'wonderful renewal' of her life, re-opened 'springs of affection' and the 'miracle' of his love (*Letters* 7, 259–60). She told Georgiana Burne-Jones of 'a sort of miracle' (*Letters* 7, 269) and writes to Charles Lewes from Grenoble on the wedding journey, that she had 'been getting hard' but now feels 'the loveliness of a nature close to me', 'the fountain of tenderness and strength to endure' (*Letters* 7, 283). A month before she died, she told Cara Bray of 'a miraculous affection which has chosen to watch over me'. She wrote of miracles less spontaneously and more scrupu-lously in her Strauss and Feuerbach translations, and when Tom Tulliver guessed at the 'almost miraculous divinely protected effort'. She excused her sudden engagement to Georgiana Burne-Jones: 'Explanations of these crises, which seem sudden though they are slowly dimly prepared, are impossible' (*Letters* 7, 269). The novelist Anne Thackeray Ritchie, whose marriage to a much younger man George Eliot had noted with interest, told her husband, 'She is an honest woman, and goes in with all her might for what she is about' (*Letters* 7, 284).

On the wedding journey, Cross was taken ill in Venice, and is said to have jumped into the Grand Canal. We know some facts about the breakdown and the history of emotional illness in the Cross family but there is no evidence of the sensational jump, which has become as notorious as Ruskin's marital failure, indeed perhaps a little influenced by that story. In his *Letters* Haight described the story of the jump as 'vulgar, malicious gossip' (7, 301n.) but in *George Eliot. A Life*, after reading Acton, he says 'He jumped from the balcony into the Grand Canal' (544). Ashton says, 'He jumped from their hotel room into the Grand Canal' (376).They both cite Acton who wrote in his diary 'she … heard that he had jumped into the Canal', but as Ashton says 'on whose authority we do not know'. He may well have jumped, but we can't be sure, and Acton does not say where he heard that 'she heard' that he jumped. We know that Cross was treated by Venetian doctors, that his wife sent for his brother Willie, who travelled part of the way back with them until Cross felt better, and that Cross blamed his illness on bad air and the 'sudden deprivation of all bodily exercise', describing Venetian indolence in words ironically echoing her old image of drifting in a gondola with Lewes: 'it is another thing to spend all one's days in a gondola – a delicious, dreamy existence' (Cross 3, 407). They spent late summer and autumn recovering, visiting friends and family, and planning the move to Chelsea, in which Cross was active. Until she had one of her kidney attacks in September she regularly reports his improving health and his tender care of her.

She was ill for most of October, then recovered, but they had only been three weeks in the house in Cheyne Walk where Cross said 'they had meant to be so happy', when she caught cold, either at a student production of the *Agamemnon*, in Greek, or as Cross thought, at one of the St James's Hall Pop concerts she loved, and died suddenly on 22 December 1880.

Cross devoted himself to his memorial, *George Eliot's Life as related in her Journals and Letters*, which was severely criticized, by old friends like Mark Rutherford, reviewers like Gladstone, readers like Alice James, biographers like Haight. It was a labour of love, and he edited character, life, and language to construct his image. But he was not insensitive, telling Henry James the union was like that of a carthorse yoked to a racer, echoing *Daniel Deronda*'s archery scene in which Gwendolen is a racehorse amongst hacks. At the end of his book he adapts a quotation from Dante (also on her coffin), recalling their Dantean courtship and praising her genius: 'The spring, which had broadened out into so wide a river of speech, ceased to flow' (Cross 3, 438; *Inferno* 1, 79–80). It is a good ending to a life-story: Dante's archetypal image for Virgil's epic and influence suggests her development of art, the mutation of life into art, and her own water imagery[8]. Cross honours a marriage which Charles Lewes tearfully described to Anne Ritchie, saying his father would have understood, having 'no grain of jealousy in him', and 'she was of such a delicate fastidious nature that she couldn't be satisfied with anything but an ideal tête à tête' (*Letters* 7, 284). Cross says 'Her life was … a life of heart-loneliness. Accustomed as she had been to a solitude *à deux*, the want of close companionship continued to be very bitterly felt … . A bond of mutual dependence had been formed between us' (Cross 3, 387). They enjoyed some consoling companionship, and if he wrote her life his way he preserved unique memories. But whatever happened in Venice, the couple were distressed and disappointed. The best was over. Jane Eyre tells the reader, 'to talk to each other is but a more animated and audible thinking'. George Eliot had that ideal conversation with Lewes.

Notes

1 In 'Dear Cara – A New George Eliot Letter'. Kathleen Adams reports the discovery of the note by the Herbert Art Gallery and Museum, Coventry, and finds the date 1856 on its envelope correct. *George Eliot Review*, 27, 1996.

2 Nancy Paxton thinks this criticises sexism in Spencer's 'antagonism of individualism and reproduction' in this article but personal meaning seems paramount. (*George Eliot and Herbert Spencer: Princeton:* Princeton University Press, 1991.

3 In 'The Art of the Ancients' *The Leader*, 6, 17 March, 1855, George Eliot spoke of the 'terrible beauty' of the Medusa Rondanini relief from the Glyptotech in Munich: there may be an unconscious link with Spencer, especially in view of his association with Hetty's journey but I'm sure it had personal significance for George Eliot.

4 George Eliot used the name of Gaskell's subversive labourer in

Middlemarch, Barbara Hardy, 'The Two Timothy Coopers', *The George Eliot Review*, 35, 2004.

5 Saying GE's letters to Chapman and Bray from Germany 'could *easily* be characterised as the letters of a travelling companion who had been cheered up by a badly needed vacation, and they seem intended to be read in that way' (my italics) Bodenheimer says the letter to Chapman has 'the most personal revelation, quotes Verweilen sie … ', but omits the reference to 'our happiness' and the earlier letter hoping he may 'find as much happiness, and of the same kind' (Bodenheimer, 88).

6 Ashton points out Lewes's change in 1875 from the 1855 edition's 'a dear friend of mine' (who defended the slow pace – Goethe's' retardation' – of *Die Walverwandtschaften* or *Elective Affinities*) to 'a great writer, and one who is very dear to me'. (Ashton says it was so changed in 1864 but it was not.)

7 Hughes reasonably speculates that the 'circumstances' may refer to London gossip, though this is hard to reconcile with Marian's statement that 'circumstances' did not concern her. Bodenheimer's long discussion of the relationship with Lewes omits the separation letters. Another gap in knowledge concerns a 'Painful letter' which made Marian anxious and depressed when she was in Dover between 13 March to 18 April: she notes on 9 April 1854 that it 'made reading and writing impossible'; and it may be related to Cara Bray's story about Marian's 'ultimatum': Timothy Hands's entry for 9 April is: 'Upset by her efforts to ensure that GHL and his wife would never attempt a *rapprochement*' (*A George Eliot Chronology* 44).We do not know what the letter said or who wrote it.

8 For example, in *Felix Holt*: 'So our lives glide on: the river ends we don't know where, and the sea begins, and then there is no more jumping ashore' (27).

Chapter Four
Acquaintances and Friends

… any one who discerned the core of truth must also recognise the large amount of arbitrary, imaginative addition … (*Letters* 3, 86)

In June 1859, George Eliot wrote to the Brays about *Adam Bede*, 'There is not a single portrait in the book, nor will there be in any future book of mine. There are *two* portraits in the Clerical Scenes; but that was my first bit of art, and my hand was not well in – I did not know so well how to manipulate my materials' (*Letters* 3, 99). George Eliot's pity and love shaped characters with no particular likeness to her sister Chrissey, but rather imaginary variants of a suffering woman. Personal feeling is at the heart of these stories, where so much incident and character was drawn from experience or hearsay. What we see when her 'hand was not well in' are two kinds of autobiographical inspiration, roughly corresponding to what Coleridge called imitation and copy – imitation is transformation or re-imagining and copy is replication, what George Eliot calls portraiture.

What is this portraiture in the *Scenes*? The Reverend John Gwyther was positive he recognized his portrait, 'as assured that I am intended by Amos Barton as I am of the Truth of any Fact so ever' (*Letters* 3, 84). His daughter even suggested he might have written the story himself. Tom Winnifrith said Gwyther writes 'rather angrily'[1] but in fact he writes in mild remonstrance after the 'pained feelings at the making public my private history [had] abated'. He never thought Liggins, the local candidate for 'George Eliot', 'equal to writing such a tale' but suspected WH King, curate of Nuneaton when Gwyther was at Chilvers Coton, sending him 'kind remembrances' and assurances that the pain he 'felt at the first publication is past off – although I thought it unkind and taking a great liberty with a living Character – yet I fully forgive for old acquaintance sake'. He ends on a friendly note, asking Blackwood to reprint a 'poetical and humourous article' in *Blackwoods* which amused him 'in 1830 or there about', which he would like to laugh over with his children, and thinks is called 'Skying the Copper' (*Letters* 3, 84–5). He ingenuously fails to distinguish the woman in the case, Countess Czerlaski, the object of unfounded scandal, and her innocent brother, from real people he had known: 'The Countess too and her (professed Father) the Rev. Sir John Waldron … in 1836–7 to Holyrood … since which time I have heard nothing of them' (*Letters* 3, 84). In 'Amos Barton' his English was criticized, but Gwyther was more literary, shrewd and fun-loving than his portrait, and – just for a minute, by his daughter – taken to be his own author.

This would not have ingratiated him with George Eliot, who replied through Blackwood rather heavily and evasively, that the author was not King and had written 'under the impression that the clergyman whose long past trial suggested the groundwork of the story was no longer living, and that the incidents, not only through the license and necessities of artistic writing, but in consequence of the writer's imperfect knowledge, must have been so varied from the actual facts, that any one who discerned the core of truth must also recognise the large amount of arbitrary, imaginative addition' (*Letters* 3, 86). Her apology for 'any annoyance' which she assumes must be 'brief and not well-founded', is ungracious considering Gwyther's grievance and good-tempered forgiveness, but she was always irritated by crude views of her sources, and Gwyther's very identifications reveal what she calls the arbitrary imaginative addition. It is not every day that an author is addressed by a character – outside Pirandello – but George Eliot failed to see the joke, especially as she had made Amos 'a much better man than he really was', but could scarcely say so to him (*Letters* 3, 156).

The novels she said had no portraits use fact to form their fiction. Camden Farebrother of *Middlemarch* owes something to George Tugwell of Ilfracombe, a 'nice little fellow' with 'a sweet nature', who was apparently unmarried when he met the Leweses, and a curate and naturalist who liked to show his collection, to shed 'new light on glass jars', and who gave Lewes three specimens of sea-anemone (*Journals*, 266). His book was recommended for publication, and reviewed, by Lewes, and he is sympathetically sketched in George Eliot's journal.

She lifts and varies a few of Tugwell's features for Farebrother: he, too, is small and amiable, unmarried, a clergyman, naturalist and collector who likes to show his collection and who displays at least one glass jar or vase. He preaches, though not in a small Gothic chapel like Tugwell's, and he is an entomologist not a marine biologist, and does not give Lydgate his 'lovely anencephalous monster' but swops it for a book and some sea-mice (*Middlemarch*, 17).

Her friend Frederic Harrison, who gave her valuable legal advice for *Felix Holt* and *Daniel Deronda*, tried to persuade her to write a didactic Positivist novel, and may have suggested an emotionally important detail for *Middlemarch*. On 5 June 1869, Harrison wrote to her about his cousin, to whom he had become engaged: 'My love for her has been a very old one of which I can no more remember any origin than I can conceive any close ... ever since she was a little girl we two have felt and thought and resolved and hoped – as one and not as two' (*Letters* 5, 42). George Eliot wrote back to him the next day that she liked to think of his love 'having grown imperceptibly along with sweet family affections' (*Letters* 5, 43). Fred and Mary, childhood sweethearts in *Middlemarch*, re-live Harrison's story: surprised by a delicate hint that Farebrother feels more than friendship for her, Mary replies with a delicate story of her old affection for Fred. Like her author and her tragic predecessor Maggie, she speaks up for faithful continuity in words that renew Harrison's exchange with George Eliot: 'It has taken such deep root in me – my gratitude to him for always loving me best ... from the time when we were very little. I cannot imagine any new feeling coming to make that weaker' *(Middlemarch*, 52). George Eliot must have known other childhood romances, but here is a link of emotion, image and relationship.

Novelists using models, even selectively, need differences and disguises. Real people are modified by new contexts, placed in relation to fictional characters or events. George Eliot was given the idea for *Adam Bede* by her aunt, but strenuously denied that Dinah was modelled on Elizabeth Evans, except in her being a Methodist woman preacher who heard the confession of a girl who killed her child – the original of Hetty was a 'poor coarse girl', Mary Voce, who was hanged, and whose life was indeed different from Hetty's[2]. When Harriet Beecher Stowe asked if Casaubon was Lewes,

George Eliot laughed the idea to scorn and said that 'Casaubon-tints' were not 'foreign' to her own complexion (*Letters* 5, 322). (Portrait-spotters often seek male models for female-authored male characters.) The most sensitive novelist has no access to the inner lives of her acquaintances – or even her lovers, relations and friends, though she may guess at them. Some of the portraits George Eliot admitted, and partial portraits, like Gilfil and Tryan, identified by Gwyther but not admitted, were acquaintances recalled after many years.

George Eliot said her second portrait was Dempster, based on a Nuneaton solicitor, James Buchanan, like and unlike his original in being badly but not fatally injured when a wheel came off as he was driving his carriage. He may be 'a certain person' whose 'evil habits are too rooted for marriage to cause their permanent disappearance' (*Letters* 1, 26) and is the subject of pious comment to Maria Lewis, written in ignorance of his wife Nancy Buchanan's sudden death in Margate, where she was with Maria: 'My last accounts of the poor sufferer at Nuneaton were favourable: but you will probably receive more regular and trustworthy information concerning him than I. I cherish hopes concerning the result of this scourging should God see fit …to uphold his life …' (*Letters* 1, 58). Mrs Buchanan, the daughter of Mrs Wallington, Mary Ann's headmistress, moves in and out of George Eliot's letters to Maria in messages, news and questions from Mary Ann, who shared Nancy's interest in good works. Nancy is like Janet in being charitable, bustling and assisting at a reception – Queen Adelaide's, not a bishop's – but she died just before her husband's accident, and was not childless. We do not know if Mrs Buchanan was an alcoholic and ill-treated, but she did not survive like Janet, with the comfort of an adopted child and loving memory of a curate who changed her faith and life. George Eliot told Blackwood: 'The real Janet alas! had a far sadder end than mine …' (*Letters* 2, 347). Nancy was evangelical, and died in the company of her evangelical friend Maria, who first met her at her mother's school. (She was of Maria's generation not George Eliot's: Maria was born about 1800, Nancy in 1803.)

Maria shared Mary Ann's zealous evangelicalism, though Haight puts down her religion as 'sentimental' and less austere than Mary Ann's, and was her confidante for years. The pupil outgrew the faith and friendship, but they wrote now and then after Mary Ann's religious crisis, and Maria came to visit as late as 1847, when Cara writes unkindly of 'a stupid Miss Lewis' coming to stay with the Evanses (*Letters* 1, 230n). When George Eliot received her letters back from Maria, she never returned them. They were in touch when Maria was old and poor and George Eliot sent her money. Maria observed the 'divergence in their careers': 'As "George Eliot" I have traced you as far as possible, and with an interest which few could feel; not many knew you as intimately as I once did … My heart has ever yearned after you …' (*Letters* 1, lxxiii).

Maria worked unhappily in at least one family and some schools, and may have left her mark on Mary Garth's dislike of school-teaching, Gwendolen's dread of being a governess, and on Miss Morgan and Miss Merry, the silent governesses of *Middlemarch* and *Daniel Deronda*, who are not nonentities because we are made to feel for their nonentity. Fanny Evans and Sara Hennell were governesses but, as far as we know, not downtrodden like Maria. She was important for 'Janet's Repentance' because she told Mary Ann of Mrs Buchanan's story, no doubt in piecemeal confidence. Maria and Nancy were close; she went with her to see a London surgeon and was with her when she died. Maria often visited Griff and Bird Grove, and the letters refer to intimate conversation, gossipy as well as evangelical. Janet's semi-portrait of Nancy Buchanan is a rare firm link between George Eliot's first close friend and her writing. We know a great deal about Bray and Spencer and little about the obscure Maria, except that she was hard-up, unsettled and unmarried, with strict evangelical principles and a squint, and that she loved a laugh – Mary Ann says so – and had stories to tell. One of the stories inspired her friend's imagination in 'Janet's Repentance', the first 'scene' to show powerful psychological analysis, with the first character who has nerves, feelings and an inner life. If George Eliot put Chrissey's sorrows into Milly Barton, and Nancy's into Janet's, she also drew on her own inner life for Janet's despair, hysteria, disenchantment and recovery. Perhaps this is why she was pleased when readers liked the third *Scene* best, and was so hurt by Blackwood's lack of enthusiasm that she stopped the series and never wrote about the Clerical Tutor, whose story she longed to tell.

As she moved away from Maria, it is tempting to exaggerate the break in thinking, feeling and style. Judging from Mary Ann's letters, theirs was an exchange of Johnsonian syntax and Biblical lexis. Mary Ann poured out ideas and feelings about religion, morality, family, books, affections, fears and fantasies:

> I venture to believe that the same causes which exist in my own breast to render novels and romances pernicious have their counterpart in that of every fellow-creature.
>
> I am I confess not an impartial member of the jury in this case for I owe the culprits a grudge for injuries inflicted on myself. I shall carry to my grave the mental diseases with which they have contaminated me. When I was quite a little child I could not be satisfied with the things around me; I was constantly living in a world of my own creation, and was quite contented to have no companions that I might be left to my own musings and imagine scenes in which I was chief actress. Conceive what a character novels would give to these Utopias. (*Letters* 1, 22)

Cross cut out the sentence about mental diseases, and we can see why. Mary Ann was 20 and intensely puritanical; too young to know she was making a vice out of imaginative virtue, though she was to worry about the ethics of imagination and art all her life. Her moral attitude is religious but her subjects are literature, imagination and emotions. The style isn't inflexible. The first two moralizing sentences are inert, verbose and elaborate, but the last two, simple and vivid. What is more, she writes to Maria with an awareness of style, illustrating and commenting on rhetoric as she was to do in novels and poetry. She describes troubles as clouds and meteors, then corrects the lofty banality. 'Though I have fetched a metaphor from the sky I confess that my troubles … have been of a very grovelling nature.' She uses a Pauline metaphor of bullock and yoke, tries 'lever' but finally prefers 'magnet' (*Letters* 1, 31–2). Her 'Sonnet' in a previous letter defends its own imagery of path and green prospect: 'To my poor thought, an apt though simple trope.' It discusses the conflict of fantasy and reality, a subject always close to her heart, and introduces the idea of disenchantment, which returns in a letter to Sara Hennell and is a recurrent theme in the novels: 'Visions with

which fancy still would teem / Scare by a disenchanting earthly tone'
(*Letters* 1, 30). Her awareness of language was to become more easy
and sophisticated – a quiet deconstructive force – but it starts in her
letters to Maria.

George Eliot does not draw portraits of close friends any more
than she did of lovers or relations – except for the young Isaac
– but Maria is one of three women friends who influence her novels
differently, indirectly, and strikingly. The next was Sara Hennell,
who replaced Maria as chief correspondent. She and Mary Ann had
talents and tastes in common – religion, philosophy, art, music,
books and writing. Sara shared the friendship with Cara, but when
Mary Ann knew Sara first she lived with her mother in London,
so they developed their friendship in writing. Sara was learned and
clever, about seven years older than Mary Ann, and when Rufa
Brabant passed on the Strauss translation, it was understood that
Sara would help. From January 1844 to September 1846, there was
constant discussion of ideas between them about practical problems
of the translation – what to prefer, correct, cut, add, depart from or
keep. When printing began there was regular exchange of proofs, and
Mary Ann said that without Sara she would have despaired. Sara also
helped with Mary Ann's translation of Feuerbach, published in 1854.
They had languages in common, and moved easily into German and
Latin, but they shared fun as well as knowledge. Mary Ann's joking
tone to and about Charles Bray – 'That dear unmanageable male
unit in our quaternian' (*Letters* 1, 223), also lightens the learned
letters to her 'Dearest' and her 'Beloved Achates'. Gwendolen's fond
comic compounds – 'you dreadfully careless-about-yourself mamma!'
(*Daniel Deronda*, 44) – are first seen in teasing letters to Sara:
'your never-having-time-to-write-pretty-letters potter's vessel' and
'loving-in-spite-of-people's-faults-and-deficiencies ... Sara' (*Letters*
1, 215–16). (Also, as I mentioned earlier, at least once to Bray).
The friends shared holiday pleasures of talk, theatres and music, and
Mary Ann writes to Sara about happy idling and trying 'to live in
and love the present' (*Letters* 1, 209), anticipating Ladislaw's 'sturdy
neutral delight in things as they were' (*Middlemarch*, 30).

Sara came to feel Mary Ann had abandoned their intellectual
companionship. She never stopped trying to reconcile a rationalist
critique of false history and supernaturalism with a deep feeling for

Christianity, and as she was brought up as a Unitarian, was more of a deist and less of an agnostic than George Eliot. She agonized more persistently over faith and rationality, and wrote four books on the subject, including a prize essay, 'Christianity and Infidelity' (1857), which had a prescribed format, with the case for Christianity in one column and the case for Infidelity in another. Mary Ann recognized the restrictive form but complained that Christianity was given a better say than scepticism. Sara also wrote a memoir of her beloved brother Charles, who died of tuberculosis seven years after he married Rufa, and *Present Religion as a Faith Owning Fellowship with Thought,* which the Leweses thought a terrible title.

In June 1860, Sara brought her newly finished *Thoughts in Aid of Faith* to show her old friend. They had not met since Mary Ann had become Marian, the unofficial Mrs Lewes and the unidentified George Eliot. The Leweses dined with Sara and the Brays, who were in London for a Handel festival, but at some point, perhaps before Sara could produce her manuscript, George Eliot announced that she was the author of *Scenes of Clerical Life* and the bestseller *Adam Bede*. Her friends' astonishment astonished her. Charles was delighted but Sara was stunned. It was not the first time Marian had upset her. Four years earlier, when she went to Germany with Lewes, Sara and Cara were hurt, not at the liaison, though they disapproved, but at their friend's lack of faith in their support, and her apparent willingness to give up their friendship. Sara summed up her response in a rather good phrase, 'I have a strange sort of feeling that I am writing to some one in a book, and not to the Marian that we have known and loved so many years … I mean nothing unkind' (Haight, 165). She was eloquent on this occasion, too. She had expected sympathy from her old kindred spirit but encountered 'greatness', and put her feeling that Marian had 'passed beyond herself, seemed lost to me' into a sonnet and a letter:

> I have been fancying you, as ten years ago, still interested in what we then conversed together upon – I was not sure that the writing that now occupied you was not the 'Idea of a Future Life' that was then in nubilas – that perhaps your thoughts had not been flowing in a parallel track to my own – I see now that I have lost the only reader in whom I felt confident in having secure sympathy with the *subject* … she has

floated beyond me in another sphere, and I remain gazing at the glory into which she has departed, wistfully and very lonely. (Haight, 288)

Marian and Lewes returned Sara's manuscript next day with some praise and criticism of her obscure style and weak argument, though this was followed by a more friendly explanation by Marian and, much later, a critical but respectful review by Lewes. But what the friends expected to be a renewal of friendship instead widened the breach between them. Sara's book is more interesting than Marian and Lewes made it sound, though it is only read now for the George Eliot connection. Sara's argument is often obscure, and weakened by an intense desire to be as Christian as possible. At times, her hypothetical deity is addressed as passionately as a personal God. But to read it is to see the personal reasons for Sara's painful disappointment. The book is all but literally dedicated to an intellectual coterie, with discussions of Charles Hennell, Herbert Spencer, Lewes, John Martineau, Strauss and Feuerbach, and it quotes a brilliant image from Marian Evans's translation of *The Essence of Christianity*. Feuerbach distinguishes the abstraction of God from the individual person of Christ, using the metaphor of a longing sigh: 'In God the soul is still silent as to what affects it most closely – it only sighs; but in Christ it speaks out fully; here it no longer has any reserves …' then says that in Christ 'all anxiety of the soul vanishes …' Next comes a sentence Sara praises as 'exquisitely rendered by the English translator': 'the sighing soul passed into a song of triumph over its complete satisfaction' (*Thoughts in Aid of Faith*, p 107). The friends shared a love of Feuerbach's passionate humanism and his lyrical tenderness for discarded faith. They also shared a sense of style, and discussed nuances of English and German. Sara's homage to an intellectual community is clinched by her personal tribute, and shows what she had expected, and did not get, from Marian's response. Sara wrote poetry, and a tale 'Heliados', but modestly discussed music, fiction and creative genius as a philosopher not an artist, only to discover with chagrin that her old friend, a translator, reviewer and modest poet, had not been labouring over a book like hers, the never-written *Idea of a Future Life*, but was instead a creative genius – George Eliot, the new mysterious author and subject of newspaper enthusiasm and Midlands speculation – who had found her own form of passionate humanism, her own way of moving beyond infidelity to a faith, and – the unkindest cut – who was not keen on her old friend's book. No wonder she saw Marian moving beyond her and beyond her old self.

Sara does not get into the novels any more than Maria, but her friendship helped George Eliot's writing. Her correspondence with Sara was freer and less repressed than her immature exchanges with Maria – she was growing into her vocation, released from old strictures of ethic and belief. The letters to Sara – often punningly signed 'Pollian' and playfully addressed to 'My friend of the dark eye', 'dearest friend', 'Dearly beloved spouse', 'Meine Liebe' and 'Liebe Gemahl' – have wit, sparkle and original new images[3]. George Eliot was developing her style. Sara was a writer, often obscure but also vivid, learned and intense, and an ideal reader. In letters to her, Marian finds poetry for the inner life, for momentariness and shifting emotion, brilliantly catching nuances of bright, dark or dull feeling, not exactly Joyce's stream of consciousness or Woolf's falling atoms, but something like James's fine sensitive register, edging towards the freer and more open languages of modernism.

The language of her novels resembles, but also surpasses, the style of her letters at their most articulate. It draws on their matrix of symbol and image to become a new resource for the language of thinking and feeling. George Eliot's recurrent interplay of scene and symbol is anticipated in one particular letter, written under great stress from St Leonards on Sea during Robert Evans's last illness. Its vivid particulars and self-generative imagery anticipate the fiction. Personal emotions and moods are poured out, generalized and analysed, for a close friend who will understand. The expression is profuse but controlled and the writer not so self-indulgent as to forget her correspondent:

> I wait and wait for a better mood, in which, poor moon that I am, I may shed on you some gentle, peaceful light, instead of thrusting my cold dark orb between you and the 'lux alma' which is just now shining on you from Cara's and other friendly eyes. But the better mood does not come, and if I were silent longer you might fancy that it was because I was 'full rich and reigning as a king without you'.
>
> Alas for the fate of poor mortals which condemns them to wake up

some fine morning and find all the poetry in which their world was bathed only the evening before utterly gone – the hard angular world of chairs and tables and looking-glasses staring at them in all its naked prose. It is so in all the stages of life – the poetry of girlhood goes – the poetry of love and marriage – the poetry of maternity – and at last the very poetry of duty forsakes us for a season and we see ourselves and all about us as nothing more than miserable agglomerations of atoms – poor tentative efforts of the Natur Princep to mould a personality. This is the state of prostration – the self-abnegation through which the soul must go, and to which perhaps it must again and again return, that its poetry or religion, which is the same thing, may be a real ever-flowing river fresh from the windows of heaven and the fountains of the great deep – not an artificial basin with grotto work and gold fish.

I feel a sort of madness growing upon me – just the opposite of the delirium which makes people fancy that their bodies are filling the room. It seems to me as if I were shrinking into that mathematical abstraction, a point – so entirely am I destitute of contact that I am unconscious of length or breadth, and by the time you see me again, I shall have lost all possibility of giving you any demonstration of a spiritual existence – like a poor sprite metamorphosed into a pomegranate seed or some such thing. (*Letters* 1, 263–4, 4 June 1848)

It is another extraordinary letter. As in no previous letter, rhetoric and self-awareness are the work of an artist: the allegory of passage, and startlingly mixed metaphor; images of poetry, prose, wide water, small pool, and light on everyday objects; and brilliantly articulated themes of depression, annihilation and disenchantment, restricted sensibility, inspiration, assertion, vision, and the sense of self, with reflexive awareness. Style, theme and feeling are echoed in the novels, beginnng with 'Janet's Repentance', where George Eliot first re-imagines her own personal experience of feeling and imagining. For example, as she moves through generalization back to her character: 'The daylight changes the aspect of misery to us ... That moment of intensest depression was come to Janet, when the daylight which showed her the walls, and chairs and tables ... seemed to lay bare the future too' ('JR' 16)[4].

The open poetry of this letter to Sara went into the matrix of art, and it was art – original, impassioned and self-generative. George Eliot used the spontaneous, immediate and familiar medium of the personal letter, a flexibly lyrical and narrative form for intense meditation, before she wrote novels, showing what the novels were to do. She wrote journals, but they never stimulate intensities of feeling and language, perhaps because they do not involve personal address, and are oddly reader-less. The style of her letters is not as vivid, complex and expansive as the style of the novels, and of course less deliberated and revised. Its imperative is to express the self and remember the reader, but the letters to Sara clearly anticipate the evolutionary languages of her fiction. And, like them, it shifts from abstract to the particular, and like them can be passionate as it reflects on passion.

Given the quality of their correspondence, it is surprising that Sara Hennell did not identify Marian Evans's 'great big mind and heart', the poetry as well as the learning and tenderness spotted by Barbara Bodichon when she read a review in 'an obscure paper' that quoted *Adam Bede* (*Letters* 3, 56). George Eliot replied: 'Curiously enough, my old Coventry friends ... have given no sign of recognition' (Haight, 280). If she disappointed Sara, George Eliot was disappointed by her, but without feeling lonely because she had Lewes.

Sara and the letters to her came before Lewes and the lasting, close and thoughtful exchanges between the lovers which we often infer and sometimes see. And after George Eliot started to write novels, her creative prose was engrossed by them, but she continued to write intimate and eloquent letters to many friends. One of these was Jane Senior. The letters to her have not been discussed as a series, perhaps because they have no striking biographical significance[4]. But George Eliot's acquaintance with her left more of a mark on the novels than longer or more intense friendships with Mrs Congreve, Georgiana Burne-Jones, Clementia Taylor, Emilia Pattison, Elma Stuart, and Edith Simcox. In the *Letters*, Haight referred to the *Dictionary of National Biography* entry for Jane Senior's father-in-law, Nassau William Senior, lawyer and illiberal workhouse 'reformer': it noted her Red Cross work in London during the Franco-Prussian War, her appointment as Inspector of Workhouses in 1873, and her controversial report. George Eliot's letters to her are about *Middlemarch*, ambition and goodness, Girton, problems of women, the public appointment, her Parliamentary Report 'Education of Girls in Pauper Schools' (25, 1874) and its hostile reception, Charles Lewes's article about it, and her husband's application for the Secretaryship of the Girton Foundation. But Haight's biography never mentions Jane Senior's public life, only domestic detail: she recommends a house in Spain (398), comes to lunch, sings, shops with George Eliot for a silk dress (442), and brings 'flowers or grapes' to Thornton (418) – the flowers are Haight's addition (Haight, 428). He omits George Eliot's description of her to Blackwood as 'a good woman as well as pretty and accomplished' (*Letters* 4, 404).

Rosemary Ashton briefly and perceptively refers to Jane Senior as 'this Dorothea' who did achieve public work, and quotes George Eliot's praise of her Report's 'fullness, clearness and wisdom of suggestion', along with conservative demurrings. Though sympathizing with her friend's zeal, George Eliot understood 'how the pointing out of evils under a system may be regarded by officials as "an attack"' and her doubts about public welfare and fears of 'communistic provision' are disappointing when we remember her earlier praise of Sibree's *sans-culottisme* (*Letters* 1, 252): 'Do what one will with a pauper system it remains a huge system of vitiation, introducing the principle of communistic provision instead of provision through individual, personal responsibility and activity. But what evil can be got rid of on a sudden?' (*Letters* 6, 47).

Like the Hennell correspondence, the Senior letters have intensity and style. The women met in 1866, before George Eliot had thought of *Middlemarch*, and their friendship continued until Jane's premature death from uterine cancer in 1877, at the height of her professional success. Re-reading the published and unpublished Senior letters, I was struck by the connection between the friendship and *Middlemarch*. Did George Eliot's growing acquaintance with Jane Senior's character, situation and ambition influence the composition of the novel by suggesting Dorothea for *Miss Brooke*? The letters connect with images and themes in the novel, but most striking is the link between the two women.

The journal entry for 2 December 1870 says: 'I am experimenting in a story, which I began without any serious intention of carrying it out lengthily. It has been recorded among my possible themes ever since I began to write fiction.' (We do not know to what theme this refers.) Jane Senior first met George Eliot in October 1866, when she was taken to visit her by Octavia Hill, the sister of Gertrude Lewes who married Lewes's son Charles[5]. The earliest letter we have to Senior from George Eliot is dated 11 December 1866, before she had begun her public work, and there is a group of letters written between 1867 and 1870, just when George Eliot was meditating on and writing the first version of *Middlemarch*, which did not include Miss Brooke, laying it aside for *Miss Brooke*, and finally incorporating the two separate beginnings in *Middlemarch*. Some of their letters after *Middlemarch* are relevant also.

Several of the letters are intense, inventively and lightly metaphorical and mythopoeic, sharing images and themes with *Middlemarch*. One is dated 22 May 1867, about six months after the women met. It addresses 'My dear Mrs Senior', but its tone is warm. She later uses what became a customary address to Jane Senior (and others), 'Dear Friend', and never calls Jane by her first name in letters, as she does to Sara, Barbara and Elma Stuart. She writes:

> You are a good angel for taking trouble to help me in millinery which is a crux to me. The angels fold their great wings to enter through very small door-places, and help the old women and little children. And sometimes they spare a little attention for me. I am very full of wings – I mean my mind is full of them, for we went to the Brit. Museum yesterday, and saw all sorts of winged creatures that were seen perhaps by Ezekiel … (*BL add. mss.* and *Letters* 4, 365)

Millinery, angels and wings are links with *Middlemarch*. Jane was more than a shopping adviser, even at this time before she worked for the Red Cross or in her government appointment. And George Eliot had help with clothes, as well as presents of shawls, scarves, handkerchiefs and underwear, from several other friends, including one man, the architect and designer Owen Jones, who persuaded her to dress more aesthetically to match his décor for the new house, The Priory. Millinery was 'a crux' for a woman indifferent to adornment – though I have mentioned the two Jane-Austen-like letters to Fanny about muslins (*Letters* 1, 362) – but dress was important to the novelist. It is dramatized and discussed by narrators and characters, who show or know, like Thackeray's Lady Kew in *The Newcomes*, that 'we belong to our belongings'. Millinery is a sartorial sub-genre in all the fiction: social and historical in 'Amos Barton'; wonderfully comic in *The Mill*; and subtly symbolic in *Middlemarch*, which has dress in the first sentence and first page of its first chapter. Dress is a crux for some of its characters. George Eliot's personal indifference is validated as it is transferred to her austere heroines or reversed in characters who are too keen on dress. The costumes of Dorothea, Celia, Rosamond and Mrs Bulstrode are historically remembered, researched and expressive. There are dramatic and moral acts of dressing up and dressing down, and if the narrator provides anthropological comment, it is backed by solidly specified fabric, texture, colour, cost, washability and accessories like the quilling in Rosamond's expensive bonnet round which her aunt's fine eyes 'rolled' observantly with appreciative envy. The drama of Chapter 43 would lose much without its costume: Dorothea wears a dress of 'thin white woollen stuff soft to the touch and soft to the eye' – an admiring androgynous or sartorially inexpert narrator does not know 'exactly what stuff it was' – and Rosamond a 'pale-blue dress of a fit and fashion so perfect that no dressmaker could look at it without emotion', with a large expensive embroidered collar. Dress is essential to the psycho-sociology and patterning of the great period piece. The millinery in the letters signals differences between dress in fact and fiction. In life she need not bother, unless Owen Jones makes her buy the grey moiré silk, in fiction she attends to dress with imaginative energy.

Angels return to the letters again after *Middlemarch*, when George Eliot welcomes the workhouse appointment, 'May all blessings attend you in it, over and above the affectionate wishes of your friends, wishes which you will carry with you like a host of encouraging guardian spirits' (*BL add. mss.* and *Letters* 5, 372). The last angel is Jane, told to 'lay herself up for two or three years at least', and 'like a white angel in her little bed' when the Leweses visit her in November 1874, 'to get the character of a new servant', (*Letters* 6, 90n), a fortnight after George Eliot wrote to Blackwood about Charles Lewes's article on the report[6].

Middlemarch is full of angels and wings. Milton's 'affable archangel' is in the motto to Chapter 3, identified ironically with Casaubon, and unironically recalled in Chapter 29. In Chapter 3, the prospect of marrying Casaubon thrills Dorothea, 'as if a winged messenger' is greeting her. In Chapter 21, Will thinks her an angel beguiled. Wings are classical as well as Biblical: in Chapter 20 the Casaubons exchange an urgent, nervous question and a bland, pedantic answer about the Cupid and Psyche frescoes; and the story of Psyche is implicit in Dorothea's labours, revised as the earnest narrator says Dorothea has been visited unawares by 'Love … with the hues of morning on his wings' (55). Even the flying insect, 'a winged visitor' in the innocent amorous drawing room of the previous chapter, is on the verge of being magnetized by the myth', especially when we find its wings were added during a revision. Dorothea's west-facing boudoir becomes a spiritual sanctuary populated by moral memories like 'a cloud of good or bad angels' (37). In Chapter 70, Bulstrode's conscience is 'soothed by the enfolding wing of secrecy, which seemed just then like an angel sent down for his relief'.

Wings and angels are not exclusive to this novel or these letters – 'Janet's Repentance' is full of them and Daniel Deronda is a stern angel for Gwendolen. In her letter for their joint birthday on 22 November (in 1872, after *Middlemarch*), George Eliot wishes she could fly to Sara on 'the wings of the morning' and 'fly back on the wings of the wind' (*Letters* 5, 330). Before the 'angel' letter of 22 May 1867, George Eliot twice describes Bessie Parkes as Barbara Bodichon's guardian angel, and on 19 November tells Barbara that Julia Smith is her guardian angel (*Letters* 4, 362–3, 399). Angels are un-Victorianly associated with socially energetic women who were not exactly angels in the house. Two of them speak of angels: Barbara Bodichon jokes about her 'angel and devil' (*Letters* 3, 56), and in March 1852, Bessie Parkes writes of her new acquaintance to Barbara Leigh Smith, not yet Bodichon: 'Large angels take a long time unfolding their wings; but when they do, soar out of sight. Miss Evans either has no wings, or, which I think is the case, they are coming, budding' (*Letters* 2, 9n).

On 14 March 1868, George Eliot effusively compliments Jane Senior's fine contralto by calling her 'the sweet bird-visitor', and says: 'I am writing a book, and when it comes out you may think it pitiable and want to have no more to do with me' (*Letters* 4, 422–3). The book is the original *Middlemarch* without Miss Brooke. On 13 March 1870, she thanks Jane for a scented sachet:

> The sachet came to me quite safely, smelling like the garden of Eden in its most desirable spots where the violets grew. So you will be hovering about me like an invisible angel with violet-scented wings. Very delicate scents make me feel happy, but I find it too troublesome to get them for myself. So such a present as this is really a greater addition to my pleasure than it would be to most people's. (*BL add. mss.* and *Letters* 5, 82)

George Eliot can be a tactful giver, as when offering financial help to Sara and Cara, but her thank-you letters are not graced by understatement. Her thanks to Oscar Browning for a chair, George Smith for a dressing-case, John Blackwood for real and china 'Pugs', and Elma Stuart for carved furniture and well-designed undergarments, are all gushing. But though the Edenic violets and violet-scented wings are too sweet, they come with an interesting admission: 'very delicate scents make me feel happy' and we are alerted to the sensitivity in the fiction, where scents are imaginary, their sweetness drained of excess to be subtly savoured. Fictional scents are significant in a society where hot water was expensive and there were no easy-care fabrics, dry-cleaners or deodorants, and of course the novels draw attention, ironically or simply, to social fact. There is the class-significance of rose-scents in Arbury Hall, Freshitt Grange and Rosamond Vincy's imaginary great houses, and in rose-scented gentlemen such as Anthony Wybrow in 'Mr Gilfil's Love-Story', Arthur Donnithorne, Stephen Guest and Sir James Chettam. Scents are erotic, too. Rosamond's 'delicate' handkerchief is lifted, with Lydgate's fourth finger, to be delectably sniffed after she says he has the advantage of visiting houses with 'the scent of rose-leaves everywhere' (31). Scents are refined in metaphor, sometimes ironically: Dorothea 'takes in' one of Casaubon's pamphlets 'as she might have taken in the scent of a fresh bouquet' (4). In a strange comparison where the intense vehicle seems disproportionate to tenor, 'prejudice' is as subtle 'as the twentieth echo of an echo, or as the memory of hyacinths which once scented the darkness' (43). Like flowers and presents, perfumes gushed over in letters are imaginatively placed in novels.

Another theme of the letters is goodness, mentioned in the scented-wings letter of 13 March 1870: 'Bless you first of all for being a good woman, and next, for being good to me', a discrimination glancing at Jane's still unpractised ideals and ambition, consoling her for the lack of outlet. Just after *Middlemarch*, in 1873, when Jane had found a professional channel for her virtues, George Eliot advises: 'You have only got to be a good faithful woman such as you have always been, and then the very thought of you will help to mend things' (*Letters* 5, 372). It is a backhanded compliment to the new professional woman, with its domestic image to 'mend things', and talks of inspiration not active work: 'you have only got to be ... the very thought of you'. It is more like Dorothea and the earlier Jane Senior than the 1873 Inspector. However, the rejoicing in human goodness in the earlier letter of 13 March 1870 stresses the domestic but brings in the metaphysical: 'Keep a little love for me till we come back, for I shall think of you as one of the friends who make an English home dear, and enter into my life quite out of proportion to the number of times that I see them. One lives by faith in human goodness – the only guarantee that there can be any other sort of goodness in the universe' *(BL add. mss.* and *Letters* 5, 82–3).

The idea that human goodness can guarantee any 'other sort of goodness' is extraordinary, and unprecedented in George Eliot's writings. It is explicable as rejection of religious guarantees which ignore human virtue, relying solely on divine grace, but the suggestion that human goodness 'guarantees' any other kind is strange for a Feuerbachian agnostic. What we might expect of the ex-Christian, at her most sympathetic and nostalgic, is not 'guarantee' but 'implication' or 'suggestion'.

The emphasis on domestic virtue, 'making an English home dear', may not have comforted Jane Senior, who was conscientious in the home but wanting a lot more. George Eliot's sentimental tone and words praise the 'fair bright' and imply the domestically 'useful' woman (*Letters* 6, 359) but when we think of Dorothea, who had no career, a combination of the domestic with the ideal is apt. An association of her friend with her heroine could explain the 'guarantee'. It is not like George Eliot but it is not unlike Dorothea, who stopped praying, whose lack of religion in crisis was noticed by one Christian reviewer and who, in spite of early evangelical leanings, is George Eliot's least religious heroine. She tells Will she does not want her religion labelled, 'You will say it is Persian', and her 'belief' is perfectly judged by Will and brilliantly placed by George Eliot as 'a beautiful mysticism'. Benign and humane, it comes close to Jane Senior's goodness as George Eliot saw it, but it is also tentative and hesitant, and closer still to George Eliot's 'faith in human goodness' and her metonymic – not metaphysical – vision: 'by desiring what is perfectly good, even when we don't quite know what it is and cannot do what we would, we are part of the divine power against evil – widening the skirts of light and making the struggle with darkness narrower' (*Middlemarch*, 39).

In a letter of 13 March 1870, Jane's goodness, like Dorothea's, is 'diffusive': 'See how diffusive your one little life may be. I say that à propos of your longing for a wider existence' (*BL add. mss.* and *Letters* 5, 83). The idea of *diffuse* influence is central to *Middlemarch*, and strongly emphasized at the end. George Eliot may have this in mind when she says her response to Jane Senior was 'quite out of proportion to the number of times' they had met. In the novel's last paragraph we have – and it is all we have – Dorothea's 'incalculably diffusive' influence.

The 'wider existence' has resonances too: 'wider' and 'width' recall Dorothea's dream of wider scope, large vistas and wide views, Ladislaw's artistic and political aspirations, Naumann's joking 'wi-ide', Casaubon's constricted and constricting concern for narrow Egyptian dwellings, and other positive or negative metonymies of windows, rooms, houses and views. Dorothea's plans for village housing are implemented by Sir James and his land-agent, but her plot of land for an ideal community comes to nothing. Jane achieved more but she had confided to George Eliot that she wanted 'a wider existence' and may have inspired George Eliot to write about diffusive powers and the influence of 'one woman's' lot' on another – as she does with no other heroine.

Writing to her, George Eliot remarks on the diffuse influence of women in ways that are sensitive to gender, using language close to that which *Middlemarch* uses to speak of women, their influence and their 'lot'. After *Middlemarch*, the 'lot' of women comes into the congratulatory letter of 24 January 1873 when George Eliot says Jane Senior had 'entered into' and strengthened her beliefs:

> The influence of one woman's life on the lot of other women is getting greater and greater, with the quickening spread of all influences. One likes to think, though, that two thousand years ago Euripides made Iphigenia count it a reason for facing her sacrifice bravely that thereby she might help to save Greek women (from a wrong like Helen's) in the time to come. There is no knife at your throat, happily. You have only got to be a good faithful woman such as you have always been, and then the very thought of you will help to mend things. Take it as a sign of that, when I tell you that you have entered into my more cheerful beliefs and made them stronger because of the glimpses I have had of your character & life … *(BL add. mss.* and Letters 5, 372)

These 'glimpses' are significant: perhaps George Eliot was inspired to incorporate aspects of this friend's character and life because she strengthened her 'beliefs' and because her life was not thoroughly known, so was more usable. In a letter after the death of one of Jane Senior's brothers, George Eliot says she hopes to learn more about the Hughes family, one of whom, Thomas Hughes (*Letters* 5, 285), was famous as author of *Tom Brown's Schooldays*.

The references to Iphigenia, sacrifice, women's lives, faithfulness and womens' influence on each other effectively form a reprise of the last page of *Middlemarch*, where George Eliot uses another Greek heroine, Antigone – morally rather than psychologically apt for Dorothea – and speaks of 'the lives of many Dorotheas, some of which may present a far sadder sacrifice than that of the Dorothea whose story we know' (*Middlemarch*, Finale). Other words echo, too: 'Comfort will gradually come in your activity for others, which never leaves you long in the power of your own particular lot' (*BL add. mss.* and *Letters* 5, 285), which repeats 'lot', the 'particular' of *Middlemarch*'s famous particular web, and Dorothea's impulse away from self. If George Eliot did not model Dorothea on Jane Senior, she must have come to see her friend as like her heroine.

Middlemarch ends with men as well as women: those around 'her', 'you and me', and 'the number who lived faithfully a hidden life'. Mentioning Girton in a pre-*Middlemarch* letter of 4 October 1869, George Eliot says the 'Women Question' seemed 'to overhang abysses, of which even prostitution is not the worst' and alludes to a recent conversation:

> I write these hasty words to show you that I valued what you said to me. But do not let anyone else see this note. I have been made rather miserable lately by revelations about women, and have resolved to remain silent in my sense of helplessness. I know very little about what is specially good for women – only a few things that I feel sure are good for human nature generally, and about such as these last alone, can I ever hope to write or say anything worth saying. (*Letters* 5, 58)

This relates to George Eliot's fears about publicizing her views on women and their education, which were also expressed in her correspondence with Emily Davies. Looking ahead – 'about such as these last alone, can I ever hope to write' – it also emphasizes her concern in *Middlemarch* with the education, vocation, frustration and misdirection of men as well as women – 'why always Dorothea?' This was not new in her work: Tom's wasted education is criticized and critical, as well as Maggie's. But at times, a woman's lot is jealously compared to men's. The energetic, talented, altruistic and frustrated Dorothea shames and shows up the indolent Mr Brooke, impotent Casaubon and tragically compromised Lydgate. In this, it resembles the contrast between zealous, idealistic and radical Jane Senior, and her conservative father-in-law, Nassau William Senior, responsible for Poor Law miseries, and her lethargic husband. Jane Senior's family situation may have encouraged George Eliot's feminist placing of the novel's able woman among less able men. On 2 January 1871, George Eliot wrote cautious and perhaps embarrassed testimonials for Jane's husband, unsuccessfully, to Emily Davies and Thomas Huxley. The following is from the slightly longer letter to Huxley:

> I trouble you with this letter for the sake of a very good, sweet woman – Mrs Nassau Senior. It is true that her goodness is not a sufficient reason for her husband's appointment to the chief secretaryship of the Educational Board. But you, I imagine, are especially bound to regard it as a presumption in a man's favour, and a becoming background to

his other advantages, that he has chosen an excellent wife … I only know that Mr Senior has had all the experience implied in having been Secretary of Commissions for four years under three Chancellors, and I have reason – chiefly in the unsought indirect testimony of those who know him intimately – to believe that he has some of the moral qualities which help to make a good public servant and fellow-worker. (*Letters* 9, 5–6)

To repeat, George Eliot's fictional characters are hardly ever portraits, and it is impossible to be sure that this reality even suggested this fiction. I can only point out resemblances between the language and themes in letters and novels, and propose that Jane's frustration, altruism and talent, may have inspired these aspects of the original Miss Brooke, who significantly interrupted the *Ur-Middlemarch* then solved its problem by joining it[7]. The two beginnings – of the first *Middlemarch* and *Miss Brooke* – had a common subject, but this was no simple thematic fusion: *Miss Brooke* brought centrality to structure, and meliorism to moral conclusion, radically altering the earlier three-plot novel in which Lydgate was the most important character. We do not know exactly how the novelist originally meant to end *his* story, but if she intended anything at all like the Lydgate–Rosamond marriage, it would have the defect, for a George Eliot narrative, of concluding in tragic failure. Dorothea's end is not ideal success but not failure either, and her diffuse, benign influence contrasts with Lydgate's failure in an ending disappointing to some feminists but congenial to George Eliot the meliorist.

And to George Eliot the historian. *Middlemarch* is a novel of reform, its narrative scrupulously set in the early part of the century but written from an authorial viewpoint of the late 1860s, when the woman's movement started. It needed a woman character, an untragic Maggie with larger vision and more defined talent, to be urgently ambitious and socially frustrated. The annexation of *Miss Brooke* gave centrality and realism to the project of *Middlemarch,* in a heroine whose restrictions and powers could be dramatized with historical accuracy as well as feminist regret. George Eliot invites or promotes an historical reading and creates an open ending by the Finale's plural, 'many Dorotheas': Dorothea is briefly but conspicuously defictionalized, like Maggie Tulliver – 'not the only girl' – and

Jo in *Bleak House* – 'dying thus around us every day'. Such shifts from fiction to the real, raw life outside it do not suggest simple origins. If Jane Senior's life and character nourished Dorothea's, they were experimentally transposed to an earlier generation in an act of historical distancing common in Victorian fiction. Perhaps the differences between famous George Eliot and frustrated Jane Senior, for whom public work was perhaps not yet imagined, were inspiring. A lack of full knowledge may have made the encounter suggestive, like a *donnée* or 'germ' for Henry James.

Jane Senior was born in 1828, nine years after Mary Anne Evans. In real time she was a baby and Mary Anne Evans a child, when in fictional time Dorothea was a marriageable, immature 19 year old, a woman dreaming, like Mary Ann and Jane, of wider scope for her energy and idealism, but unlike both in not finding it. Foundress of nothing, Dorothea could only 'diffuse' influence in the private life. She is unlike George Eliot, whose lot was the career of an exceptional artist, and unlike politically active women, Barbara Bodichon, Emily Davies, Bessie Parkes and Octavia Hill, who widened their own and other women's lives, provided 'lots' more available to ordinary women than an artist's career. Dorothea is unlike the Jane Senior who became the first English woman public servant, 40 years after Dorothea's young frustration, at a time when it was possible to be a foundress of something. But she is not unlike Jane Senior when George Eliot first met her. Dorothea is a fictional character born of, and belonging to, a real, beloved sisterhood, but representing an early stage in its aspiration, not the achievement of Barbara Bodichon, Octavia Hill and Florence Nightingale. George Eliot's early acquaintance with an aspiring Jane Senior could have suggested Dorothea, whose relationships, talents, tastes, looks and personality have nothing in common with Jane Senior's, but whose ideals, powers and frustrations and virtues do. And George Eliot was, by this time, adept at what she called 'manipulating' her 'models' (*Letters* 3, 99).

In Dorothea's situation, not her character or lack of career, George Eliot was re-imagining her own frustrated past as well as the present of the unfulfilled Jane Senior in 1869. If Jane Senior's frustrated ambitions merely resembled Dorothea's, as George Eliot was imagining *Miss Brooke*, the link with a fictional fellow has its poignancy. A real woman's career proved that George Eliot was right about Dorothea's capacity, not so much as a Saint Theresa – the novelist looking back, but as a Jane Senior – the novelist looking ahead.

Dorothea is an historical experiment, a displaced Saint Theresa. She may have prompted George Eliot's reading of Jane Senior, but if it were the other way round, and Jane Senior were the prompt character – as I think likely – her character and her story made it possible for George Eliot to re-imagine herself by historical displacement. She did not want to tell her own story of sexual subversion or artistic success. She created Janet's psyche by fusing her own experience with Nancy Buchanan's, and she needed to edit her own creative autobiography in order to dis-empower Dorothea. It is as prompt, not prototype, that I imagine Jane Senior. Whatever she is, she is fact resembling fiction. Fiction particularizes and generalizes, too, not often so boldly and bluntly as at the end of *Middlemarch*. Its particularities come out of a process in which real lives are abstracted and re-particularized. Carlyle said history was composed of innumerable biographies, and so is this novel. It is not disguised autobiography or portraiture, but an imaginative recom-position, concentrated and diffuse, direct and indirect, public and private, psychological, social and moral.

Of course, it is dangerous to infer sources from style. Angels, wings, perfumes and millinery came before and after the Senior letters. We speculate about origins and inspirations, but only know about adhesions and affinities. George Eliot's language develops in literature, and feeds back into letters to regenerate. Worries about the education of women and men, hopes for progress, faith in virtue and loyalty, and themes of ambition, power, frustration and success are distanced and brought close in fiction. Life and art grow together.

Gwyther, the Buchanans, Tugwell, Frederic Harrison, Maria Lewis, Sara Hennell and Jane Senior are all acquaintances or friends who get into her novels. She was less deeply and complexly involved with them than with her father and brother, or Spencer, Lewes and Cross, but they were important to her writing, some as models, some as story-tellers, all as inspirations.

Notes.

1 Tom Winnifrith's 'Subtle Shadowy Suggestions: Fact and Fiction' in *Scenes of Clerical Life*, George Eliot – *George Henry Lewes Studies*, Nos. 24–6, September 1993.

2 In her edition of *Adam Bede* (2002) Toronto and Plymouth: Broadview Editions, Broadview Press, Mary Waldron includes a broadsheet account of 'The Trial and Execution of Mary Voce', 1802, and other useful material (Appendices C and E).

3 I discuss this and other examples in 'The Moment of Disenchantment', *The Review of English Studies*, 19, 5, 1954 and *NGE.*

4 In December 2000 a batch of letters to Jane Senior from George Eliot was auctioned at Sotheby's. In March 2001, a proposed export was deferred by the Department of Culture, Media and Sport, in accordance with the Waverley guidelines for considering the export of cultural property, which specify historical, national, aesthetic and scholarly value. The letters were bought by the British Library. The auction, export stay and purchase drew attention to the series, three of which had already been published by Haight, with others to Jane Senior not in the new series. For those letters I discuss which are now also in the British Library, I quote the manuscripts, which differ slightly from Haight, who standardizes punctuation and abbreviations: *BL add. mss.75298. BL add. mss.*

5 For information about Octavia Hill's introduction, Jane Senior's religion, and her husband, I am indebted to Sybil Oldfield.

6 See *Letters*, 6, 87 and 157. His article, 'The Education of the Children of the State', which defended her report against attacks by Edward Carleton Tufnell, former Inspector of Schools (*Edinburgh Review*, 142, July 1875) was sent to Blackwood while GE and Lewes were away, and she asked for its return, apparently expecting Blackwood to find it politically unsuitable, as he apparently did. Charles Lewes was glad Jane Senior approved of it.

7 Jerome Beaty (1960) *Middlemarch, From Notebook to Novel: A Study of George Eliot's Creative Method*, Urbana: University of Illinois Press; and David Carroll's use of Beaty in *Middlemarch*, World's Classics, Oxford: Oxford University Press, 1988.

Chapter Five
Illness and Death

... that terrible handwriting of human destiny, illness and death ('Amos Barton', 9)

Illness in George Eliot's novels is serious, thrilling, illustrative or symbolic, important for plot, and usually fatal – Dempster's and Raffles's *delirium tremens*, Tryan's consumption, Tulliver's strokes, Baldassare's amnesia, Casaubon's heart disease and the terminal illness of Daniel's mother. There are almost none of the everyday malaises, headache, toothache, rheumatic twinge and bilious attacks she and Lewes suffered chronically or acutely, but which are too random, accidental and petty for novels, where detail seeks significance. Even more inclusive modern fiction doesn't give bad colds, headaches and indigestion much of a look in.

She sometimes introduces minor ailments into domestic scenes, making experience serve her purposes. One chronic invalid is the energetic but 'pale' Mrs Poyser in *Adam Bede*. She is less lugubrious about her health than Mrs Pullet, but harps on it: 'and the dairy thralls [stone slabs] I might ha' wrote my name on 'em, when I come downstairs after my illness, as the doctor said it was inflammation' (6); 'if trouble was to come an' I was to be laid up i' my bed' (20); and 'an' me th' only aunt you've got above-ground, an' am brought to the brink o' the grave welly every winter as comes' (49). She is conveniently laid up to provide cover for pregnant Hetty's symptoms and terrors: 'soon after Christmas Mrs Poyser had taken another cold, which had brought on inflammation, and this illness had confined her to her room all through January' (35). If there is truth in the tradition that Mrs Poyser is based on the second Mrs Evans, her milder ailments may be memorials of the mother's real pains and death from cancer. Amos Barton's Mrs Hackit, her predecessor in sharp wit, kind heart and possible indebtedness to Mrs Evans, has a chronic liver complaint.

A dutiful womanly woman asking after her betters, Mrs Poyser is told by the Reverend Irwine that his sister Anne has 'one of her bad headaches', and sickly Anne makes her appearance in a scene which gives domestic detail of the gentry for this novel where class barriers are crucial, making its social fabric more dense. She brings out the sympathetic character of her brother, too: 'It was a small face, that of the poor sufferer; perhaps it had once been pretty, but now it was worn and sallow.' Her sister Kate explains she cannot bear to be spoken to, her 'brow contracted as if from intense pain', Irwine kisses her hand, and 'a slight pressure ... told him that it had been worth coming up-stairs for the sake of doing that' (5). Irwine leaves her, treading gently, having 'taken off his boots and put on slippers before he came up-stairs'. Anne is able to attend Arthur's Coming-of-Age, where Kate is mysteriously absent, perhaps from authorial oversight, though she returns later in the book. The narrator wryly calls Kate and Anne dull and insignificant and, like characters in *Scenes of Clerical Life*, they are shown, briefly, to possess their centres of self. Their roles as grateful invalid and patient nurse give an entry to the minor bad headaches that plagued their author, and the sickroom sympathy is the other side of the hilarious good-natured fun and caricature of Mrs Pullet's pills, medicine-bottles and hypochondria. George Eliot could laugh at her own ailments, too, as on the occasion when she wonders if a pill or a prayer would be more efficacious in the treatment of 'the Bile' (*Letters* 1, 263).

She visited the poor and sick at Griff and after she moved to Foleshill, and her good works and knowledge of humble living are reflected in Janet's charities, and rather strikingly in one of her narrator's rare personal anecdotes, in *Silas Marner*, exceptional at this period in sounding more like a woman's experience than a man's. It is like the narrator's talk with Adam in old age: ' "Is there anything you can fancy that you would like to eat?" I once said to an old labouring man, who was in his last illness, and who had refused all the food his wife had offered him. "No", he answered, "I've never been used to nothing but common victual, and I can't eat that" ' (*Silas Marner*, 1). Here sympathetic memory brings language and narrative into sharp focus after the generalization about narrow lives where imagination is 'almost barren of images that feed desire and hope'. The digression is in keeping with the calm tone and simple narrative and opens a narrow shaft of light into the author's life.

Bereavement is most fully observed in Lisbeth Bede's domestic rites after her husband's death. This episode reflects the style of Wordsworth's *Excursion*, the poem which presides over the novel in an epigraph, but every solid, specific detail reflects George Eliot's experience of rural habits and the domestic round, not just as a cottage visitor but as someone who has lived the life and is acquainted with habitat, furnishing and act. The relation of inner and outer life is delicately observed and composed:

> She had brought out her little store of bleached linen, which she had for long years kept in reserve for this supreme use. It seemed but yesterday – that time so many midsummers ago when she had told Thias where this linen lay, that he might be sure and reach it out for her when *she* died, for she was the elder of the two. Then there had been the work of cleansing to the strictest purity every object in the sacred chamber, and of removing from it every trace of common daily occupation. The small window which had hitherto freely let in the frosty moonlight or the warm summer sunrise on the working man's slumber, must now be darkened with a fair white sheet … Lisbeth had even mended a long neglected unnoticeable rent in the checkered bit of bed-curtain … Our dead are never dead to us until we have forgotten them: they can be injured by us, they can be wounded; they know all our penitence, all our aching sense that their place is empty, all the kisses we bestow on the smallest relic of their presence. And the aged peasant woman most of all believes that her dead are conscious. Decent burial was what Lisbeth had been thinking of for herself through years of thrift … (10)

Individual emotion and motive are tracked minutely and warmly in domestic actions and objects, placed and analysed by sympathetic anthropology and art. There is a swerve to generalization as we move from Lisbeth's respect for her dead to the common habits of memorial, then back through the general subject of keeping the dead alive in memory to particulars, to this aged peasant woman. It is felt experience, not portraiture, which makes this mourning scene and its sacred objects self-analytic and impassioned, as poignant in George Eliot's rhythmical prose as in Thomas Hardy's lyric poetry.

The fatal illness of Featherstone, an 'inward complaint', chest weakness and dropsy, is important to the Garth–Vincy plot of *Middlemarch*. His chronic cough and swollen legs evoke varying responses from his lachrymose sister Mrs Waule, who knows 'The doctors can't master that cough, brother. It's just like what I have …' (12), Fred Vincy, who walks him round the room, 'in spite of his irritation … a little sorry for the unloved, unvenerated old man, who with his dropsical legs, looked more than usually pitiable' (12), and Mary Garth. Both housekeeper and nurse, Mary Garth is always at hand, providing syrup for Vincy's fits of coughing, approved by Trumbull as she carefully measures the drops of his medicine. She feels hurt but puts up with his rude humours, and watches by his bed, as Mary Ann had done for her father and no doubt for her mother in their last illnesses. George Eliot's fiction assimilates the author's experience of caring for the sick: during her mother's last illness Robert Evans suffered a severe attack of kidney stone and of course his daughters cared for him then, just as Mary Ann nursed him in his last years. She was reported by Cara Bray to be worn, sickly-faced, strained, suffering terrible headaches, and pathetically grateful for rare kindness; but her nursing had its positive side. She told Sara Hennell, whose sister Mary was dying of tuberculosis: 'You have need of all your cheeriness and energy, and if they do not fail I think it almost enviable as far as one's self is concerned not of course when the sufferer is remembered, to have the care of a sickroom, with its twilight and tiptoe silence and helpful activity. I have always had a peculiarly peaceful feeling in such a scene' (*Letters* 1, 156). She revives this peculiar peacefulness for her Mary:

> That night after twelve o'clock Mary Garth relieved the watch in Mr Featherstone's room, and sat there alone during the small hours. She often chose this task, in which she took some pleasure, notwithstanding the old man's testiness whenever he demanded her attentions. There were intervals in which she could sit perfectly still, enjoying the outer stillness and the subdued light. . . . Mary was fond of her own thoughts, and could amuse herself well sitting in twilight with her hands in her lap; for, having early had strong reason to believe that things were not likely to be arranged for her peculiar satisfaction, she wasted no time in astonishment and annoyance at that fact. (33)

The image of twilight, in a scene starting just after midnight, alerts us to personal origins: George Eliot is adapting her experience of nursing her father for different characters and a different situation. There is her own repose and quiet in the intervals of attendance. Mary's acceptance of a world not arranged for her peculiar self, too, is in harmony with her author's young experience and mature ethic. The drama that breaks the peace, when the dying man tries to bully Mary into destroying his will and she exerts her will in resistance, is fine contrast to the meditative calm which has shown the source of Mary's firm integrity.

'Amos Barton', as I have said, turns on a woman's suffering and death from chronic child-bearing, drawing on George Eliot's knowledge of Chrissey's life. The subliminal eloquence of this woman's story, its gender-significance shown everywhere rather than discussed, may explain why several readers, most famously Dickens, felt sure the anonymous author of the serial and the masculine-named author of the book, was a woman. The story describes woman's work like sewing, darning, repairing and contriving to make ends meet, but the woman's physical fatigue, deprivation and stress are sub-texts, the stronger for being subdued. As a father of a distressingly large family, though he resented rather than sympathized with his prolific wife, Dickens may have been alert to the 'bad illness' that made Milly pale, exhausted and in need of the iron-rich meat and wine supplied by wise Mrs Hackit. Unlike that other great childless English novelist, Jane Austen, whose remarks on married women's sufferings are sharp and clear in her letters, not novels, George Eliot says little on the subject in her letters, but writes that first story about a woman dragged down by childbearing, miscarriages and malnu-trition, setting tone and theme for the *Scenes* that follow.

As an adolescent and woman, George Eliot suffered from severe periodic headaches, toothache, rheumatism, depression and the occasional fit of crying. There are so few references to this kind of chronic suffering in her novels that the exceptions stand out. 'Janet's Repentance' contains an unusual reference to a woman's physical cycle. It is folded away in the drama of event, slipped in quietly in contrast to the strong action of brutal Dempster and his violent hallucinations. Janet has been asked to look for some papers and searching her husband's bureau, she unexpectedly comes across a brandy flask and is shocked by temptation. But what the narrator emphasises just before this episode is a woman's susceptible state of feeling, especially interesting in view of Mary Ann's tendency to weep: 'she could not help bursting into tears. It is such vague indefinable states of susceptibility as this – states of excitement or depression, half mental, half physical – that determine many a tragedy in women's lives' (25).

Preserved equally from didactic dryness and sensationalism, the comment is diagnostically brilliant in refusing diagnostic precision. Its cool firm insistence on elusive symptom: 'vague indefinable', 'excitement or depression', 'half mental, half physical', is emotionally particular in its knowing, compassionate fellow-feeling. Of course it draws on a woman's self-observation – her letters and journals are full of headaches lasting for days, pain, tears and depression. (Attempts to find menstrual patterns, in spite of asterisks in the diary, seem defeated by frequency and irregularity of symptoms[1].) Dickens and Thackeray create some wonderful women characters, but Amy Dorrit, Bella, Becky Sharp and Amelia have inner lives and no menstrual cycles.

Milly Barton's death has been called sentimental, but if her death is sweetened by loving word and distant music, the feelings are not stereotyped, and the elusive griefs of the children and widower are finely done. Caterina's death is softened by the flower-image but foreshortened, and the hardening, sad solitude of eccentric Gilfil is too particular for sentimentality. Janet nurses Tryan, and her response is more complicated than anything in the first two stories in both presentation and emotional content. It seems to draw on George Eliot's experience in several ways. She may have seen people die of the common social disease of tuberculosis, or heard from Chrissey about her brother-in-law Charles Clarke who died young of 'galloping consumption' in 1841. There is clever avoidance of the actual death and, on the whole, the decline is done matter-of-factly, with medical detail of a second doctor's opinion, and the (early) use of the stethoscope, which reappears in *Middlemarch*. Symptoms and emotion are straightforwardly described: 'The strange hallucinations of the disease which had seemed to take a more decided hold on him just at the fatal crisis, and had made him think he was perhaps getting better at the very time when death had begun to hurry on with more rapid movement, had now given way, and left him calmly conscious of the reality' (27). A similar observation is made in *Daniel Deronda* when Mordecai is dying of tuberculosis.

The feelings of Janet as she nurses Tryan are analysed rather than dramatized, but the narrative is sufficiently personal and impersonal too.

> She felt no rebellion under this prospect of bereavement, but rather a quiet submissive sorrow. Gratitude that ... almost silenced regret. Janet had lived through the great tragedy of woman's life. Her keenest personal emotions had been poured forth in her early love – her wounded affection with its years of anguish – her agony of unavailing pity over that deathbed seven months ago. The thought of Mr Tryan was associated for her with repose from that conflict of emotion, with trust in the unchangeable, with the influx of a power to subdue self.

George Eliot re-imagines for Janet what she experienced herself – waiting for death over a long period when she nursed her father from the summer of 1848 until he died in the spring of 1849. She leaves out the tumultuous phases of her own watching and nursing and gives repentant Janet the comforts of religion, but she allows her to feel, as she had, the end of egoism and conflict, a welcome, if painful, reduction to simple human bond and duty. In April 1848, Robert's bed was moved downstairs into the dining room, and Mary Ann told Fanny she was going to sleep on a 'sofa in his room until he is better' (*Letters* 1, 257). She wrote: 'I am enjoying repose strength and ardour in a greater degree than I have ever known and yet I never felt my own insignificance and imperfection so completely' (*Letters* 1, 269), and 'These are very precious moments to me; my chair by father's bedside is a very blessed seat to me' and 'Strange to say I feel these will ever be the happiest days of life to me' (*Letters* 1, 283–4). In September 1848, Cara told Sara:

> We are very anxious about MA and shall be very thankful to hear that all is over. Her father gets rapidly worse. The doctors expect his death to take place suddenly, by a suffusion of water on his chest; and poor MA, alone with him, has the whole care and fatigue of nursing him ... with this constant nervous expectation. She keeps up wonderfully

mentally, but looks like a ghost. It is a great comfort that he is now quite aware of his situation, and was not in the least discomposed when Isaac told him he might die suddenly. It was quite a pleasure to see him sitting in his chair looking so calm just after known this. (*Letters* 1, 272.)

Robert's calm repose becomes Tryan's 'divine calm'. The finality and farewell of the traditional death-scene, like those of Dickens's Little Nell, Smike, Paul, and Jo, or Thackeray's Colonel Newcome, is replaced in this story by a short exchange of broken sentences. The religious feeling is conventional, unappealing to most modern readers but with no deathbed sublimities. The pathos is rather good: the dying man and the woman he has come to love have a real, simple, allusive conversation: 'you will have a long while to live after I am gone'. (He wonders if her abstinence can last.) There are halting speech-rhythms and long pauses: she is breathless in fear that he is dying, he is breathless from the illness. A single kiss is made particular, his lips 'wasted' and hers 'full life-breathing'. Emotion is shown as turbulent, solemn and uncertain, as it is for Milly's children and Amos in trying to keep grief alive. Janet's new love is muted and unidentified: 'the time was not yet come for her to be conscious that the hold he had on her heart was any other than that of the heaven-sent friend' (27)[2].

The most interesting and most biographically specific dying in her fiction is in *Middlemarch*, into which George Eliot put so much of her experience. In December 1869, she recalls her father's death, 'Death had never come near to me through the twenty years since I lost my Father', as she wrote to Harriet Beecher Stowe about the death of Thornton (or Thornie) Lewes, her foster-child, young, creative, vital and amusing, on 19 October 1869 (*Letters* 5, 71). It was not only a bitter grief in itself but brought very close the thought of her own and her partner's death. She had spent another six months waiting for death, a young man's not an aging parent's, and records hope, fear, pity and ignorance. On 19 October 1869, Thornton died in her arms, suffering from an agonizing, wasting spinal complaint which may have been tuberculosis. She told Cara Bray: 'Thornie is dead. He died last night, very gently. Nurse and I raised him and his last breathings were quite peaceful' (*Letters* 5, 60). Lewes wrote to TA Trollope: 'She had lavished almost a mother's love on the dear boy, and suffered a mother's grief in the bereavement. He died in her arms … But she will get to work and *that* will aid her' (*Letters* 5, 69). She wrote to Barbara Bodichon after the death, 'I have a deep sense of change within, and of a permanently closer companionship with death' (25 November 1869, *Letters* 5, 70). (Haight prints this sentence a second time, dating it 1878, five days before Lewes's death [*Letters* 7, 84] and giving his source as the Anderson Galleries Catalogue 983, January 1913, item 271, presumably in his or the catalogue's error. It was Thornton's death, not Lewes's illness, which began George Eliot's companionship with death.)

On 9 September 1869, George Eliot answered Jane Senior's enquiry by describing Thornton's improvement but mentioning a 'mental inertness which has taken the place of his former vivacity and ready interest' (*Letters* 5, 55). On 4 October 1869, she is hopeful but adds: 'His face has more than ever of the wizened look that has come instead of its old beauty, and that pains me to see. I cannot shake off the impression it creates in me of slow withering' (*Letters* 5, 57). Mary Garth meets Fred after the reading of Featherstone's will, plucks up courage to look at him and sees 'that withered sort of paleness' (35)[3]. Fred is pale with disappointment, and also frail and convalescent after typhoid, when he was said to be vulnerable, feeble and childish. The withered look in reality and fiction is dwelt on as a peculiarly dreadful image of death in life, and is part of a pattern of death-imagery new in her work, a sign of new and profound apprehension. For her, the look of slow withering had meant death, and though Fred's withering is healed, it came into the novel by an unusually fast passage from life to art, as if experience demanded to be made articulate.

In Chapter 42 of 'Three Love Problems' (Book 4), after 'Waiting for Death', Lydgate gives his prognosis honestly and directly as Casaubon asks, and leaves the patient alone. The narrative tracks the inner responses of a man taking in the fact that he has a short time to live. Outer scene and inner action are introduced by a solemn poetry, in ordered sound and in imagery of sympathetic nature: Casaubon is alone, the yews providing 'a mute companionship in melancholy'. George Eliot shifted her letter's metaphor of death's companionship from a bereaved survivor to a man about to die, and from personified death to personified melancholy. Companionship with death is at the heart of the scene, but it does not engross it. The novel transplants 'companionship' to revive its vitality and make it intense, sensuous and strange, for a while:

> … the black figure with hands behind and head bent forward continued to pace the walk where the dark yew-trees gave him a mute companionship in melancholy, and the little shadows of bird or leaf that fleeted across the isles of sunlight, stole along in silence as in the presence of a sorrow. Here was a man who now for the first time found himself looking into the eyes of death – who was passing through one of those rare moments of experience when we feel the truth of a commonplace, which is as different from what we call knowing it, as the vision of waters upon the earth, is different from the delirious vision of the waters which cannot be had to cool the burning tongue. When the commonplace 'We must all die' transforms itself suddenly into the acute consciousness 'I must die – and soon', then death grapples us, and his hands are cruel; afterwards he may come to fold us in his arms as our mother did, and our last moment of dim earthly discerning may be like the first. To Mr Casaubon now, it was as if he suddenly found himself on the dark river-bank and heard the plash of the oncoming oar … (42)

The narrator moves from Casaubon 'looking into the eyes of death', ponders humanity in general – 'we', 'I' and 'us' – and animates death grotesquely and grandly with eyes, hands, and arms. Mysterious death becomes cruel death then kind death, but it is all one figure with different features. And a solemn music: many falling feet, a balance of long and short words, lofty latinate diction with Anglo-Saxon monosyllables, her usual subtle prose alliteration, and fine assimilated iambic pentameters, such as 'when the commonplace '"We must all die"', 'cannot be had to cool the burning tongue', 'heard the plash of the oncoming oar', and 'earthly discerning may be like the first'. There are also variants: 'mute companionship in melancholy', 'to fold us in his arms as our mother did'. This is George Eliot's best poetry, its rhythms asserted but approximated to speech-rhythm as they hardly ever are in her smooth verses[4]. The occasion is dignified with images of the Styx and Charon, more ominous for being unnamed, then with manipulative skill, George Eliot returns from myth to everyday, undignified life for undignified dying:

> In such an hour the mind does not change its lifelong bias, but carries it forward in imagination to the other side of death, gazing backward – perhaps with the divine calm of beneficence, perhaps with the petty anxieties of self-assertion … Mr Casaubon's immediate desire was not for divine communion and light divested of earthly conditions – his passionate longings, poor man, clung low and mist-like in very shady places.

The modulation from elegy to moral fact slowly arrives at a shocking bathos for the reader, as we come to Casaubon's jealous thoughts of the future while contemplating varieties of imaginative dyings.

Resuming her novel, which was being written before and during Thornton's fatal illness but interrupted by the dying and death, she emphasized her ironic imagining of Casaubon's imagination with particulars coloured by recent experience. Companionship with death after Thornton's suffering, and his gentle dying in her own 'almost' motherly arms, are impersonalized and re-ordered in the novel's rhetoric, placed and displaced, and figured and disfigured with craft and intense feeling. George Eliot's arms held a young man, her foster-son, the universal mother in the comparison holds her own child, or rather 'folds' it. 'Folds' is a layered image of comforting warm cover and sheltering sheepfold used in another *Middlemarch* personification: 'Destiny stands by sarcastic with our *dramatis personae* folded in her hand', which in its turn echoes the conceit of a gift 'close-folded' in the hands of the New Year, from a letter to Emilia Pattison (*Middlemarch*, 11; *Letters* 5, 74)[5].

As she remembers and fictionalizes, George Eliot imagines one thing she did not experience, the certain expectation of imminent death; but she had seen this knowledge at work, not in Thornton but in her father, whose calm after Isaac told him he could die at any moment was remembered for Tryan, and may echo in the 'divine calm' of one of the imagined responses to death in the Casaubon garden scene.

She takes us into the sublime, with awe and fear recollected from the two crucial deaths in her own life, but she returns us to the far from sublime world of her novel, and Mr Casaubon, 'poor man', not exalted but degraded by the prospect of death. The novel's language resembles or repeats real events and words, but its palpable process from general to particular and its branching elaboration is a generative form in action, creative passionate growth of life into art, and in art. It shows her back in life, back 'to work', as Lewes had expected.

Thornton's death also got into her poem 'Jubal', or so Lewes thought. He wrote to Alexander Main in October 1871: 'What a passage that is about Death! It was written under the shadow of a great grief, when our second boy in his 25th year passed away from us after six months of frightful agony' (*Letters*, 5, 205):

The wings upbore him, and the gazing song
Was floating him the heavenly space along,
Where mighty harmonies all gently fell
Through veiling vastness, like the far-off bell,
Till, ever onward through the choral blue,
He heard more faintly and more faintly knew,
Quitting mortality, a quenched sun-wave,
The All-Creating Presence for his grave.

This has the defects of her rhapsodic poetry, attempting the sublime in language and attitude but lacking felt particulars. (It is shown up by the hard truthfulness of the *Middlemarch* passage.) After assuring Jubal that he will live on in his art – a thought George Eliot consoled herself with in 'O May I Join the Choir Invisible' – Death, his angel, lets him die beautifully. A little earlier, the verse has presented death as his bride, 'thine alone, a dear dead bride / Who blest thy lot above all men's beside?', in contrast to that wry 'companion' in the novel. Jubal is the artist who has known bitter rejection and isolation but dies the painless death Keats imagined in the 'Ode to a Nightingale' – though Keats knew he was only imagining, knowing the pain and waste of real death-beds. George Eliot the novelist also knew dying is not always sublime, as she shows in Casaubon and later, wonderfully imaging what egoistic Gwendolen could not imagine, 'not a woman who could easily think of her own death as a near reality, or front for herself the dark entrance on the untried and invisible' (*Daniel Deronda*, 48). If it seems strange that critical Lewes could admire the sweet, soft death-poetry of 'Jubal' we must remember his love for the poet and grief for the son.

Lewes died on 30 November 1878 after a long period of pain and weakness. The death caused Marian unspeakable pain and changed her life. She never wrote any more poetry or fiction, or wrote about the death at length. Some reactions we know through Edith Simcox: the maid told her George Eliot had been screaming in agony, and Charles Lewes warned the demonstrative adoring friend that 'she would never be able to endure any caress' and wanted the world to think of her 'as a dead friend' (*Letters* 9, 250, 251). After two months she wrote briefly to friends in simple or striking words: to John Blackwood of 'a sorrow which has broken my life' (*Letters* 7, 93); to Barbara Bodichon, 'I am a bruised creature' and 'The sorrow deepens down' (*Letters* 7, 93, 113); to John Cross, 'what used to be joy is joy no longer' and 'Each day seems a new beginning – a new acquaintance with grief' (*Letters* 7, 99, 102); to Elma Stuart, 'I am gone into a far country' (*Letters* 7, 100); to Georgiana Burne-Jones, 'my everlasting winter has set in' (*Letters* 7, 101); and to her half-brother Robert's widow, 'My joy is buried' (*Letters* 7, 106). For several months she wrote about her grief in laconic diary entries while reporting inability to work, fatigue, headache and renal pain: 'Head miserable and heart bruised'; '*la mort dans l'âme*' (twice); 'weary and heavy laden'; 'lived with him all day'; 'head-weak as well as heart-fainting'; '*alone*'; and, four months after his death, 'Moved into our Bedroom' and '*his presence came again*' (*Journals* 157; 159; 162; 166; 167; 175). He is 'my darling' or 'my loved one'.

She wrote to Mrs Robert Lytton whose child had died: 'learning to love any one is like an increase of property – it increases care, and brings many fears lest precious things should come to harm ... under the pressure of grief, I do not believe there is any consolation' (*Letters* 5, 106–7). She let other writers speak as companions not consolers. The *Journals* editors write of 'a substantial anthology of morbid verse'[6], but it is only a handful, and I think morbid only in being about death, a selection not obsessed or indulgent but intelligently ordered like the extracts themselves, models of elegiac genius.

At the beginning of January 1879 there is a cluster of 11 quotations, between January and mid-March six more, and on 17 December, two months after the love-letter to Cross, Emily Brontë's winter poem about faithfulness and forgetting, 'Have I forgot, my only love, to love thee?' (*Journals*, 154–6, 158–9, 160–1, 162–3, 188).

Most of the writers had special associations. She and Lewes loved Shakespeare on the stage and read him together; Heine was admired by both and introduced to English readers by her articles in the *Leader*, the *Saturday Review* and the *Westminster*, and the quotation for Lewes had appeared with translation in her essay of 1856 (Pinney, 17); an extract from Goethe was in Lewes's biography; Tennyson was a friend who had read to them and whose poems, except for *Maud*, she loved, whose *Locksley Hall* she mislineated and corrected for an epigraph in *Daniel Deronda*, which also refers to William Browne's *Pastorals*, perhaps read with Thornton for the India Office examination. She slated Young for hypocrisy in 'Worldliness and Other-Worldliness' but praised 'the unmistakable cry of pain' in lines she repeats here (Pinney, 366) and which is also in 'Wild Decembers', by Emily Brontë who was said by Charlotte Brontë to look like Lewes.

The subjects too are strictly relevant to her situation and passions, in poetry that is as self-aware as it is articulate. Performing the tasks of bereavement, editing *Problems of Life and Mind*, coping with letters, wages and bills, she quotes Chaucer's awareness that grief can be disabling. She and Lewes had been lovers, so she takes Tennyson's image of a widower's physical loss, imaged in dream's embrace and the shock of empty-handed waking. She was re-reading and finishing Lewes's work, scrupulously reading his critics as he used to read hers, greedy for tributes of obituaries and letters, feeling the need to exalt her dead lover's work and mind as Tennyson had needed to praise Hallam: 'Thy likeness to the wise below, / Thy kindred with the great of old'. She wants to hug her grief close and make it last but is fully aware of so-called excess and indulgence, quoting Tennyson's 'she loveth her own anguish'. She grieved for former happiness so she repeated Walton on the 'commensurable grief which took possession' of the bereaved Donne 'as joy had done', perhaps seeing the pun Donne and Lewes would have liked. The affinity celebrated in 'By the Fireside' is articulated by the ecstatic abstraction of *In Memoriam*:

When Each by turns was guide to each,
  And Fancy light from Fancy caught,
  And Thought leapt out to wed with Thought
Ere Thought could wed itself with Speech.

Browning spoke for living love; Tennyson about love for the dead, and even his 'weddings' were congenial since her 'marriage' to Lewes had been metaphorical. She did not write grief while she grieved but even in her diary used critical tact and reserve and carefully chose familiar voices and appropriate words to mourn for her.

Notes

1 *Journals*, 95–147.

2 I now think there is more control in the account of Tryan's dying than I had judged when I wrote *NGE*.

3 The link was pointed out by Hilda Hulme, without reference to Jane Senior, in 'The Language of the Novel' in *Middlemarch: Critical Approaches to the Novel*, edited by Barbara Hardy, London: Athlone, 1967.

4 I discuss George Eliot's prose in 'George Eliot for the Twenty-First Century: *Middlemarch* and the Poetry of Prosaic Conditions' in *The George Eliot Review*, No. 32, 2001.

5 See Chapter 6 for further discussion.

6 *Journals*, 151. The editors, Margaret Harris and Judith Johnston, who comment on the neglected 1879 and 1880 diaries, and who note significant quotations from Heine and Goethe, say: 'GE's mourning was mediated by her intellect' and the use of other writers was 'controlled' but judge the collection morbid, the quotation from *King John*, 'Here I and sorrow sit', 'simply lugubrious', and say the 'affective response may seem excessive even by Victorian standards'.

Chapter Six
Objects, Words and Metaphors

> ... a combination of subtle shadowy suggestions with certain actual objects and events ... (*Letters* 2, 459)

Henry James said *Middlemarch* was 'a treasure house of details but ... an indifferent whole' and he looked forward to writing novels with less brain but more form (*Galaxy*, 15 March 1873; quoted Haight, 444). We may think George Eliot's novels have enough form and still treasure their detail. One of the pleasures of relating her life to her novels is to see things, words and images which appear isolated, random or casual in the life-records turning up again in her novels and poems. They are mostly deep-rooted in plot, character, thought and feeling, microcosms, parts that stand for the whole, small things transformed to ends in art's teleology, in company, but sometimes on the surface, still casual and isolated. The processes are complex and the details are what John Livingstone Lowe calls 'hooked atoms', images equipped with 'hooks and eyes of the memory', fine threads in imagination's web and links with lived experience[1].

In 'Recollections of Berlin', 1854–55 George Eliot quoted Zechariah to record 'a day of small things' when she and Lewes 'made much of little' (*Journals*, 243). Observing small things in her life changed in her art – odds becoming ends – is to focus on lived moments often ignored in the broad narrative sweep of biography, and fictional moments neglected in theme-and-pattern-seeking criticism. When we spot and spotlight the words, things and metaphors of everyday life – furniture, endearments, food, scents, pens, windows – we recall the solid sensuous particulars of real lost yesterdays.

There are some word-links which are or seem random and arbitrary, like names she picked up in life and used for her characters, Farebrother and Lemon, for instance, though these

147

names are vivid and suggestive. They are often hooked to other links, as in Shakespearean image-clusters. We meet 'Mrs Farebrother' as a friend of Maria Lewis and Nancy Buchanan, a source for Janet Dempster (*Letters* 1, 26), and the name of Miss Lemon, the head of Rosamond's finishing-school, is comically fixed for George Eliot in St Mary's, Scilly: 'I was repeatedly told, in order to make me aware who Mr Hall was, that he married "a Miss Lemon"', about the time she meets Mr Buckstone, with his contempt for curs, 'O, I wouldn't have a cur', recalled in Maggie's 'You don't call Mumps a cur, I suppose?' and Bob Jakin's pitying smile (*Mill*, 4, 3; *Journals*, 278–9: the editors note the *Middlemarch* and *Mill* connections).

Sometimes the link is an object which may become a poetic image or symbol. Many of George Eliot's domestic metaphors were ordinary objects before they became resonant and illustrative in the novels, in an unconscious process brilliantly described in her account of Wagner's symbolism: it 'rushes in on … imagination before … slower reflection has seized any abstract idea embodied in it' (*SCW*, 88). Real chairs, tables and looking-glasses become illustrations in a letter to Sara Hennell about disenchantment, and are further adapted for different characters in fiction – rose-coloured satin chairs and curtains for Mrs Transome, blue-green tapestry for Dorothea, a hard bed and crucifix for Savonarola, piano and music for Gwendolen, and so on. Some objects can be traced back to a real source like the attic window in Griff from which Mary Ann looked over at the 'college' or workhouse and restores for Dinah's and Dorothea's far-reaching vision[2].

Many ordinary objects in life are ordinary objects in fiction. George Eliot would have learnt from Saint-Preux's rural anthropology in *La Nouvelle Héloise*, and her cottage, farmhouse or grand dining room tables register social fact as they dramatize the cooks, servants, housekeepers, families, hosts and guests. But first, Mary Ann ate or ordered or supervised or cooked the food, and it is put on fictional tables with knowledge and appreciation. She knew it all: Mrs Poyser's stuffed chine, cold potatoes and lettuce; butter finished by Hetty's neat hands and wrapped in dock-leaves; pork-pies, some with 'the taste of the fire in them'; Lisbeth Bede's potatoes heated up in meat gravy; Mary Garth's fine ham in cut; Fred Vincy's grilled bone; potato-pie slowly cooked or warmed in front of a fire by Eppie or Mrs Holt. She writes about making damson cheese inaccurately, glossed by Haight as 'plum jam' (*Letters* 1, 68) and mince-pies – when Mrs Steene, the vet's Byron-reading wife in 'Brother Jacob', at last manages to make light mince-pies, the author speaks from a cook's experience. She knew taste and texture: Mrs Tulliver's cheese-cakes would blow away in 'a puff o' wind', and her puddings and pastries include Tom's favourite apricot roll-up, tipsy-cake ('good the day after'), the famous jam-puff, and the 'brandy-cherries and cream-cakes' Stephen Guest prefers to her company (*Mill*, 6, 1). People play with food: Ben Garth kneads crumbs for Mary to make a bread peacock but she is sewing handkerchiefs for Rosamond's trousseau.

The exotic Sabbath meal with unleavened loaves, thin fishtails and sweet-cake at the Cohen's is perceived because Daniel is there as guest. Cottage economy and a mother's devouring need to feed her child are registered as Lisbeth presses chopped meat, potatoes and gravy on Adam, which he at first rejects and then accepts; her flavours for porridge, mint or marigold, are commended in passing, most naturally. Two good cooks are critics of cooking: Bartle Massey, who dismisses intuitive bread-making and, to balance his misogyny, Priscilla Lammeter guaranteeing her pork-pies. George Eliot's ceremonies of food are less elaborate and less fraught than meals and feasts in Dickens and Thackeray, but like them she uses the table as theatre, and knows more than them about what goes on in the kitchen. She cared about food. At St Mary's in the Scillies she complains about 'loin of mutton ... all fat' and 'fowls ... of patriarchal toughness' (*Journals*, 276). And you can see where Bartle Massey's criticism comes from 'every morning': she gave a culinary lecture to the St Mary's landlady, who 'like almost all peculiarly domestic women, has not more than rudimentary ideas of cooking' and 'seems to think eating a purely arbitrary procedure' (*Letters* 2, 314).

She does not describe many great tables, but a real peacock is cooked for a dinner in the Rucellai Gardens, and the gourmet dish is cleverly and amusingly described through the solutions of various diners, who push the uneatable flesh under other viands or flourish it on a fork – George Eliot, who described the tough fowls, could adapt experience. The most solidly specified foods in *Romola* are a cup of fragrant milk, plenty of bread and 'a mountain of macaroni flavoured with cheese' (33), undated everyday food and drink the writer tasted at home or abroad.

There is a recondite joke about venison fat on another high-life occasion, *Daniel Deronda*'s Archery dinner where the men and women dine apart. (I know of no other Victorian example of this separate dining.) There is drama at breakfast on Grandcourt's yacht as he speaks dismissively then chooses an orange all in a half-sentence; social precision when he says they must put in somewhere for fresh fruit. Gwendolen likes chocolate made by the housekeeping governess Miss Merry, but at another breakfast with her husband dallys 'prettily over her prawns' and faces 'the boiled ingenuousness' of their eyes rather than his lizard look (*Daniel Deronda*, 48).

In the funny moral episode where Maggie enjoys the bigger half of the jam-puff, watched and reproached by Tom, the narrator observes that her 'palate was not at all obtuse': it is an odd, witty personification, giving taste a mind (*Mill*, 1, 6). It had a history. She had used a weaker adjective when explaining that she and Lewes need a good cook because he is 'dyspeptic' not because he is 'epicurean (for he is stupid of palate)' (*Letters* 3, 22). Even earlier, in the 1856 essay 'Woman in France: Madame de Sablé', the narrator discusses Madame de Sablé's '*friandise*' and uses the *Mill*'s phrase, claiming not to be one of those 'spiritual people … who pique themelves on being obtuse of palate' (Pinney, 69). George Eliot was not obtuse of palate, or wasteful of wit.

Like the things, her words have histories. Writing for the first time to Sara Hennell in autumn 1842, she is amused by a request to write about herself: 'Do I not live with myself and tire of myself until I have no need of metaphysics to make me believe that there is nothing certain but that *self* exists? And you … would keep me on a spot where I have already pirouetted until I am giddy, until I am one of the most egotistical speakers and writers in this world of egotists' (*Letters* 1, 144–5). The 'pirouette' returns 30 years later when Dorothea refuses to wear her mother's jewellery, saying if she wore a necklace like the amethyst and gold one round her sister Celia's neck: 'I should feel as if I had been pirouetting. The world would go round with me, and I should not know how to walk' (*Middlemarch*, 1). A ballet term for spinning on points, the French 'pirouette' is conspicuous in the abstract moral lexis of the letter and novel. It may express a dislike of dancing and lack of physical confidence: she disparages opera-dancers and rope-dancers, and had headache and 'hysteria' at Mrs Thomas Bull's party where there was dancing (*Letters* 1, 41). Invited to a ball, she writes to Bessie Parkes that she has no ball gown and only likes dinner parties. There are dances at Arthur Donnithorne's coming-of-age, at the Guests, where Maggie is briefly belle of the ball, at New Year in *Silas Marner* and *Daniel Deronda*, and for the Archery Club at the Arrowpoints, where Gwendolen refuses to waltz or polk and dances a cool quadrille with Grandcourt. But there are hardly any details of movement or music. Some of her beauties dance but never pirouette: 'pirouette' is her image for unthinkable moral motion. The image of brilliant vertiginous dance joins two witty arguments about egotism and frivolity.

Another word moved from letters to fiction is the thundering nonsense-word 'fee-fo-fum' from the story 'Jack the Giant Killer' and Poor Tom's chant in *Lear*: 'fee-fo-fi-fum I'll smell the blood of an English man'. It is also first used to Sara Hennell, as Mary Ann wonders whether to translate some Hebrew in a note to Strauss: 'I do not think it well to give the English in one place and not in another where there is no reason for such distinction – and there is not here for the note sounds just as fee-fo-fum-ish as the other, without any translation' (*Letters* 1, 204). This is the irreverent style of many letters to Sara and 'fee-fo-fum' is used with the same scorn of learned nonsense by another irreverent speaker, Mr Cadwallader the fishing Rector, who also shrugs his shoulders at dry scholarship: 'I know no harm of Casaubon. I don't care about his Xisuthrus and fee-fo-fum and the rest; but then he doesn't care about my fishing-tackle' (*Middlemarch*, 8).

Some words move from novel to letter, like a phrase in the sentence: 'We are all of us born in moral stupidity, taking the world as an udder to feed our supreme selves' (*Middlemarch*, 21). Less striking than the yoked 'obtuse' and 'palate', 'moral stupidity' also mimics zeugma – but after all, reason should apply to ethics and ethics to intellect. In December 1874, it recurs in a letter to Mary Ponsonby, disagreeing with something unspecified George Sand said about individualism, 'What sort of "culture of the intellect" is that which, instead of widening the mind to a fuller and fuller response to all the elements of our existence, isolates it in a moral stupidity which flatters egoism … ' (*Letters* 6, 99). The phrase moves back into fiction as Daniel contemplates Mordecai's claim on his future and duty: 'It was his characteristic bias to shrink from the moral stupidity of valuing lightly what had come close to him, and of missing blindly in his own life of today the crises which he recognized as momentous and sacred in the historic life of men' (*Daniel Deronda*, 41). In each repetition the grand image-attachment, 'the world as an udder', is dropped, but the subject of imaginative egoism has imprinted one key phrase.

There is a real object and a metaphor link with *Middlemarch* and a Christmas day letter of 1870 from Lewes to his son Charles. He describes a practical joke played when he and Marian were staying at Swanmore with Barbara Bodichon, in a 'parsonage … so intensely ritualistic that there is even a *scourge* hanging up in the priest's study'. Lewes told his hostess he had taken the liberty of ordering a new dish for dinner, 'only met with at recherché tables': 'Ann brought in the huge dish and set it before Barbara, then solemnly removed the cover and revealed the scourge lying in a most uncanny aspect – the thongs which had been pressed inwards by the cover gave a slight outward movement which startled Barbara as if a live eel or so were there. Immense laughter!' (*Letters* 5, 126–7).

In the third chapter of *Middlemarch* conversation turns to rural housing and Dorothea 'energetically' answers Sir James's mild goodwill: 'I think we deserve to be beaten out of our beautiful houses with a scourge of small cords …' The image is just right for Dorothea's flouting of ladylike decorum, religiosity, repressed sexuality, emotional excess and the Saint Theresa context. It has developed beyond the source in the dish but seems sensitive to that source – not funny, but shockingly irreligious, erotic and violent. George Eliot knew about scourges and flagellants from the Bible, saints' lives, Dante and Christ expelling the money-lenders from the Temple, but she is unlikely to have come across many actual scourges and I am sure the physically particular scourge of 'small cords' derives from the dished-up wriggling thongs of Lewes's bizarre bad-taste joke. Earlier that December, George Eliot interrupted *Middlemarch* to begin work on *Miss Brooke*, as she records (*Letters* 5, 124). Real scourge and fictional image are substantial sensed objects, the real one startlingly visual, Dorothea's startlingly tactile. The real scourge was startling for Barbara Bodichon and memorable for George Eliot. The figurative scourge startlingly rushes out of Dorothea's imagination. The use of this fact for this fiction may suggest something about George Eliot's erotic and religious imagination. When Lewes told Robert Lytton about the scourge in the parsonage, he hoped it was 'more for show than for use' (*Letters* 9, 6). I don't know if his remark looks more or less innocent when we read in Daniel Waley's introduction to the catalogue of a George Eliot exhibition held in the British Museum in 1980, that on the day Gladstone finished *Adam Bede* he 'had recourse to the scourge'.

Biblical scourges are common in letters and novels. George Eliot writes to Maria Lewis about James Buchanan's being scourged by God (*Letters* 1, 58), and in a later letter of August 1863, says 'my own books scourge me' (*Letters* 4, 104). The scourging of Christ comes in Dinah's sermon 'they scourged him' (*Adam Bede*, 2). It is frequent in *Romola*, associated with Savonarola's purifications and his warnings of the scourge of God. Rosamond's 'vagrant fancy' comes back 'terribly scourged' by Will's 'utterance' (like 'the cut of a lash'), and the image is physical (81, 78). 'Scourge and Renovation' is a chapter-title in *The Impressions of Theophrastus Such*, Theophrastus likes to keep 'the scourge' in his 'own discriminating hand 'and thinks 'indignation and scorn' the 'proper scourges of wrong-doing and meanness' (*ITS*, 'How We Come to Give Ourselves False Testimonials, and Believe in Them'). The scourge reminds us of Dempster's and Tulliver's slashing horsewhips, Dunsey Cass with Godfrey's gold-handled whip, as rider and skeleton, Gwendolen's dropped whip and the sadistic Squire who whipped his dog in front of his wife, recalled at the Grandcourt wedding.

Another key object and image is a pen. Pens, paper and ink, those archaic tools of our trade, have been active and reflexive in novels from *Robinson Crusoe* to *The Count of Monte Cristo* and *A Tale of Two Cities.* Not as prominent as Pamela's or Clarissa's pens, parts of their survival kits, or Valmont's amusingly pornographic pen used with a woman's back for desk in *Les Liaisons Dangereuses*, but slyly powerful is the independent pen of Mr Brooke. George Eliot uses it to make a serious joke about the power of small causes, with an author's awareness that composition is not simply conscious. Long before she thought of his pen she writes about the physical act of writing. She has a steel pen that scratches, a pen made by Herbert Spencer, and a gold pen bad for 'scribbling' but good for writing slowly (*Letters* 1, 354). When she and Lewes were poor and had to write in the same room, the sound of his pen nearly drove her mad. She varies writing positions, at a table, on her knee, in a special chair. She was fussy about ink and paper, apologizing for bad paper and disliking 'that large blue paper' on which Rufa Brabant had begun the Strauss translation (*Letters* 1, 171). In the early letters she is always apologizing for illegibility, often with no reason. Some letters anticipate Mr Brooke's pen by casual allusion to the physically creative writing act. Mechanical handling is creative, movement and rhythm facilitating the unconscious generation of word and meaning. She writes to Maria Lewis, 'I generally let my feelings flow to the end of my pen as soon as I begin to write to you' (*Letters* 1, 57). She jokes to Sara Hennell about the writer's double problem – the reluctance to write and the urge to write: 'My letter-writing pen is entirely at the mercy of a host of little sprites, more tiny and ethereal than the train of Queen Mab, and it is only when they come tickling my forefingers and thumb, making them itch for this same pen, that the strong repulsion from it is overcome' (*Letters* 1, 228). Shakespeare is not invoked as mere mock-solemnity but in creative recognition of Mercutio's brilliant comic demonstration of creative dreaming. Another letter to the Brays makes an excuse for high praise: 'I have not yet found *any one* who can bear comparison with you, not in kindness to me – ça va sans dire – but in solidity of mind and expansion of feeling. This is a very coarse thing to say but it came to the end of my pen and – itera scripta manet – at least when it comes at the end of the second page' (*Letters* 1, 310).

Writers love to write about writing, in every genre, and amusing self-conscious comment is common in George Eliot's letters. Like Jane Austen, though with less wit and elegance, she finds it a useful way to begin, as humble apology, invocation of the Muse, and a signal of what Richardson calls writing to the moment. Her epistolary self-consciousness gets lighter and smoother. She tells Bray her pen is not 'of the true literary order which will run along *without* the help of brains' (*Letters* 2, 233) and uses a perfect phrase to Sara Hennell: 'talk from the end of the pen' (*Letters* 4, 135). She has fun with pens in the essays – in 'Silly Novels by Women Novelists' (*Westminster Review*, October 1856) her 'mind-and-millinery' novelists 'write in elegant boudoirs, with violet-coloured ink and a ruby pen' and she laughs at the pen of a 'superior authoress' in *Laura Gay*, said to move 'in a quick decided manner when she is composing' (Pinney, 304, 307). Her own first novel begins with pen and ink: 'With this drop of ink at the end of my pen I will show you … (*Adam Bede*, 1).

By the time we come to *Middlemarch*, the conceit is seasoned, or to borrow George Eliot's kitchen metaphor, has 'simmered' to perfection. Mr Brooke's is not the only pen in *Middlemarch*. Captain Lydgate is not 'a great penman' and never answers Rosamond's letter (64). She writes a charming and unsuccessful begging letter to Lydgate's uncle. Dorothea is conscientious about legibility and writes out her acceptance of Casaubon's deadly proposal three times. Featherstone and Casaubon re-write wills and codicils with their grasping hands. University-educated Fred Vincy forms blotted and illegible letters with the pen of Caleb Garth, which Caleb examines and hands to Fred, 'well-dipped' (51).

But the crucial pen-stroke comes in Chapter 30, when Mr Brooke's pen – the letter is written by 'it' rather than by him, without his plan or intention – invites Will Ladislaw to come back to Middlemarch. The pen's impetuous strokes bring about the attachment of Will and Dorothea; the jealousy of Casaubon; the discovery of Will's parentage by Raffles and Will himself; the blackmailing of Bulstrode; the passive murder of Raffles; the scandal about Lydgate and his exile; and Will's career – just about everything in the intricate plot of the large novel. Mr Brooke's pen stands in for the author's pen, in more ways than one:

> But the end of Mr Brooke's pen was a thinking organ, evolving sentences, especially of a benevolent kind, before the rest of his mind could well overtake them. It expressed regrets and proposed remedies, which, when Mr Brooke read them, seemed felicitously worded – surprisingly the right thing, and determined a sequel which he had never before thought of. In this case, his pen found it such a pity that young Ladislaw should not have come into the neighborhood just at that time, in order that Mr Brooke should make his acquaintance more fully … it also felt such an interest in the young man … that

by the end of the second page it had persuaded Mr Brooke to invite
young Ladislaw … to come to Tipton Grange. (30)

A light, brilliant touch in this understated perception is a writer's
self-satisfaction: he finds his letter 'felicitously worded', like the
delighted and surprised artist looking at the finished work, or God
on the seventh day. At the end, Mr Brooke's thinking pen gets
to work again, with a new plot-point, another joke, and elegant
symmetry: 'Mr Brooke could not resist the pleasure of corresponding
with Will and Dorothea; and one morning when his pen had been
remarkably fluent on the prospects of Municipal Reform, it ran off
into an invitation to the Grange …' (Finale).

Mr Brooke's pen is a sly intricate image of reflexive art. George Eliot
reflects and reflects on creativity in a joke about a creative writer. His
pen also has a biographical source, in the active pen of Mr Bracebridge
of Warwickshire – bumbling squire, amateur archeologist, aspiring
magistrate and unsuccessful Liberal candidate, and a credulous
busybody who was positive that Joseph Liggins of Nuneaton wrote
Adam Bede. John Blackwood described him as 'a distinguished member
of the Fogie Club', 'an old foozle' and 'not a bad fellow' (*Letters* 3, 57).
George Eliot had once dined with him, said he came from an old
family, and was 'kind-hearted, and patronising', but when he persisted
in backing Liggins, she grew very much less tolerant (*Letters* 3, 53).
Mr Brooke is an original, an individualized character and unlike
Bracebridge in many ways, especially in not being a gossip, but there
is a link. Haight does not go beyond saying he was tempted to think
of him as a source for Mr Brooke (*Letters* 3, 53; *George Eliot's Originals
and Contemporaries*[3]) but his suggestion is supported by word and
object. The 'muddle-headed magistrate' of the letter grew into witty
alliterative metaphors, 'motes from the mass of a magistrate's mind'
(*Middlemarch*, 2). The pen was hooked to the muddle and mind:
George Eliot jokes to Bray about 'some slip of the pen – the extremely
slippery pen – of that muddle-headed magistrate Mr Bracebridge',
metamorphosing dead metaphor for a trail of wit that leads to Mr
Brooke's creative slippery pen and his leaky-mindedness (*Letters* 3,
147). And, as Empson said of *Alice in Wonderland* in *Some Versions of
Pastoral*, you don't need to push an erotic reading: etymology, shape
and slipperiness make these pens fine gifts for Freudians.

There is a back-up source for the creative pen in Goethe's *Elective Affinities,* where it is also a self-generative instrument and crucial in the plot. When Eduard writes to his wife Charlotte 'on the spur of the moment', he intends to promise only a tentative parting from his beloved Ottilie but, in the process of writing, he finds himself offering more than he intends, and in words which surprise him: ' "I for my part will not resist recovery should the power to recover be given me …"' This last phrase came from his pen not his heart, and when he saw it he began to weep bitterly. He had promised in some way or other … It was only now he realised what he was doing' (1, 16).

I have mentioned the evolution of a playful friendly greeting to Emilia Pattison on 28 December 1869, while George Eliot was working on *Middlemarch*: 'I was going to write just to express my affectionate wishes for your happiness in the coming year, which brings some close-folded gift in its hand for each of us' (*Letters* 5, 74). A witty, half-figurative New Year wish and image of festive donation, is darkly mythologized in the alliterative, rhythmical portentous pronouncement, 'Destiny stands by sarcastic with our *dramatis personae* folded in her hand' (*Middlemarch*, 11). The novelist metamorphoses the New Year to Destiny, no genial present-giver but made strange as presenter of a play, ominously holding in 'her' – not 'its' – hand, no small parcel but a cast of characters who will perform our unknown future, Lydgate's and Dorothea's in particular, but with general application. The sentence keeps the 'folded' and the 'hand' of its benign source but surprise and donation turn grotesque and sinister.

The image turns mild again when George Eliot writes to Elma Stuart about 'the old, old poet' who says 'the lingering years bring each something in their hand to every mortal – having in his mind perhaps something good rather than the many things evil' (*Letters* 6, 327). (Haight notes Emerson's poem 'Days' but he cannot be the old old poet.) A later letter to Elma Stuart says Lewes 'liked to keep in mind that the year brings in its hand much unexpected good as well as ill to us mortals' (*Letters* 7, 210). Yet another image from the cluster goes back to when she was 20 and wrote to Maria Lewis: 'We are each one of the Dramatis Personae in some play on the stage of life' (*Letters* 1, 23). In an 1855 review of Geraldine Jewsbury's

Constance Herbert, detesting the argument that virtue is rewarded, she dismisses 'Duty with her hand full of sugar plums' (*SCW*, 121). In *Adam Bede* Arthur's destiny 'disguises her cold awful face behind a hazy radiant veil, encloses us in warm downy wings, and poisons us with violet-scented breath' (12), a wonderfully corrupt version of the conceit, its wings and breath perverting George Eliot's favourite pure angel and scent images. Like Mr Brooke's pen, the image of Destiny has a complicated history.

Mary Ann and Isaac played by a stream and brown canal, and a recurring image-cluster combines mud, water, green slime and falling, and draws explicitly on Bunyan's Slough of Despond where Help pulls Christian out of mud and bog, and perhaps on the mud, marsh and filth of Dante's *Inferno*. George Eliot writes to Sara Hennell 'in high displeasure' with herself, finds her life 'the shallowest, muddiest, most unblessing stream', but has got her 'head above this slough of Despond' (*Letters* 1, 150). In a later letter to Sara she speaks of herself as 'a horrid stagnant pool' (*Letters* 1, 244), jokes to Charles Bray about his 'little half-drained puddle of a soul' in comparison to her own 'great Atlantic', (*Letters* 1, 268), and tells Sara, 'Poor pebble as I am left entangled among slimy weeds I can yet hear from afar the rushing of the blessed torrent …' (*Letters* 1, 274). Soon after *Middlemarch,* she tells Mrs Cross she dare not 'count much on fulfilling any project, my life for the last year having been a sort of nightmare in which I have been scrambling on the slippery bank of a pool, just keeping my head above water' (*Letters* 5, 301).

The imagery is varied for the novels but always with moral significance. Janet half-dreams of slipping down to a lower level and later thinks that if her feet slip she can cling to Tryan, and later still is afraid she will 'slip back into that deep slimy pit from which she had been once rescued' ('JR', 25). In *Adam Bede*, Arthur is on the brink of confessing to Mr Irwine but while he 'was hesitating, the rope to which he might have clung had drifted away – he must trust now to his own swimming' (16). In *The Mill on the Floss*, where water-images are dominant, Maggie pushes Lucy into real 'cow-trodden mud', and in one of George Eliot's rare dreams and dream-anticipations, Philip dozes in his studio after he has told his father about Maggie and then gone for a row, and 'fancied' her 'slipping down a glistening, green, slimy channel of a waterfall, and he was looking on helpless' (6, 8). In *Silas Marner* Dunsey Cass turns out of an 'unpleasantly slippery lane', as mist passes into rain, to rob Silas and fall into the Stonepit; Eppie cuts her linen tether and is found by a pond, her foot 'on a cushion of olive-green mud'; Silas's soul is a 'shrunken rivulet …' with 'its little groove of sand … blocked up' (10); and 'Instead of keeping fast hold of the strong silken rope by which Nancy would have drawn him safe to the green banks, where it was easy to step firmly', Godfrey 'had let himself be dragged back into mud and slime, in which it was useless to struggle' (3). There is unpleasant mud-and-slime association in the 'rank green stems' where Baldassare waits for Tito and kills him, 'a sloping width of long grass and rushes made all the more dank by broad gutters which now and then emptied themselves into the Arno' (*Romola*, 67); in *Middlemarch* when Lydgate feels his life is 'as noxious as an inlet of mud to a creature that has been used to breathe … in the clearest of waters' and feels 'he was every day getting deeper into that swamp, which tempts men towards it' (63); and there is a trace in *Daniel Deronda* when Gwendolen is compared with a heroine of 'genteel romance where … if she wanders into a swamp, the pathos lies partly, so to speak, in her having on satin shoes' (6). There is also a more abstract variation: 'Liszt, Wagner, and Weimar' refers to Liszt being like 'ordinary men … who pass through so many "mud-baths"' before they are 40 (*SCW*, 83), which is echoed in *Daniel Deronda* when Mrs Meyrick tells Daniel that 'the mud has only washed' Mirah, who is 'a pearl' (20). Bunyan's Slough is a muddy, miry and dirty bog but George Eliot's nightmare disgust with slime, dirt and pollution, like Sartre's dread of viscosity, suggests an obsessive distaste and fear.

Reviewing *Maud*, Marian Evans criticized Tennyson's intense expression of morbid feeling: 'These hexameters, weak in logic and grating in sound, are undeniably strong in expression, and eat themselves with phosphoric eagerness into our memory …' (*SCW*, 173). A more convoluted image of chemical poison and eating describes Tito's fast deterioration: 'Having once begun to explain away Baldassare's claims, Tito's thought showed itself as active as a virulent acid, eating its rapid way through all the tissues of sentiment'

(*Romola*, 11). Phosphorus and eating return in *Middlemarch* for Mrs Cadwallader's egocentric creativity, 'as active as phosphorous, biting everything that came near into the form that suited it' (6). Over the years, the image-cluster presents morbid poetry, moral self-corruption and a sharp, shaping mind.

Mrs Cadwallader is pre-figured in *Felix Holt*, her blue blood and other features of her history and character sketched in one of the aristocratic 'novelettes' Mrs Transome relates to Esther: 'how the brilliant Fanny, having married a country parson, became so niggardly that she had gone about almost begging for fresh eggs from the farmers' wives ...' (40). The brilliant Fanny starts off as the mere stuff of gossip and anecdote (perhaps memory) but solicits her author (like Christina Light beckoning Henry James) for a small speaking part in *Middlemarch* with her high rank, wit, country parson, and niggardliness, to make matches and scrounge fowls from Mrs Fitchett the lodge-keeper, inheriting Mrs Transome's taste for genealogies and high-life scandal. Perhaps her husband's benign character and 'rough exterior' is foreshadowed by sympathetic Mr Cleves in 'Amos Barton' with his 'roughly-cut mouth', though we know nothing about Cadwallader's sermons and Cleves's sound rather like Farebrother's.

There are smaller links. In George Eliot's first fiction, *Poetry and Prose from the Notebook of an Eccentric*, the artist Adolphe says his greatest calamity has not been the loss of his beloved but something 'far more withering': 'I have ceased to love the being whom I once believed that I must love while life lasted' and compares the experience to cherishing 'a bright amethyst' and seeing it 'lose its lustre day by day' (Pinney, 19). Romola has similar fears of ceasing to love Tito, and Lydgate dreads the end of his loving more than the end of Rosamond's love for him, and gives her a marriage present of fine amethysts, which she offers back coldly when they are in debt. The visual memory of 'red drapery' in St Peters, to recur 'all' Dorothea's life in 'states of dull forlornness', is startlingly compared to 'a disease of the retina' (*Middlemarch*, 20), and it is one of the small back-hints George Eliot subtly uses, implying for those who notice that Dorothea's future was not to be free of dull forlornness. The image dates back to Mary Ann's 20th birthday when she wrote that 'objects in which we have long gazed remain on the retina when we would fain be rid of them' (*Letters* 1, 34). The image must go back to childhood, when we first observe such optical phenomena, and both letter and novel emphasize not science but involuntary imprint.

The narrator of *Middlemarch* observes Lydgate's awkward position on the library steps as he excitedly reads about the valves of the heart in an encyclopedia: 'somehow, one is apt to read in a makeshift attitude, just where it might seem inconvenient to do so' (15). John Fiske, a disciple of Herbert Spencer, repeats with an author's gratification George Eliot's story about: getting his 'myth book' as 'she was sitting on the floor fixing a rug, or something of the sort, and she got so absorbed in my book that she sat on the *floor* all the afternoon, till Lewes came and routed her up!' (Haight, 468). Art did not really anticipate life – George Eliot passed on one of her reading habits to her character, to particularize a key moment. In *Daniel Deronda* she passed on something more personal. As I mentioned in Chapter One, Hans Meyrick's endearment for his small mother is 'little mother', the address used for George Eliot by Lewes and his sons in family intimacy, with 'Mutter', 'little Mutter' and Mater as alternatives to 'Mamma', who was Agnes Lewes. 'Little Mutter' was used in Bertie's letters, rather pathetically, and later by his widow Eliza ingratiatingly, and perhaps irritatingly, to the famous woman she had never met, to whom Bertie was not close, and on whom she and her two children, one called Marian, were to depend utterly.

Sometimes an object or image only exists in repetitions and links within the novels. The tempting dagger in 'Mr Gilfil's Love Story', which Caterina takes from a cabinet but never uses, turns up for a more subtle study in *Daniel Deronda*. The dead hand with which Featherstone and Casaubon try to grasp the living becomes a benign dying hand in *Daniel Deronda*: 'There was a foreshadowing of some fateful collision: on the one side the grasp of Mordecai's dying hand on him, with all the ideals and prospects it aroused; on the other, this fair creature in silk and gems, with her hidden wound ...' (45). George Eliot turns from the clutching power of Featherstone and Casaubon to Mordecai's grasp of dedication and faith. A vinaigrette is rudely rejected by Caterina in 'Mr Gilfil's Love Story' when her rival patronizingly offers it and by Hetty in *Adam Bede* as the kind servant Kitty sees her tears when Arthur does not turn up in church, but accepted when Denner, George Eliot's most individualized servant, proffers with 'the instinct of affection' 'a gold vinaigrette which Mrs Transome often liked to carry with her, and … put it into her hand gently' (*Felix Holt*, 39). Rosamond's large embroidered collar is first worn by a dissenting ex-beauty, Mrs Muscat, while waiting for a clerical debate that never took place (*Felix Holt*, 24). Mary Burge's pink ribbon that makes her look 'as yellow as a crow-flower' (*Adam Bede*, 9) is changed for Priscilla Lammeter to silver-coloured silk making her 'look as yellow as a daffadil' (*Silas Marner*, 11). There is no known life source, though repetition implies one, but we can think of George Eliot using smelling-salts, closely observing and pricing embroidered collars, and disliking the clash of certain colours.

Dorothea's joke about her plans for labourer's cottages, 'I shall think I am a great architect, if I have not got incompatible stairs and fireplaces' (1), repeats an illustration from a *Leader* essay of 1855, 'The Future of German Philosophy': 'an intelligent neighbour comes in, and you show him your plan … He is not an accomplished architect, but he sees at once that you have put a door and a chimney in incompatible positions' (*SCW*, 133–4). This comes in handy for Dorothea without much change. In 'Liszt, Wagner, and Weimar' the essayist observes that most 'London concert-goers' think of Liszt as 'an erratic, flighty, artistic genius' (*SCW*, 82) and one of these adjectives comes back for the philistine peer Mr Bult, who thinks of Klesmer's opinions as 'flighty' (*Daniel Deronda*, 22), and a small point reinforces the possibility that Liszt, as well as Rubenstein, Haight's candidate, was one of the sources for George Eliot's fictional composer and pianist.

If Mr Brooke got his impulsive pen from Mr Bracebridge, his fear of 'going too far' echoes the speech of a 'general reader' scathingly sketched in George Eliot's *Fortnightly* essay of 1865, 'The Influence of Rationalism': 'he does not exactly know what distance he goes; he only knows he does not go "too far"' (Pratt and Neufeldt, 11; Pinney, 398). This gentleman has a sloppy speech-habit – 'say that black is not so very black, he will reply "Exactly"' – which is adapted for Sir James Chettam, whose 'Exactly so' exasperates Dorothea. The journalist's clever thumbnail sketch helps to characterize a man and his mind (as editors note). The 'noose of matrimony' which Mary

Ann jokingly wishes for herself, so that she might give a home to Maria Lewis, and no doubt for other reasons (*Letters* 1, 54), echoes for Mr Brooke as he feebly attempts to warn Dorothea off marriage, and tells us something we didn't know about himself, 'I never loved anyone well enough to put myself into a noose for them. It *is* a noose, you know' (*Middlemarch*, 4).

One fascinating metaphor links friendship and a favourite book. During 'the Liggins nightmare', as she calls it, Cara Bray uses a fine phrase from Bunyan, 'the shining ones', in love and admiration. Her letter is important because it leaves a mark on *Middlemarch*, and because doubt has been cast on the strength of their friendship after Marian went to live with Lewes: 'It is so grievous that works like yours should bring anything to you but pure good. I suppose it is in the nature of things that such annoyances should cluster about a great fame as the toadstools grow at the foot of the oak and the shining ones of the earth always get crucified somehow' (*Letters* 8, 248). George Eliot was delighted by Spencer's praise of *Adam Bede* and must have been moved at being named a shining one by Cara. The image went into *Middlemarch*, where an aspiring provincial doctor is placed, sadly and sympathetically, with Herschel and other 'great originators': 'Each of those Shining Ones had to walk on the earth among neighbours who perhaps thought much more of his gait and his garments than of anything which was to give him a title to everlasting fame' (15). Lydgate inspires the category, but turns out to be one who might have shone. The Shining Ones walk in Beulah's perpetual sunlight on the borders of Heaven, radiating faith for pilgrims toiling behind, in both parts of *The Pilgrim's Progress*. Cara's allusion to Bunyan was intimately knowing. He was a childhood favourite of George Eliot's and provides a key text in *The Mill on the Floss* and *Middlemarch* – and her imagination was saturated in his landscape and myth. Cara's personal use of his radiant humane vision may have extended George Eliot's celebration of the famous, to include makers, progenitors and teachers who were not famous: Adam and Caleb, builders, surveyors and planters of trees; Rosamond's piano teacher; and Dorothea, foundress of nothing, whose anonymous works have an 'incalculably diffusive' influence (*Middlemarch*, Finale). The image of Shining Ones was faithfully and unforgettably re-imagined by Cara Bray whose work and life is remembered for the George Eliot connection, but who left a small trace in her friend's great novel[4].

Notes

1 *The Road to Xanadu*, Cambridge, Mass: Riverside Press, 1927, p 344.

2 I discussed some of GE's windows in 'The Woman at the Window' in *Perspectives on Self and Community*, Patricia Gately, Dennis Leavens and D Cole Woodcox (eds) (1997) Lampeter: Edwin Mellen Press.

3 Edited by H Witemeyer. London: Macmillan, 1992.

4 For drawing my attention to George Eliot's development of Bunyan's 'Shining Ones' I am indebted to Dyan Elizabeth Wade's *A Study of the Authorial Commentary in 'Scenes of Clerical Life', Felix Holt, Middlemarch and Daniel Deronda, by George Eliot*, M.Phil. thesis, Birkbeck, 1975. She quotes a real example in George Eliot's tribute to George Simpson, manager of Blackwood's printing office, which praised his 'good work … the kind that goes on without trumpets' (*Letters* 5, 165).

Index